TRANSCRIPTS OF THE SACRED IN NIGERIA

TRANSCRIPTS OF THE SACRED IN NIGERIA

Beautiful, Monstrous, Ridiculous

Nimi Wariboko

INDIANA UNIVERSITY PRESS

This book is a publication of

Indiana University Press
Office of Scholarly Publishing
Herman B Wells Library 350
1320 East 10th Street
Bloomington, Indiana 47405 USA

iupress.org

© 2023 by Nimi Wariboko

All rights reserved
No part of this book may be reproduced or utilized in any form or by any means, electronic or mechanical, including photocopying and recording, or by any information storage and retrieval system, without permission in writing from the publisher. The paper used in this publication meets the minimum requirements of the American National Standard for Information Sciences—Permanence of Paper for Printed Library Materials, ANSI Z39.48-1992.

Manufactured in the United States of America

First printing 2023

Cataloging information is available from the Library of Congress.

ISBN 978-0-253-06642-8 (hdbk.)
ISBN 978-0-253-06643-5 (pbk.)
ISBN 978-0-253-06644-2 (web PDF)

Robin W. G. Horton (1932–2019)
"Abaji wula,"
Okolobio-obi of Kalabari Ekine Sekiapu Society

CONTENTS

Preface ix

Acknowledgments xv

Introduction: Ambiguity of the Sacred 1

Interlude: Methodological Matters and a Theory of African Postcolony 26

1. The Sacred as Im/possibility 41
2. Demons as Guests: Aesthetics of Pentecostal Prayers 67
3. The Pentecostal Incredible 94
4. Production of Violence in the Postcolony 130
5. Chosenness, Spirituality, and the Weight of Blackness 148
6. Disruption and Promise: The Religious Powers of Development 168

Conclusion 189

Notes 197

Bibliography 215

Index 223

PREFACE

> The sacred leaves transcripts of itself in social practices, transcripts comparable to graphic representations of an EKG machine that are imprinted on paper. The present alone possesses philosophers perceptive enough to read the graph paper for the rhythm of the sacred for their time, to grasp its dynamics in concepts. Who can correctly scan the sacred in Africa?[1]
>
> —Nimi Wariboko

A VIOLENT INTERACTION HAPPENED BETWEEN THE PRESIDING BISHOP of one of Nigeria's most powerful Pentecostal churches and a young woman—probably a teenager—in late 2011. For insisting that she was no witch or that her purported witchcraft was instead for Jesus Christ, the bishop had lifted his palm high up and struck her on her face. "You are a foul devil!" he had declared to her, before the congregation that had filled the massive auditorium and the members of the public who would witness the clip of the event when it landed on social media shortly after the incident. As he continued to speak, his voice carried over the whole church—both inside and outside—where thousands of people had congregated to worship. Into the face of the young woman, who must have been stunned by the violence she had suffered in the safe haven of God's house, the bishop shouted, "Do you know who you are talking to? You are a foul devil. You are not set for deliverance. And you are free to go to hell!"

Stories of violent subjugation like this one are common, and I consider them to be symbols of the African postcolony in the sense that they not only point beyond themselves to the degrading and dehumanizing character of the postcolony but also participate in the absurd reality of the postcolony to which they point. The bishop is one of the nation's wealthiest pastors and one of the most powerful preachers in Africa. Months before he slapped the young woman, he had reportedly bought a Gulfstream V jet for US$30 million, the newest addition to his collection of four aircrafts. The juxtaposition of stupendous wealth and abject poverty or of power and powerlessness is not the only thing that frames the bishop's entanglement with the young woman. There is the contestation of identity, forms of recognition of the "who" of a person in the public square. It was not an accident when the esteemed bishop shouted, "Do you know who you are talking to?" It is common to hear "Do you know who I am?" even in minor confrontations in Nigeria. In the dire, humiliating, and traumatic living conditions of the postcolony, Nigerians are quick to assert the "who" of their persons in order to grasp any scraps of human dignity and respect they can gather for themselves in intersubjective encounters. Another juxtaposition that frames the bishop's entanglement with the poor young woman is the acute coexistence of spiritual knowledge and empirical, verifiable knowledge in everyday life.

The bishop—or his church, as they claim—owns well-run universities where professors and students seek empirical knowledge through scientific, rational methods. Moments before he struck the young woman, the members of the congregation were in the midst of long, drawn-out praise, worship, and fervent prayers, raising their holy hands unto God and entreating God for knowledge production through the invisible realm to allow them to transform their human conditions. This glimpse into an interaction between a powerful man of God and a relatively unknown young supplicant on the church altar reveals something about the triune assemblage of the good, the bad, and the ugly of the African postcolony. The three converge in the man of God and the young congregant, and the event is symptomatic of the deep contradictions in the postcolony. More importantly, it also speaks to the transformative, destructive, and in-between possibilities of human existence in Africa.

But how does one make sense of the possibilities in the Nigerian or African postcolony? The purview of these possibilities exceeds what we ordinarily call religion. In this book I develop a new theory of the sacred to make sense of the range of possibilities in Africa and the ways they craft subjects, their experiences, institutions, and human conditions. The sacred is the constellation of possibilities and impossibilities in any given community—it is informed by the experiences of subjects in the African postcolony. The sacred is the universe of possibilities (beautiful, monstrous, and ridiculous im/possibilities) available to a community. The interaction between a rich, powerful bishop and a poor young woman displays some of the dimensions of the working of the sacred in Africa. And what we have read of the interaction between the bishop and the girl is a record of the traces of the sacred as it is *created* and coursing through Africa.

I will develop the conceptual framework of "transcripts of the sacred" to enable us to track, analyze, and evaluate movements and impacts of three dimensions of the sacred—the beautiful, the monstrous, and the ridiculous—so scholars and public policy makers can understand their progressive and destructive influences on human flourishing.

By *transcripts of the sacred* I mean the network of practices, ideas, orature, symbols, objects, social memory, and persons that documents, interprets, speaks to, theorizes about, and allows us to understand a culture's engagement with the sacred. By *sacred* I do not mean the usual categories of gods, deities, and spirits, natural or supernatural forces, or the ultimate concern of a people. All these names and many more (secular or nonsecular, spiritual or nonspiritual) that people usually consider to be sacred matter only to the extent that we can conceptualize them as contributing to, hampering, or being part of the universal set of possibilities available to a group. In every society there are three sets of possibilities: (a) one that is open to all individuals; (b) another that is available to only a few and excludes the rest; and (c) the universe of possibilities that are yet to be fulfilled or are not available to all persons and institutions. The sacred is the web of possibility and impossibility a community has spun as its ground of existence (being). The sacred is the realm of possibility and impossibility. It is the primordial locus of possibilities, the floating site of im/possibility, impossible possibility that unfolds, folds, and enfolds within communities.[2] Transcripts document not only the expansion or constrictions of the range of possibilities at different periods, the play of im/possibility in reality, but also their distribution into the three sets. Transcripts are the form of the sacred, the form that the realm of im/possibility takes in everyday life. They capture the dimension of meaning as possibilities unfold, fold, and enfold themselves, expressing a community's interpretation of life.

In other words, transcripts of the sacred are the archives of the actualization, movement, iterability, and novelty of possibilities in a community.[3] *Transcripts* serve as a name for order and disorder, meaning and meaninglessness, orientation and disorientation to human flourishing that appear and disappear as a people generate and manipulate possibilities of their existence. As archives, transcripts are neither objective-photographic descriptions nor subjective descriptions of the movements of the sacred. They are *symbols* that enable us to interpret a community and its culture, and they refer to "the scientific and artistic, the economic, political and ethical forms in which they express their interpretation of existence."[4]

While it is customary to think of archives as past cultural knowledges, achievements, and histories, in this work I expand the meaning to include ongoing contemporary experiences of the sacred. I accessed the archives or transcripts of the sacred through philosophical analysis, social-ethical interpretations, and tools of cultural criticism as applied to a community's creative self-interpretation at a particular historical juncture.

Let us further explain the temporality of transcripts by resorting to the analogy of earthquakes, more precisely seismography. There are at least two types of transcripts relating to earthquakes. We can study the shock waves as recorded by seismometers days or years after the incidence of an earthquake. Or we can try to make sense of the needle as it moves on the face of the meter. A focus on the contemporary or historical movements of the needle is never to the exclusion of the other. They complement one another in any study of earthquakes.

I have named related general movements of the sacred, seismographs of the "divine," the *transcripts of the sacred*. In this book, I pay more attention to interpreting contemporary movements of the sacred in Africa, tracing circumstances and events that they initiate or forestall. To guide my focus on the contemporary movements, I have categorized the manifold of transcripts into three categories: beautiful, monstrous, and ridiculous. The beauty of the sacred is its capacity to initiate something new amid ongoing social automatism. Beauty is the appearance of something new, something that affirms life and enhances human flourishing in human communities. Beauty of the sacred speaks to the processive opening of a community to the not-yet.

There is a tension between the beautiful (natality) and the monstrous (destructive fury) in the sacred. Possibilities (potentiality), in actualizing themselves, might initiate something new in a community, increasing its level of human flourishing, or they might, in the same process of actualizing themselves, lead to the contraction of the impulse for progress, solidarity, and communality, threatening to annihilate human flourishing. The beauty of the sacred wants "something," and the monstrous of the sacred appears to want "nothing."[5] Though possibilities are still in play, the positive impulse, the orientation toward beauty (expanding human flourishing), cannot overcome the antagonism of the negative (contractionary powers of the monstrous), and in this tension the beautiful and the monstrous frustratingly move in rotary form; the positive is not able to break out. In this monstrous state (dimension), the sacred, as the locus of possibilities, cannot withdraw completely into impossibilities and stasis or open itself up to forward movement. In many places in Africa, what I have named *the sacred* is caught in this dimension, in the grip of the monstrous sacred. Africans are still generating possibilities, trying hard to actualize their potentialities, but it appears they are caught in an impenetrable ground of self-limitation. How do they put a distance between this ground and themselves? How do they overcome the contractive, anti-human-flourishing dimension of the sacred and welcome the expansionary, pro-human-flourishing dimension of the sacred?

The ridiculous is an indication of a possibility that might break the destructive fury of the sociality caught in the monstrous. It is nothing more than having confidence (*con-fides, with-faith*) in the very people caught by monster to free themselves.[6] It seems ridiculous to hope that the very people causing, coursing through, caught in, and conserving the destructive fury will be their own saviors. It is indeed ridiculous to hope for otherwise possibility, for an alternative world amid the destructive fury. This is nothing more than grasping the sacred as it is, tarrying at its dimension of the impossible possibility until the new is birthed, perceiving and discerning the constructive potentialities within the core of destructive possibilities. Africans are daily creating spaces for such expansionary possibilities of the sacred.

Africans envision a lifeworld that at its core "bespeaks the ongoingness of possibility, of things existing other than what is given, what is known, what is grasped."[7] They draw from a philosophy of life that emphasizes possibility in the face of all impossibility, even as it highlights the commingling of the visible and invisible realms. Everyman's everyday form of philosophy is a philosophy of possibility, and the scent and accent of possibilities sustain the grit and energy of the rejected, oppressed, and marginalized masses. The ordinary folks who espouse this philosophy are always demanding in their words and deeds, "Is there a creative alternative to the current regime of obstacles, to the forces that thwart human flourishing?" Their answer is always "Yes, and soon there will be an opening, a space for a miracle." They believe that to succeed or grasp a miracle, they only need to deploy their imagination and show fidelity to their cause and course of enhancement of life.

The goal of this book is to lead us to a rich and profound understanding of how the sacred plays itself out in contemporary Africa. It offers a creative analysis of the logics and dynamics of the sacred in religion, politics, epistemology, economic development, and reactionary violence. Through the deployment of the tools of philosophy, social sciences, and cultural criticism,

I lay bare the intricate connections between the sacred and the existential conditions that characterize disorder, terror, trauma, despair, and hope in the African postcolony. In this discourse, I develop and defend the thesis that the transcripts of the sacred provide the best key to interpretatively engage the dynamics of the present political moment. The sacred here is not about religion or divinity but about the set of possibilities opened to a people or excluded from them, liberatory potentials for the transformation of selves and the structures of society, and the sum total of possibilities conceivable given their level of social, technological, and economic development. These possibilities profoundly speak to the present political moment in sub-Saharan Africa.

The political is at the core of the sacred. The political, rightly or broadly understood, is the set of transcripts of a community that reveals the "liberating opening and closing, and continual opening and reopening, of existence to itself, to and through its many singularities and pluralities."[8] When politics celebrates the continual opening and reopening of existence to itself, it marks the beauty of the sacred. But when politics locks down existence in one place, when citizens in their singularities and pluralities are "'locked down' in systems that resist opening and reopening," it has become a site for the monstrous sacred.[9] The ridiculous is the surprising, revivifying hope that the singularities and practices that are locked down will have "the surprising power to haunt, and at times also to dismantle and erode, the forces that freeze and subjugate."[10] Reflecting on such a hope, on such a possibility of the future that breaks the fever of the destructive fury, foretells of the critical space for radical, emancipatory politics and freedom that conduce to higher levels of human flourishing.

Nimi Wariboko
Westwood, MA
January 5, 2021

ACKNOWLEDGMENTS

Five months before she passed, on March 16, 2019, I had a telephone conversation with my mother. I asked her how she was doing, and she replied, "*Wa biokpo na balafa ke angari,*" we are living with hope and fear. The context for this answer was the violence political thugs visited on her home during a gubernatorial election on March 2, 2019, part of the deadly armed struggles between two political parties in Abonnema, Rivers State, Nigeria. They broke the doors and windows in her house, and the eighty-seven-year-old woman became very restless after that violent episode. Her response to my question conveyed the restlessness that had settled over her, which might have led to her death on August 11, 2019. In the scholarship of researching and writing about Nigeria, I bear on my mind the marks of hope and fear—in addition to hers.

Scholars also live with hope and fear. Ideas also invade their homes, the sanctuaries of their bodies. Once ideas invade them, they also live life in hope and fear. They live in the hope of perfecting and birthing the ideas. They agonize over their ability to be the proper embodiments and midwives of cutting-edge ideas. The day of ideas comes like a thief in the night. The idea is this night, this luminous darkness that contains everything beautiful in its generosity—an unending pageantry of parts and wholes—of which none is fully formed. One is raptured by this beauty of the night when one looks the thief, the invader, in the eyes—into a night that becomes day.

Once a scholar has caught a glimpse of beauty in the darkness of the night, she longs, burns to see the whole form clearly in the brightness of the day. This is like the mother who discerns the beauty of the fetus in the darkness of her womb and desires to see it in the daylight of its birth. Such beauty nourishes the soul of any scholar who catches a fleeting glimpse of it. In my short life filled with trouble and common enchantment, I have been blessed beyond measure with glimpses of such beauty—and with high magical moments of idea-inflected restlessness.

Indeed, ideas render me restless once they invade my inside, even as I am drinking from the nectar of their beauty. Sometimes my restlessness is caused by seminal ideas that become visceral and hysterical inside me. My restlessness is also caused by imaginations that have been shaken loose from their states of indolence, and they begin to wander violently in my bloodstream and other bodily fluids, all the time unable to ejaculate their seminal fluids into my dark womb of creativity. The bulls cannot pour themselves into the golden chalice. The bulls have a way of bulldozing their way through a pathless path to the womb. Often it takes the *weak force* of a good book to set such powerful beings right on their journey. For instance, in the days of June, July, and early August 2020, I had the bulls behaving as if they were in a china shop. Their behavior put me in a fog: errant ideas oppressed me in their prolonged gestation. These were days of distress, as when ideas come to the time of their birth without the concomitant strength to bring them forth. The waves of the womb's waters were pounding on the shores of the birth canal, but nothing was coming out. But on the morning of August 7, 2020, I woke up and read a brilliant economic essay, and it blew my mind—and everything was diffused. The water broke. The waves calmed down. And my insides became sweet (*I biobelem*). What a wonderful world!

The people who provided me with the care and attention after the delivery of the idea to bring this particular book to you are many and varied. Permit me to mention only a few of them—with hope and fear, with fascination and trembling. Gary Durham, Anna Francis, David Miller, and Stephen Matthew Williams of Indiana University Press were wonderful in their magnanimous assistance and professionalism.

When my mother uttered, "*Wa biokpo na balafa ke angari*," she was signaling the restlessness limited to possibilities of hope that can only exist within the domineering and hegemonic structures of the death-dealing Nigerian postcolony. I would like to believe that when I am ecstatically grasped by ideas, I am tapping into imaginative possibilities of the *novum* (genuine newness) that are beyond the prevailing postcolonial order. In this juxtaposition of hopes, I am audaciously intuiting that my form of restlessness can bring some respite (or an expectation of genuine newness) to those who are subjugated by the de-energizing turmoil that thwarts human flourishing in the African postcolony. This juxtaposition of hopes implies the imbrication of the predatory, monstrous, and ridiculous restlessness that marks existential conditions in Nigeria and the relative beautiful restlessness of the Nigerian scholar thinking about Nigeria.

TRANSCRIPTS OF THE SACRED IN NIGERIA

INTRODUCTION

Ambiguity of the Sacred

POSTCOLONIAL AFRICA IS BURDENED BY THE SACRED. It is this burden that this book will examine. The sacred is not made of gods and spirits but themes, forms, signs, constellations, and languages of possibility. The sacred is the universal set of possibilities available to a community or people. I propose that we can only adequately grasp the present sociopolitical predicament of Africa if we reread the sacred as no longer under the sign of divinity or the numinous but on the basis of the symbol of possibility. Africa is being crushed by the weight of unfulfilled possibilities, yet these possibilities inexorably draw, fascinate, and interpellate Africans because of the hope of new birth or renewal.

The sacred is the ultimate possibility to which we journey, but it is also the undying possibility within us that journeys side by side with us as our power of self-transcendence. It is not difficult for any casual observer of people in sub-Saharan Africa to note the predominance of high belief in or fervent pursuit of possibility in everyday life. There is, in the thick of suffering and deprivation, this almost palpable belief that everything is possible. Life is an unrelieving performance of the "theology of possibility."

Africans, especially millions under the sway of Pentecostalism and other charismatic forms of religion, believe that they can squeeze possibility from the abyss of impossibility. The African postcolony is above all else marked by profound uncertainty, precarity, and disappointment. Where nothing is certain, where one's neighbor is poor at one moment and rich beyond imagination at the next, everything is possible. The sacred in such a context becomes the infinite urn of im/possibility, the *chora beyond God*. But by seeking to go beyond the uncertainty and precarity of existence in the postcolony, Africans necessarily expose the burden and insidiousness of the sacred in Africa. And in exposing it, they expose the lack of certainty and normality in the postcolony and proclaim, paradoxically, their helplessness, vulnerability, and predicament in the very praxis by which they claim to manifest the omnipotence and wisdom of the sacred. The condition of subjugation to the sacred is daily renewed and repeated.

Now, since it is impossible to secure from the sacred all the possibilities they will need for flourishing life once and for all, the appropriation and consumption of possibilities are executable only in repetition. The joyful pursuit of possibilities must be endlessly renewed. Herein lies the compulsion to engage the sacred, an engagement that in other times and climes is the source of discovery, innovation, and creativity. In Africa the repetition is accursed, so far as it is counterproductive to human flourishing, broadly defined.

As we shall demonstrate throughout this book, religion has badly distorted Africans' engagement with the sacred. The sacred is now predominantly seen as a deus ex machina, power outside of history. Religion in Africa is one giant desiring machine, a gigantic apparatus for the production (of illusions) of possibilities, vast and unbound. Yet in this seeming addiction to impossible possibilities, Africans touch the kernel, the core of what the sacred is all about, even as they expose the sickness, death, and smell of decomposition of the postcolony. Today, to properly understand the logic and dynamic of the sacred in Africa is to gain an entrée into the heart of Africa's present predicament, enabling us to expose and critique the darkness and contradictions, entanglements, and excretions of religion that easily trap African communities in the vise of mucky underdevelopment. (In chapter 1, I will explain in detail the conceptualization of the sacred, the universe of possibilities, that drives this book.)

I argue that the notion of the sacred developed in this book constitutes the best conceptual framework by which the religious-political forces of antiflourishment are best interpreted, rendered meaningful from the lens of everyday folks, and subjected to critical review. The critique of the sacred is the premise of all criticisms of Africa. The critique of the sacred is also the end/*end* (goal) of criticism in contemporary Africa. The mystery of the sacred distorts and deforms desire. There is this abiding illusion that the sacred can support, produce, or authorize what the heart desires. This desire translates into the desire to possess the powers to sustain one's existence and make it flourish. In Africa, existence is a process of power exchange. Personal existence is a militant site of the agonistic transfer and control of power. Often existence is considered a spiritual warfare, a struggle between one *power of being* against another that determines the "who" of the contestants' humanity. The spiritual is the inner dynamics of existence and the politics that inevitably attends it. To succeed in the workings of existence, individuals must command the mystery of power.

The mystery of power is revealed as the mystery of possibilities, possibilities of freedom or of the actualization of potentiality for human flourishing in any given context. Thus, the mystery of the sacred is ultimately revealed as the mystery of possibilities. As it is in the nature of the sacred, as the universal set of possibilities available to a people or community, that we can find the red thread that connects most of Africa's sociopolitical problems, linking most of its religious and nonreligious issues and their possible solutions. The critique of the sacred is the critique of the possibilities that support or thwart human existence (flourishing). Put differently, the critique of the sacred is the critique of the *situation* in Africa—that is, it offers a diagnosis and evaluation of the existential conditions of historical or contemporary periods for Africans. Paul Tillich argues that the "situation cannot be neglected in theology [or critical studies] without dangerous consequences. Only a courageous participation [or interrogation] in the 'situation,' that is, in all the various cultural forms which express modern man's interpretation of his existence," can uncover the possibilities of freedom and human flourishing in any given historical period.[1]

This way of examining the sacred as the set of possibilities in a "situation" does not involve the (dominant) dualistic notion of reality that is common in the philosophies of the sacred. In this perspective, the fundamental contradiction or split in existence is not one of transcendence or immanence but of life versus death. Possibilities are either life enhancing or death dealing. Possibilities are beautiful, monstrous, or ridiculous, either acceptable or unacceptable, depending on how they defend life (human flourishing) against death and the degradation of human dignity.

Beauty of the Sacred

The beauty of the sacred (as the universal set of possibilities available to a people at any given period) is the unity of form and power, a dynamic union of power and meaning of possibilities that conduces to human flourishing.[2] The form is the set of social practices, activities, and processes or contents that make any possibility what it is. This is to say that possibilities have structure as they are discerned or generated, appropriated, and deployed in social practices. The *form* of possibilities, the meaningful structures that create and sustain the site of the appearance and working of possibilities are in turn created by the possibilities. This is to say the *contexture* of possibilities, the structure of possibilities are themselves generated by possibilities. The *contexture* has the power to establish all things in it. It is the ground of being of the actions and interactions of humans and objects.[3] When the union of form and power that moves, coordinates, and enhances human flourishing in a community manifests, we have the beauty of the sacred. The beauty of the sacred is born amid and transpires in social practices that create and sustain a way of being for the good. Possibilities alone do not constitute the beauty of the sacred. If possibilities are structured—that is, if they are tied to a social site and have a form that frames and sustains them while moving them toward human flourishing—then we have the beautiful, the beauty of the sacred. A plausible judgment about what constitutes human flourishing or human good involves judgments about the virtues of justice, love, and hope. A community whose thoughts (ethos) are truly directed toward loving the creative realization of human potentialities will aspire to be just, loving, and hopeful. Justice, love, and hopefulness are particularly good ways of being for the beauty of the sacred—that is, a way of being for persistent creative realizations of human potentialities. (Conceived in this way, the beauty of the sacred is not oriented toward aesthetics. This conception avoids the aestheticizing of sacred, which "depoliticizes" it as a profoundly "political" concept.)

Justice, as a way of being good for the sacred, idealizes the actualization of potentialities for the *other* that is universal in scope in the community. Love gestures to the profundity and intensity in caring for the possibilities of the creative realization of human potentialities for *some persons* in the community, including the self. Hope is a way of being good for the actualization of human potentialities for its own sake. It is a way of "intending" the future that is *structural* rather than *motivational*.[4] It involves organizing one's motives, values, commitments, and goals for the birth of the new. One does not value human flourishing—and the sacred, for that matter—as one should if one does not care about the persistent creative realization of human potentialities for its own sake.[5]

Beauty is the harmony of love, justice, and hope in the universe of possibilities available to a community. It is the weaving of the erotic braid of love, justice, and hope to draw human existence to strain toward the not-yet, ever weaving the elastic braid with new threads in the fabric of social existence in resistance to the limits and obstacles that constrain human life or flourishing.

Put differently, the beauty of the sacred is the manifestation of the good and truth in social existence as discernible through the opaque lens of immanent human transcendence. Beauty is the eros of the good and truth, drawing members of the community into a whole only to step on the pathway outward again. What then are the good and truth of the sacred, which when combined give us beauty? The good of the sacred is the endless sequence of approximation to eudaemonia, enrichment of life, which is embodied in the humans' engagement with the actualization of potentialities. It is the movement toward the good as defined by each community. For the mere actualization of potentialities without any goal commitment toward human flourishing (life enhancement) cannot be used as a general formula in place of the good. Actualization is ambiguous on its own because of the human proclivity to use their capabilities for both good and evil. This is why in this study we will continue to examine the sacred within the context of human flourishing, the enhancement of life.

The truth of the sacred is the working out of possibilities that forever cannot arrive at the ultimate possibility, the possibility of all possibilities, the ultimate truth. Truth is the one (or the many counted as one) possibility that many types of possibility try to approximate through fidelity to realized possibility and its potential future becoming. Possibility is the link between potentialities and actuality, between potential infinities and actual infinities in the movement toward the Absolute, whatever that is. Truth is ultimately about the existence of Absolute Infinity. All a truth procedure (as in the faithful pursuit of "internal transcendence") can do is put us on a path between potential infinities and actual infinities as we approach the rationally unknowable, unconceivable Absolute Infinity. But because of what is known as the *reflection principle* in modern set theory, we can find partial truths that satisfy the truth of the Absolute Infinity.[6]

The beauty of the sacred is the fabric of good/truth, the interface of good and truth that runs through all experience of life. It gestures to the integrity, harmony, and wholesomeness of dense relationality that enables the process of actualization of potentials to go on. Beauty refers to the set of mediating relations between persons, objects, and ideas around, with, and in which good and truth happen. Each relation in turn stands in a higher-order relation to other relations, persons, objects, and ideas. This process can go on ad infinitum.[7] The eros—which I mentioned above when I defined the beauty of sacred as the eros of the good and truth—is about the power and enhancement of this mediating relation that enables life to hang together. Let me quickly add that the mediating relation (or the sacred and its eros) can turn from the beautiful to the monstrous, from the fascinating to the terrifying.

Monstrosity of the Sacred

Monstrosity refers to the terror, terrifying excesses, and terrifying formlessness of possibilities. The monstrosity of the sacred is discernible when the possibilities being generated in a community destroy its world, causing terror, violence, and domination. The unity of power and meaning, the dynamic union of form and dynamics, is violently torn apart. This is when it appears that the movements and dynamics of the sacred have stopped and turned into a terrifying stasis. Here history is considered as neither a record of the past nor the (purposive) movement of events but as a form of perpetual present, a *demonic*, dumbfounded "eternal now." History is now an abolition of both the past and the future—these temporal segments have been *deactivated*. This is history as a traumatic encounter that signifies both the loss of temporal coherence and the loss of *world*. (In such a condition of existence, time and space and self asymptotically approach *singularity*, so to speak.) The sacred has turned into an "eternal now" of nightmare. It seems the sacred has contracted within itself, in a rotary motion of destructive fury, inflicting perpetual curses on the members of the community. This monstrous manifestation of the sacred is traumatic for the community. In the pain and agony of the sacred, it appears to the community that its past and future have been abolished—leaving behind only a painful, perplexing present. Amid trauma or the unconcluding remains of a traumatic event, conceiving the future seems impossible.

It seems that the sacred, which inhabits (secrets) the place of the possibility, has withdrawn from this very place, abandoned it, and it is remembered in absence. This (non) place represents a distortion that at the same time delivers, conceals, and disguises the ontological terror that undergirds or attends the sacred. It is an anti-flourishing order, a place of erasure of human flourishing for members of a community. Unlike the beauty of the sacred, it does not pave the way for human flourishing; it paves pathology. It is ultimately a place of abandonment or absence because it is a site of nonmovement and concealment, perpetual waiting and deferral of the type of possibility that emancipates and frees for flourishment of the members of the community.

Let me deliver the point differently. In the sacred, as a terrifying stasis, possibilities exist not to exist.[8] Possibilities are held in an interval of temporality where movements of becoming are denied and the unlivingness of "nothing" that is something is affirmed. The monstrous possibilities are *something*, but they exist to negate *other* possibilities, to decenter, destabilize, or pulverize them into impossibilities, to render null or conceal all other possibilities for the movement of Being. The monstrous possibility gives no phenomenological resistance to disaster. It is already disordered in the view of beauty, the dimension of human flourishing. Monstrous possibility reflects the nothingness of the sacred's core. Monstrous possibility is nothing, but the nothingness is projected onto human organization and form as a disordering, destructive, destabilizing, castrating, rupturing, terroristic force. Monstrous possibility is like a sign that has lost its proper referent (the referent of human flourishing). Such possibilities are specters of the sacred.

Ridiculous Dimension of the Sacred

A ridiculous possibility is a correction. It does not create or destroy human flourishing at all. Its primary operation is to arrest the growth and development of monstrous possibility and redirect its energy to the beautiful. It paves the way for the return of beautiful possibility and a community's awakening toward human flourishing, for monstrous possibility must slip away under the powerful course correction it provides, under the miracle of natality (initiating something new amid ongoing social processes) it inaugurates.

Ridiculous possibility contains the gift of grace. Grace here is not some supernatural realm zapping its power of redemption into a system from outside to right things. Grace is what interrupts the chain of cause and effect that perpetuates the working of monstrous possibilities. This is done not by shunting the chain into a separate nonhuman or nonphenomenal realm but by creating a split within causation itself such that possibilities, which are either retroactively activated or become freshly legible, come together with ongoing automatism of the social processes of the now to form a new constellation.

Grace is an event. It is disruptive. Grace is the concerted immanent power of some citizens acting together in ways that radically challenge and unsettle monstrosity and cultural presumptions of why and how monstrosity perdures, and it redirects the trajectory of the sacred to align with human flourishing. Grace is an appearance of something new in human life, human condition, that breaks into the order of things. It allows freedom (not unfreedom) to appear, to flourish as such. It is a movement toward openness to future possibilities, dislocating human lives and situations toward their future (beautiful) forms, nudging them toward full actualization of their potentials. In its dislocating movement, it has a *novum* character signaling it as a response to the current order of things in which potentialities exceed the current structuring of individual and social existence. Grace expresses the hidden potentials of a situation, existence, or life as well as transcends them. Grace is the animating force of the ridiculous.

The ridiculous is the possibility for thinking otherwise. It is neither fascinating nor monstrous. It deactivates the monstrous, renders it *inoperative*, and puts it to new possible uses. It empties monstrous possibility of its profound destructive fury and relieves it of its ability to harm flourishing of life. It counteracts the effects of monstrous possibility on natality, the capacity to initiate something new, not by negating and annihilating them but by fulfilling and recapitulating them in the figure of the beauty of the sacred. Under the power of citizens' cooperation and hope, the monstrous possibility is separated from its end of condemning a community to destructive fury, and it is also delinked from its power to lock a community in stasis.

The monstrous possibility, as an integral part of the sacred, is not gone, but citizens' concert of generated power opens it to a new possible use.[9] It no longer works toward the destruction and anti-flourishing of life but toward the beauty of the sacred, which shows us how to live and live well in our common existence. The ridiculous severs the monstrous from its original instrumentality or purpose. It is in this nature of losing its purpose and moving us to realize the moral imperative of our lives—demanding that we become what we ought to be, to support human flourishing—that it becomes like the beauty of the sacred. Through the power of radical hope, playful imagination, and creativity, citizens reimagine and reconceptualize monstrous possibility to extract and displace it from its usual context and put it to good use. Ridiculous hope works to rupture the logics of monstrous possibility and constitute an alternative trajectory of the sacred.

Ordinarily, Africans are reasonably good at treating monstrous possibility as deactivated, inoperative. They are used to carving out fragments and creating forms that suit their needs, sometimes inventing new uses for the monstrous sacred within their own *assemblage* of fragments.[10] They invent, create, or carve pathways among the monstrous possibilities. Each community or group carves different pathways depending on its roots, its starting cultural identity, and its worldview. But these are not roots that are static and reified; instead, they are very adaptive, dynamic, searching for other roots to establish connections and be transformed. Africans have roots that work as routes. Africans are *radicants*, to use the neologism of French philosopher

Nicolas Bourriaud for today's "postproduction" artists. He writes that *radicant* "is a term designating an organism that grows its roots and adds new ones as it advances. To be radicant means setting one's roots in motion, staging them in heterogeneous contexts and formats, denying them the power to completely define one's identity, translating ideas, transcoding images, transplanting behaviors, exchanging rather than imposing."[11]

Devaka Premawardhana in his brilliant 2018 text, *Faith in Flux: Pentecostalism and Mobility in Rural Mozambique*, provides empirical evidence of the theorization of the ridiculous hope via fragments, the carving out of pathways amid difficult circumstances.[12] His generative book maps well onto many of my key arguments of radical hope amid monstrous possibilities. He tells the story of spirituality, modernization, and globalization through the lens of existential mobility as played out in a rural Mozambican community, Makhuwa-Kaveya. He rightly portrays the Makhuwa people, living in a very difficult situation, as those whose roots serve as routes.[13]

Premawardhana, in this fast-paced, brilliant book, maps the singular story of mobility. As a category for sociophilosophical analysis of Pentecostalism, mobility can be seen through its literal and allegorical uses as a significant factor determining and defining Makhuwa's culture, religion, religious conversion, economy, and social practices. Mobility is not only about changing geographical location or reach (movement) or finding one's way in institutionalized relationships or networks. It is also about a subject's ability to move spatially and socially in a field of possibilities—intentionally accessing possibilities, appropriating them, and developing the skills to use them to accomplish his or her mission.[14] Mobility or flow in the traditional Makhuwa-Kaveya world is a form of obligation to express (actualize) a person's or a community's potentialities.

Life in Kaveya is figured as a flow. Living is all about negotiating fluxes and flows. Personhood is fundamentally about nurturing the power to be free and float, to circulate within a network of relationality.[15] Persons circulate. To be a person is to be a capillary in life's circulatory system. Ethics, which is entirely dissimilar from the ancient Greek notion of ethos, is not about fences, barriers, and guardrails. For life to flow, ethics must be about motions and movements overcoming fences and borders. Ethics is about circulation.

Premawardhana captures the spirituality of the Kaveya people of rural Mozambique as the circulatory logic of motion and movement. Spirituality is the practice of initiating something new, the capacity to begin or be in circulation. Religion itself is merely a specific segment of circulation, or it is also circulation regarded in its totality.[16] Circulation is the overarching framework or ideological matrix within which life, qua religious life, happens in Kaveya.

The theme of the circulation of the body and self in Kaveya's culture is linked with the circulation of blood. The circulation of human beings in Kaveya is what "the circulation of blood is to the human body."[17] Paulino, a research assistant to Premawardhana, said, "*Mikakari sahu* [our veins/ roots] make our blood to circulate. . . . And that makes *us* to circulate."[18] Bodies flow through spaces; blood also flows through spaces. Blood moves through the capillaries of space. Constructed spaces, in all their roundness, enact and perform circulation. Spatial forces rotate through axes and arcs of existence. Existential mobility is, in a sense, the circulation of blood through the capillaries of space. More precisely, existential mobility is the blood of the Kaveya people as flesh and bone moving through land and mountain. In this culture of high mobility, all that is solid melts into the circulation, dissolution, and liquefaction of constructed space. In Africa, the path from the monstrous dimension (phase) of the sacred to the beautiful sacred passes through circulation; sheer existential mobility motivates and moves the ridiculous dimension of the sacred into being.

Theologian Emmanuel Katongole has a haunting image of Africa: "Churches and coffins are perhaps the two most prevalent images associated with Africa."[19] By this disturbing statement, he means Africa is bracketed, caged, or sandwiched between hope and despair, dreams and tragedy, effervescent praise and threnody, possibilities and limitations, the womb and the grave. Should we say the connection between the church and coffin is akin to that between the beautiful and monstrous sacred, if you are willing to allow me, for a fleeting moment, to use the metaphor of the beauty of the sacred for the church?

I am hesitant to unequivocally name the church in Africa as the beauty of the sacred. The church in Africa, by and large, has not exhibited enough capability of imagination to even metaphorically stand in for the beauty of the sacred, to qualify as a metonym for the fount of possibilities for the transformation of society and human flourishing in Africa. The church is yet to become the womb or site that can help Africans to realize those hopes, satisfactions, and "pleasures created and enjoyed in [their] imagination" or dreams, to create a ceaseless push for the advancement of the human condition on the continent.[20] What we have is Pentecostal churches giving us a simulacrum of this capability by driving their members under the whip of the prosperity gospel for ceaseless consumption of consumer items (novelty) and eagerness for new experiences as created and enjoyed in their exuberant magical imaginations.[21]

This is not to say that such community-transforming imaginative capability is lacking on the continent. Thomas Sankara (1949–1988), the late president of Burkina Faso, demonstrated such a vision or capability. He became the president at the age of thirty-three in a military coup in 1983, and in a mere five years, he dramatically cut the infant mortality rate, empowered more women than his predecessors ever did, and implemented popular reforms that gave hope to peasants and other oppressed and marginalized groups. All these accomplishments infuriated the elites that had made the country a "paradise for some and hell for others."[22]

At the fourth anniversary of the revolutionary coup that brought him to power, he cast a powerful vision for the transformative changes he was working out in Burkina Faso's economic, political, and cultural spheres. It was a vision of increasing possibilities for advancing levels of human flourishing. And to get this right, he wanted to *invent* a future that would usher in the beauty of the sacred. He wrote, "You cannot carry out fundamental change without a certain amount of madness. In this case, it comes from non-conformity; the ability to turn your back on old formulas, the courage to invent the future. It took the madmen of yesterday for us to be able to act with extreme clarity today. I want to be one of those madmen. We must dare to invent the future."[23]

Because he dared to dream, to gaze upon the beauty of the sacred and to seek human flourishing in its immanent frame, his friend and confidant Blaise Campaoré colluded with other turncoats to assassinate him and took power. And the small country of seven million people was dragged back into the embrace of the monstrous sacred. But the memory of the beauty of the sacred, which flashed across the sky of Burkina Faso as a midsummer lightning, lives on. Katongole sums up the legacy of Sankara with these words:

> Indeed, for Sankara the whole project of seeking to "invent the future" was a form of madness. For instead of shaping the future according to predictable patterns of the past and realities of the present (the rational thing to do), inventing the future required reshaping the present according to a vision of a future yet to be born. Sankara, for example, rejected the notion and inevitability of poverty and was one of the first proponents of the idea of "food security."

In the five years of Sankara's leadership, through agricultural reforms, and mobilization of the population, his country achieved food sufficiency, which shows that Sankara's "madness" was quite sane indeed. Inventing the future requires the audacity to live in the present with the energy and visions drawn from the future.[24]

As its stands today, the church in Africa cannot invent the future, or live in that coming future that Sankara sought and reached out for, without reinventing itself. So far, the church lacks the courage to become the decisive force for change, new energy, and new story. There are, however, Africans within and outside the church who are working to make their countries into communities of invented future, distinctive politics, and new, uplifting stories. Africa is not only a site where the grotesque hands of the monstrous sacred come out from the interstices of the beautiful to smother the child of promise or possibilities, as happened in Burkina Faso. There are also instances of creativity arising out of utter, abysmal ugliness to fashion the beauty of the sacred, to fashion new sets of possibilities for human flourishing.

Despite all the negative news about the monstrosity of the sacred in Africa, the continent is also a temple of the beauty of the sacred. Improvisation, resourcefulness, grit, ingenuity, innovation, and creativity are the liturgy of the temple. The sermon is *e go better*, things will improve. The preacher and the congregation, the everyday people who are experts in doing more with little resources, are one. Nigerian American writer Dayo Olopade, in her book *The Bright Continent*, calls this capacity of Africans to create a strategic trajectory of possibilities amid the ongoing ferocity of perils and limitations *kanju*—"the specific creativity born from African difficulty. As it turns out, uncertain electricity, clogged roads, nonexistent social protections can make life tough, but they also produce an extraordinary capacity for making do. . . . Like the sand in an oyster that creates a pearl, hardship produces an attitude that can be leveraged to attack the same."[25]

Transcripts of the Sacred

The ridiculous, the monstrous, and the beautiful are forms of modes and movements of the sacred. Do the movements of the sacred in any community leave "fossils" or "fossil matter" that indicate a particular engagement of a community with its sacred, pointing to the existence of realities and events prior to the present period? In a crude analogy, does the past life of the sacred provide information like the radioactive decay of isotopes that may enable us to infer its pattern, style, and rhythm before our contemporary time? More importantly, what kind of ongoing evidence may enable us to infer the very movements of the sacred today? I have crafted the terminology of transcripts to name such fossil matter or information of the past and present.

As the sacred manifests in the modes of the beautiful, the monstrous, and the ridiculous, it leaves deposits, remains, imprints, traces, features, and social records that when collected and analyzed will reveal the "spirit" (that is, the totality of a group's creative self-interpretation of itself or its moral life) of an era in any given community. Let us call these records transcripts. The transcripts exist relationally between the sacred and the people (community of practice). This statement is important to make because the features or traces that make up transcripts are neither in the sacred itself nor in the community itself alone. As we shall demonstrate in chapter 1, the sacred and the community coexist and arise together.

Transcripts of the sacred are the experiences and understanding of actualization of and ways of being for potentialities and for the actualization of potentialities that allow a people to engage with the dynamics of the sacred. They provide the stratigraphy of social relations, axiologies, epistemology, ideas, and practices a people (a community of practice) have crafted to carry forward the changes in the form and substance of their social existence in their continuous encounter with the sacred.

The transcripts are the public yet intimate autobiography of the sacred. If we know how to read the transcripts, we should be able to decipher the inner stories and character of the sacred in its particular instantiation in any given context. The sacred is not the same in every community. It is housed differently in each one. Each community is like a body that holds life, the fount of possibilities. Each body has its own experiences, memories, and inner stories. Each body is capable of beauty, monstrosity (terror), and ridiculousness (hope) because of the inner world, mysteries, memories, experiences, and holes and cracks within it. The study of the transcripts of the sacred provides one way for us to discern, decipher, and disseminate the autography of this body.

A set of well-organized transcripts is an icon of the sacred. This implies that transcripts are like the sacred the way a map is like the territory it refers to. Yet the map is never confused with the actual territory. Transcripts are not constructed to accurately describe the sacred and its situation but to orient the reader to what is important in a society's encounter with the sacred and to carry what is valuable in respect to the encounter over into critical social analysis. Thus, transcripts more often refer indexically to the sacred. They point us to what is important in the sacred in respect to which the transcripts indexically refer to the sacred.[26]

We can also characterize a transcript as a sacrament of the sacred. It is a visible, tangible sign of an otherwise invisible mystery of undying possibility housed in the body of the community. When properly collated, organized, and (indexically) interpreted with poetics and alertness, a transcript becomes the mirror where the movements and substance of the unseen world of the sacred (the *horizon of unfilled possibilities*) come to expression. Any time we set forth a set of transcripts with nuance and power, we unveil the unity and rhythm of the music of the sacred in the community. The signature of the sacred becomes legible.

A transcript does not only point to the sacred but also participates in the reality of the sacred to which it points. The relation between transcripts and the sacred is not always that of effect to source or signifier to its point of reference. Transcripts participate or subsist in, recreate, redirect, and repurpose the sacred. Transcripts share in the "being" of the sacred; their connections to the sacred are participatory, not merely external. Transcripts *tradition* community members through rhythms, rituals, beliefs, affections, witnessing, consciousness, thinking, and ethos in the sacramental participation in the sacred, the universe of possibilities opened to them.

Transcripts enable possibilities to assemble, cluster, and coalesce around key persons, groups, or institutions in the community. This is similar to what hashtags do around trending or viral topics in the social media world. While hashtags do this with memes that have powerful semiotic charges, transcripts as "texts," as "objects," as foci of emphasis and concentration of potentialities, promote and provoke interactivities and dialogues across social spheres of existence. Transcripts as hashtags are forms of apparatuses that collect and organize human potentialities to instantiate, enable, drive, or inhibit natality (initiate something new, opening up a path of blocked or etiolated possibilities, providing the capacity to begin). In this role (functioning), an assemblage of transcripts does not work in a unidirectional style, only receiving inputs and impulses from the sacred. The assemblage is dialectical and mutually correlational with the sacred. The questions, insights, and answers concerning human experience it gathers are a factor in the conditioning of the nature, logics, and dynamics of the sacred. An assemblage of transcripts constitutes a critical realistic bundle that operates empirically, imaginatively, and theoretically to enable the sacred to respond to existential situations. An assemblage of transcripts as a visible realization of possibilities in a community, as an efficacious conveyer of the power of the universal set of possibilities, demonstrates both the (re)making and the response of the sacred to cultural forms, finite persons, and abyssal depths of the incompletable actualization of human potentialities.

It is important to reiterate that the transcripts of the sacred are not about gods, deities, or spirits but about people—their patterns of thoughts, practices, institutions, ideas, and experiences—as shaped by the quest to actualize their potentialities that will make life meaningful for them. Simply put, a transcript is a narrative and analysis of a community's historical and contemporary engagements with its *horizon of unfulfilled possibilities*.

As sociologist Richard Fenn puts it, the sacred is the embodiment of unfulfilled possibilities: "Because the sacred embodies only *unfulfilled* possibilities, it always points beyond itself to the full range of possibilities for either salvation or destruction. This set of all possibilities, both actual and hypothetical, I call the Sacred, and it is to the sociology of religion what dark matter is to astrophysicists, or 'the god above the god of theism' is to theologians."[27]

My interpretation of the movements of the sacred in Africa will focus on a rhizome or network of transcripts that gives a long-term history and transversal view of a community's encounter with the *horizon of unfulfilled possibilities*. This orientation to the past will be balanced with an inclination to the present, as I have already indicated. Transcripts are not a "timeless creation or a product of one big-bang event. Instead, they were compounding products of several historical processes, originating from different junctures of time."[28]

There is another important methodological issue to mention at this juncture of our discourse of transcripts of the sacred. Every transcript must be explained by the theory of knowledge of its originating community of practice if we are to understand the lived experiences, meanings and meaningfulness of self-realization, and spirit it represents. Indeed, a transcript is an interpretation of the *traces* of the sacred, used as historical or social ontology relative to the social-ethical question being investigated.[29] It reveals how a society bears witness to the sacred—indeed, to itself—and the social and ethical implications of such witness. A transcript bears witness to a community's encounter with its own spirit, the totality of its creative self-interpretation.

Mapping the Fragments of the Sacred in Africa and the Arguments of the Book

This study is about Africans' particular mode of bearing witness to the sacred, their particular mode of being amid the possibilities of existence. It tells the story of the multidirectional openness of the social life of Africans without presuming a constrictive universalizing framework. In this way, it directs readers' attention to the fragmentary nature of African postcolony or *situation*. Africans' engagement with the sacred is an assemblage of practices, ideas, theologies and philosophies, and interpretations of reality, whose tangled roots burrow deep into the three segments of African temporality. Africans' quest for human flourishing, like any other human endeavor, is full of fragments, and to understand it scholars must think in parts and not in unified cultural wholes that can be narrated as a single story. Chinua Achebe once said:

> I believe in the complexity of the human story and that there's no way you can tell that story in one way and say, This is it. Always there will be someone who can tell it differently depending on where they are standing; the same person telling the story will tell it differently. I think of that masquerade in Igbo festivals that dances in the public arena. The Igbo people say, If you want to see it well, you must not stand in one place. The masquerade is moving through this big arena. Dancing. If you're rooted to a spot, you miss a lot of the grace. So you keep moving, and this is the way I think the world's stories should be told—from many different perspectives.[30]

And it is in its *dancing* fragments that one has sought to understand Africa deeply. The assumption is that the transcripts in their fragments—moving, localized, particularized, or crosscutting—will enable us to discover general patterns, themes, logics, and dynamics of the sacred and the sociopolitical in Africa.

How do the fragments coalesce to give us an interpretative perspective, which is always incomplete and incompletable, on the processes that are relentlessly shaping and redefining a community's particular mode of being African? Many factors have worked to engender the dynamic imagery of Africans' social existence that this study examines. One will not be able to examine all of them, but here it will suffice to provide an in-depth look at six of the underlying factors, or "fragments of social life," that will enable us to gain a perspective on the larger social life or cultural wholes.[31] Africans' engagement with the sacred is not a system or a unified whole, and by concentrating on its fragments, this writer seeks to interpret what Africans "are up to, or think they are up to" without essentializing any dimension of their social existence.[32] The creative interpretations of fragments of social life only gesture to the ways Africans themselves think the various fragments or parts make up the whole. If I am successful, the reader will gain some sense of the African culture's way of thinking—a way of thinking and responding to the world that is always subject to endless internal debate.

The first of the fragments one will discuss is the key idea of the sacred. Chapter 1 ("The Sacred as Im/possibility") argues that the sacred emerges from how we understand, relate, treat, and divine im/possibilities in our everyday life. The sacred is near all human beings at all times. The understanding of the sacred that I am putting forward here will inform us about how the practices (such as discernment and worship) Africans perform help them to wrest the necessary possibilities they need to live, move, and have their being in everyday life. The notion or theory of the sacred is a powerfully integrating and structuring force for the currents of ideas presented in each chapter of the book, as well as being their "ground." Chapter 2 ("Demons as Guests: Aesthetics of Pentecostal Prayers") explores how this particular understanding of the sacred drives African Pentecostals to war against demons (or personifications of the monstrous sacred), who they believe are hindering their progress in life. This war that I analyze takes place in the worship services that incorporate prayers of the spiritual-warfare type. Demons are invited to such services as "guests," and in the ensuing combat Pentecostals create what I called the aesthetics of hot prayers. The chapter speaks to how Pentecostals are trying to redistribute possibilities available in the sacred given their understanding of the sacred as the universal set of possibilities, vast and unbound, actual and hypothetical. The desire to distribute, redistribute, or restage possibilities is the primary reason they engage in hot prayers.

These two fragments (chapters) give us a glimpse of the beauty of the sacred—or at least of the attempt to bend it to serve human flourishing. But in this very endeavor, we also get the hints of the monstrosity and ambiguity of the sacred. The very epistemology and worldview that found and drive the aesthetics of hot prayers not only create and feed into the dreary disorder that is the African postcolony but also negate possibilities for human flourishing.

The next two chapters examine the religious and political fallouts of the deary disorder of the African postcolony. This is a disorder that has enthroned political (temporal) chaosmos that annihilates possibilities for human flourishing and installs necropolitics and traumatic governance, among other macabre outcomes. Governance in the African postcolony, just like the daily existential condition, is an incredible phenomenon, a situation of perpetual crisis—crisis as the norm. Pentecostalism in the country is a struggle to survive the perpetual trauma of national political governance. Caught in this agonistic struggle, Christianity (especially its Pentecostal variant) has become part of what the Nigerian scholar Tejumola Olaniyan calls the *postcolonial incredible*. "The incredible is not simply a breach but an outlandish infraction of 'normality' and its limits."[33]

Chapter 3 ("The Pentecostal Incredible") examines how Christianity/Pentecostalism participates in the reign of the incredible in the Nigerian postcolony. The incredible anomie of the postcolony feeds into the cesspool of violence that renders most Africans perpetually vulnerable to death, wayward and rogue death, at any given instant.

Chapter 4 ("Production of Violence in the Postcolony") examines the relationship between the religious sphere and the secular sphere in the production of violence in the African postcolony. There are seven dimensions to the relationship between the religious/secular and violence: (a) the relationship between religion and the secular being imbricated in the production of violence; (b and c) each of them acting separately to produce violence; (d) violence conditioning the relationship between the secular and the religious; (e and f) violence in its multiplicity of forms reproducing or conditioning either the secular or the religious; and (g) violence, religion, and the secular sharing a mutual context in relating to one another. A context of mutual relevance enables anyone of violence, religion, and the secular to relate to or impact the others in postcolonial Africa. This chapter maps these seven dimensions across historical, political, and economic terrains to reveal how constituted or constituting violence affects Africa's development and the possibilities for human flourishing. Chapters 3 and 4 clearly demonstrate how religion has badly distorted Africans' engagement with the sacred. The stories and analyses in these two chapters exemplify the monstrosity of the sacred in the African postcolony.

Monstrosity is not the last word in the African story. There are indications of emerging possibilities that might break the destructive fury of the postcolony caught in the monstrous.

Indeed, there is a ridiculous hope for *otherwise possibility*, for an alternative world amid the fury of the monstrous. Chapters 5 and 6 attempt to discern the constructive potentialities within the core of the monstrous possibilities. Chapter 5 ("Chosenness, Spirituality, and the Weight of Blackness") explores Nigerian Pentecostals' projection of their spirituality outside the shores of their country, which allows them to shore up the possibilities that their nation will become the arrowhead of Black people's scientific, technological, and economic liberation. Nigerian Pentecostals are claiming that their nation has been specially chosen by God to lead the *final* evangelization of the world before the second coming of Jesus Christ and to draw the Black race into global economic and technological supremacy. Their understanding of chosenness is not just limited to the view that God has cut a special deal with them to establish God's kingdom in the foreseeable future; they believe he has also opened the structure of hope and expectation for the future to the Black race as a whole. The belief in chosenness amid increasing race consciousness and national poverty is driving Nigerian Pentecostals to redefine what it means to be Black and how Blacks should bear the weight of Blackness in a world of historical disregard for Black people. They think they are carrying the burden of all Black people and believe God uses their nation and its successes to not only spiritually uplift Africa but also trigger its economic and technological takeoff. They consider themselves to be the trigger handle of Africa's emancipation. In a sense, the invention of the tradition of chosenness is meant to buoy up their sense of dignity in the midst of the terror of the postcolony, which eviscerates possibilities for human flourishing. They hope in this way to reverse the negativity of monstrous possibilities that has settled not only in their own nation but in most of sub-Saharan African countries.

Now, if some Pentecostals are looking toward the projection of the soft power of spirituality to combat or circumvent the hard reality of monstrosity, there are others among them whose hope of liberation starts from home, from the Pentecostal churches themselves in the country. This latter group are working to undermine the very structures of Pentecostalism that are integral to the disasters of thought and order that constitute the postcolony. This group represents forms of internal resistance within Nigerian Pentecostalism. Its emerging story disrupts the present dominant narrative of apolitical, social-justice-averse African Pentecostals. I must admit that their stories that I narrate in chapter 6 ("Disruption and Promise: The Religious Powers of Development") are not capable of dislodging the regnant narrative of African Pentecostals as being politically lethargic, but they represent the efforts of Africans attempting to wrestle the pathogen of the sacred that is ravaging their communities. The latent optimism of this chapter should not make us lose sight of the fact that religion is often hostile to the development of possibilities relevant to economic development and peace in Africa. The promise of human flourishing that religions in Africa possess has not materialized for the masses. Rather Islam, Christianity (Pentecostalism), and African traditional religions are Grim Reapers of possibilities crucial for the socioeconomic emancipation of Africans.

This insight, among others, led me to put this chapter and the one before it under the rubric of "Ridiculous Hope." This is the kind of hope that makes you say to yourself, "I cannot believe it, but I must believe it." I sincerely believe that Africans can start something new amid their ongoing social automatism. Like Hannah Arendt, I believe that human beings always have the capacity to act, to start something new, even in the unlikeliest of circumstances. This is the fact of natality. She writes:

> The life span of man running toward death would inevitably carry everything human to ruin and destruction if it were not for the faculty of interrupting it and beginning something new, a faculty which is inherent in action like an ever-present reminder that men, though they must die, are not born in order to die but in order to begin.... The miracle that saves the world, the realm of human affairs, from its normal, "natural" ruin in ultimately the fact of natality, in which the faculty of action is ontologically rooted. It is, in other words, the birth of new men and the new beginning, the action they are capable of by virtue of being born.[34]

Chapter 7 offers brief concluding thoughts on the whole study. It reminds us of the crucial lessons of this book. There are three that bear witness in Africa—beautiful possibility, monstrous possibility, and ridiculous possibility—and these agree as one, the sacred. The sacred, properly defined, matters only to the extent that it is the site for the creation and destruction of possibilities for human flourishing. The sacred in this regard has not been fair to Africans. The set of possibilities that enhances human flourishing on the continent is at best very fragile. Monstrous possibilities that thwart the good are growing stronger by the day. Ridiculous possibility that could craft or stir up alternate worlds or configurations of potentialities amid current predicaments of life badly needs strength to thwart the working of the monstrous.

These six fragments (the six chapters of the book, excluding the conclusion) will collectively give us a portrait of the dynamic imagery of social existence in the African postcolony this study examines. These "fragments of social life" enable us to analyze and interpret the sacred, which is in a sense a perspective on existence in Africa, an interpretation of how human life and institutions stand in and stand out as participating in pure potentiality.

Existence and the Sacred

The sacred is existence at play with itself. It is the inherent dynamism or relationality of existence, the mode of free evolving potentiality imbued with an eros toward open future, the to-come. One perspective from which to understand the sacred as existence at play with itself, as the diffusive ebullience of fundamental relationality, is to situate it in the context of human cooperative act, complexity, and interdependence. One of the fundamental impulses that drive human creativity and interactions to approximate catholicity and to express an openness to and straining toward the inherent dynamism or relationality of existence is the energy of non-zero-sumness, according to Robert Wright in his book *NonZero*, where he applies his logic of non-zero-sumness to moral imagination.[35] Non-zero-sumness is the kind of transactional payoff that animates history and human sociality and moves human existence to increasing communality and the building and sustenance of communal structures. Where does non-zero-sumness come from? It is human cooperativeness (the process of mutuality and reciprocity) that produces and sustains non-zero-sumness. Play is a paradigmatic form of cooperation, and it is a suitable metaphor for or even a reflection of the dynamic creativity and participation that drive existents to *act*, to actualize themselves by exchanging resources with one another in the process of mutuality and reciprocity. And play in this way points beyond itself to the "sacred depths" of human culture.

Wright's specific theory of human cooperativeness is an invitation for philosophers to undertake a serious analysis of non-zero-sumness and the materialist ideas that undergird it. There are at least three relevant places to start such an analysis. First, the idea of cooperativeness conduces to an analysis of freedom. The ability to cooperate with others to achieve one's purpose not only supervenes freedom but also is constitutive of it. Cooperativeness is one dimension of human relationality, which is crucial for self-consciousness, self-identity, and self-actualization. Second, in the world of adaptive autopoietic complexity, a world without end, *redemption* may need to be redefined as something that occurs inside the systemic cooperative process and does not come from outside at the end of time. Perhaps justice in the processual here and now has become more important than the endtime giant settlement of account.[36] Finally, the language of the beauty, ridiculousness, and monstrosity of the sacred profoundly disposes us always to see our existence as flawed, incomplete, imperfect, vulnerable, perpetually defeasible, and clearly entailing an ontology (habitus) of natality.

Morality, Religion, and the Sacred

To the attentive reader, the preceding discussions have already indicated how my conceptualizations of the sacred and transcripts speak to the morality or social ethics of the African postcolony. This does not mean that the sacred has any intrinsic morality. Its ethics or morality is all about the judgment community members make about their engagement with one another in their quest for human flourishing. The sacred maintains, furnishes, and augments social life. In its character as creative destruction, as both constructive and destructive of possibilities, it is simultaneously an offering and a sacrifice. It is at once the *host* and host of potentialities that nourishes social life.[37] The sacred comprises the material and symbolic relationships of the what-is, the not-yet, and the ought of existence grasped as participating in pure potentiality. Transcripts are nothing more than the expressions of these relationships.

Simply put, the sacred is what the communities make of their existence. Human beings and their institutions enact the sacred into being, draw from the sacred, and perform the sacred. The actualization of potentialities and the performance of possibilities by human beings change the sacred, even as they live, move, and have their being within it. The sacred does not dictate social determinism. It does not simply transmit its codes in an ironclad fashion but works through cultural adaptation and messenger triggers. In this sense, the sacred is like DNA, a network of coded information, a set of possibilities whose capability to make visible the actual "presence"—for instance, of the physiognomy of the human being—depends on both biology and environment. Just as bodies make present and visible the invisible DNA codes, transcripts make present and visible the invisible sacred, the pure potentiality. As the human body carries, stores, and transmits human DNA, the transcripts carry, store, and transmit the sacred.[38] Transcripts do much more. Present transcripts excavate, signify, and comment on past transcripts and their contexts. Present transcripts are always traces of past transcripts. Past transcripts are specters of the present. The past, present, and (imagined) future constitute the raw materials for the cultural and social construction of the sacred. The sacred is thus both a dialogue (as endless renegotiation of the cultural knowledge, generation of creativity, and episteme—a way of knowing) and a dialogical imagination. It is not an entitative being. The nonentitative is the formless reality that takes the shape of (or appears as) transcripts, which are finite or determinate, either contributing to the common good or imposing suffering on (some) members of the community. A transcript is an ongoing fulfillment of potentiality insofar as it exists potentially.

Given the preceding discussions, we can conclude that the morality of the sacred in a given community is all about the ways its members define how the transcripts they are generating enhance or thwart human flourishing. Morality here governs through the structure of the community's experience in terms of what is adjudged as enhancing or thwarting the actualization of human potentiality, the creation and destruction of possibilities for human flourishing. The emphasis of the ethical order is on the discernment of the proper relations of community members to the sacred in its beauty and monstrosity. Driving one's relation to the beautiful or monstrous dimension of the sacred determines the moral gravity, moral quality, or the comprehensive normative import of one's experiences. Here the key issue is improper experiences of the sacred. Monstrosity is a result of the improper experience or misperception—the distorted, disorganized, or dastardly engagement or perception—of the sacred.

Communities in the past and present have used rituals (interactive ritual chains of a community's everyday life) to define, induce, and drive proper experience or perception of the sacred. There is a fundamental link between ritual and moral instructions. Ritual, in the words of Ronald Green, is the "effort to use complex and symbolic group activity for the purpose of expressing and vivifying fundamental moral conceptions" that underlie a community's vision of what it is and what it wants to become.[39] This conception of ritual raises a social-ethical question: How can ritual be used to provide or impose an experience of the fundamental distinction between the beauty and the monstrosity of the sacred to liberate the parts of the African postcolony trapped or imprisoned by the monstrous sacred? This is a matter of using rituals to vivify moral commitments to the beauty of the sacred or to nudge a withdrawal of the commitments to the monstrous sacred and move such "negative" commitments into the ridiculous sacred en route to the beautiful sacred. Green argues that the rituals that vivify a community's moral defenses work best when they express the moral conceptions that underlay religious beliefs—or, I would say, undergird a community's institutions. Is the notion of the sacred as fashioned in this chapter capable of illuminating how certain transcripts or traces of sacred become religion or religious?

While the notion of the sacred as I have formulated it here is not religious, transcripts could be religious. A transcript becomes religious (or a religious object) when a certain four features characterize it. Following David Little and Sumner B. Twiss, I will state that when it (a) is considered *specially distinctive* (set apart, declared holy) by a group of people; (b) acquires *special prominence* (is considered to have an "unusual significance in relation to what human beings consider important"); (c) is "*properly determinative* with respect to the beliefs, attitudes, and practices" of the group; and (d) comes to "bear in a momentous way on the ontological anxieties of human beings, namely the problems of inexplicability, suffering and death, and the puzzles of human conduct,"[40] all these characteristics could lead to the designation or naming of a cluster of possibilities as transcendent, immanent, or, more precisely, transimmanent forces of existence.

The relationship between the sacred and the religious is roughly akin to that between *primary rules* and secondary rules of law as propounded by H. L. A. Hart.[41] Primary rules are customs and rules of obligation of a community. Secondary rules are the rules of authoritative interpretation/recognition, adaptation, and adjudication/authoritative determination of violations.[42] Religion is a set of transcripts about other transcripts that are restated at a higher level to acquire or embody the aforementioned attributes. The manifestation or positing of these attributes is the step from which the sacred enters the religious world. "All institutions of society are composed of [transcripts], but some [transcripts] are reinstitutionalized at higher levels, so to speak."[43] In this way, some transcripts, when they are transformed, restated, or raised to the status of religion, play the additional function of religion and come to "constitute yet another institution—a superintending institution."[44] Finally, it is germane to state that religion often suffers the fallacy of misplaced sacredness.[45] This is the tendency to mistake the pure possibility of the infinite sacred for concrete actualization. Religious specialists are often too quick to reduce the novum, the new possibility, to the current actuality or the already actual.

Before we actually turn the page to chapter 1, there is an interlude that clarifies my positionality in relation to the materials that I study in this book and the combination of audiences that will best benefit from reading them. I will also address how my experiences and conversations with continental philosophy affect the arguments I make here. The goal is for me to (a) clarify how I approach the scholarship of continental philosophers and put them into conversation with the examples of African thought and practice, (b) offer a methodological note on how I theorize on the "African postcolony" in a way that shows which features of the postcolony I have abstracted for theoretical and empirical analysis and how I have deployed them as a hermeneutical tool for interrogating the nature of transcripts, and (c) describe the sources and methods of the transcripts that constitute this study.

INTERLUDE

Methodological Matters and a Theory of African Postcolony

Position and Positionality

In this study of transcripts, I deploy the methods of religious studies and cultural studies to interrogate the sacred, offer reflections on religious beliefs and practices, and engage in postcolonial criticism and philosophical evaluation (appreciative and critical) of the human condition in Africa. The panoply of methods enabled me to interpret the hydra-headed dimensions of the sacred and to generate profound insights that I have synthesized to help readers grasp the nature and logic of the transcripts of the sacred. The multidisciplinary character of this study invites one or two comments about its precise disciplinary home. Since the different domains of religious studies; cultural studies; postcolonial criticism; nondogmatic, nonconfessional theological theorization; philosophy; and African studies are disciplinary stakeholders in this study, it would be wrong for me to reductively declare that the book is relevant to only one of these fields. As difficult as it is, my goal in this book is to develop a common (new) discourse for these stakeholders in the study of the sacred in the African postcolony—to craft a way of studying the sacred that bridges the regnant discourses in these multiple fields and breach the silos that lock many scholars into the incommensurable world of disciplinary discourse. This is why I reject the notion of the sacred as a transcendent other. Against the long run of religious interpretations and theological reflections, I offer an original and provocative conception of the sacred. My notion of the sacred is not theologically loaded, and, hence, it is amenable to and inclusive of the social-scientific, empirically driven phenomenological descriptions and historically reconstructionist interpretations of the sacred. The redefinition of the sacred I offer in this study is geared to enable scholars to develop a common discourse to understand the state of contemporary religion, politics, and social conditions in the Nigerian (African) postcolony. The point is to enable students and scholars to better understand how the contemporary formations of the sacred affect human flourishing and how they might be transformed.

More precisely, the book is directed to students and scholars who study the sacred and the political. What do I mean by *the political* here? The political is the common coexistence where being and *being-with* (being togetherness) are always at stake. Politics is ultimately about living well in the commons. The political is "the site where being in common is at stake" and it is about "having access to what is proper to existence, and therefore, of course, to the proper of one's own existence."[1] Thus, all political actions (words and deeds) are really about our being in common, and what is always at stake in this *in-between* where we are *ex-posed* to one another is the character of the possibilities of life. Always and above all, this boils down to the actualization of potentialities of both individuals and community. And the moral vision that undergirds it is simply this: to live best in accordance with the best of ourselves, as Aristotle once said.

This book's diverse, multidisciplinary approach and intricately textured study is relevant to all scholars and students who are interested in how an understanding of the sacred that squarely situates it in the immanent realm and grounds it in human creative activities helps us to better interpret human condition in the twenty-first century. This study, because of the richness of its methods, enables us to better respond to the question of how the sacred works in individuals, groups, and communities to promote or hinder human flourishing. The book responds to this question with care and breadth of perspective. One of the strengths of this book is that it does not analyze the sacred in reductive terms, not relating it only to the divine or analyzing it only in religious terms; rather, it broadens our understanding of the sacred to encompass all that is possible and impossible—im/possibility—in human existence.

Having said this, I am mindful of the complexity and diversity of the issues my redefinition (reformulation) of the sacred encompasses. Despite my efforts to be thorough and accurate in my descriptions, interpretations, and theorizations, I see different ways that my analyses and coverage could be challenged or questioned. For instance, in chapter 3, my description and analysis of the Pentecostal incredible is limited to Nigeria and does not engage with the operation of the incredible in other African Pentecostal contexts. Not wanting to defend myself, I venture to say that most of the weaknesses that I or other scholars can identify are largely due to the nature of this book as a transdisciplinary inquiry and to the vastness of Africa. I have risked these weaknesses for the sake of what I believe is the intrinsic value of my reformulation of the notion of the sacred and the value of transdisciplinary inquiry. The risk is worth taking for the hope of generating future communities of scholars capable of using the theory of the transcripts of the sacred in the study of human conditions in Africa. At the end, readers are the best judges to evaluate the quality of this book and decide if the risk was worth taking.[2]

It is relevant to briefly inform the reader of my positionality and its effect on my reading of the African situation. My academic location in the university is in the School of Theology, and I am a Nigerian Pentecostal Christian. A good part of my research for more than a decade has been devoted to studying and interpreting Nigerian, African, and global Pentecostalisms and carefully laying the foundations for Pentecostal philosophy. This inclination toward Pentecostalism, grounded in my years of study, is obvious in this book. It is, however, my hope that the theoretical insights scholars gain from the focus on Pentecostalism, qua Nigerian Pentecostalism, would be helpful to the study of religions in other faith communities.

Let me also clarify my use of the name Africa in the preceding and subsequent pages of the book. It is not a claim on my part that I cover all or a majority of African countries in the study. Basically, Nigeria is a stand-in for the sub-Saharan Africa, though in selected places in the book I draw examples and stories from other African countries. It is my opinion that the Nigerian story provides an important dimension of or lens into the sacred in Africa. I do not have the competence, time, or space to do what I have done for Nigeria for all African countries. At this juncture in the development of the theory of the sacred and transcripts of the sacred, I need to concentrate on my best geographical area and field of competence to flesh out and defend my arguments. This concentration demands that even in Nigeria, I limit analyses to Christianity, Pentecostal Christianity in particular. I do not tell the stories of Muslims and believers in African traditional religions (ATR). This is not to say that I do not strategically deploy beliefs and practices of Muslims and ATR followers to enhance the story I tell about the transcripts of the sacred on the continent. All I have done is in every way an attempt to provide a theoretical framework articulating how the sacred occurs and how it plays out in the political and human flourishing.

A Theorization of African Postcolony as a Constellation of Desires in the Sacred

Sacred is the universe of possibilities. It gives the postcolony the power to live, to move, and to be what it is. It is in the complex space of possibilities that the postcolony's politics, economics, culture, religion, and so on find their origins and sustenance. And the interactions of these spheres of life recreate and sustain the sacred, which is always open to emergent complexity in its growth or evolution. The beautiful, the monstrous, and the ridiculous as signatures of the activity of the sacred can be discerned using the objective (observable) behaviors and contingencies of everyday life in these spheres of social existence in the postcolony. Spheres are ways of gathering (categorizing) information about the structures and functions of the sacred.

This section of the interlude is my attempt to theorize the African postcolony so we can better comprehend its imbrication with the sacred. For the limited purposes of this study, I theorize the African postcolony as a site of interplay of three desires as Africans seek ways of improving their levels of human flourishing. These three desires cut across contextual difference in different African social milieus. First, there is the desire for knowledge, the desire to understand the physical existence or to produce knowledge through the technology of invisible, spiritual forces, to pierce the phenomenal veil over reality and to access the noumenal realm for the knowledge that can enhance human flourishing. Spiritualized epistemology gives Africans an alternative imagination to constitute or reconstitute reality, to grasp truth, and to self-govern.[3] There is, indeed, a penchant for spiritual knowledge, and it appears as the predominant mode of cognition in the culture. Many Africans maintain that to amply access the multitude of possibilities in human existence one must seek spiritual insight.

While the first desire is primarily epistemological, the second is about power, and the two are clearly intertwined. The possession and deployment of power is the key to extracting and allocating resources from the *commons* that are needed to live a full human life. Politics is a process of power exchange, akin to warfare with clear, concrete definitions of friends and enemies. The political is an agonistic struggle for power between people, who are powers of being. Politics is marked by agonistic strivings and tensions for entitative and nonentitative powers. The processes and sites for the struggles of the political are presumed to be pervaded by *spiritual presences*. The spiritual is the inner dynamics of politics in all spheres of society and public life.[4] For Africans, politics is a mode of power of being.

I need to highlight three features of power as they are relevant to my theorization of the African postcolony. First, the ultimate reason for acquiring spiritual power is to dislodge any power of being hindering the person's flourishing and to enhance the person's well-being.

Second, at the political level—that is, with respect to how leaders relate to the people—there is always a tension between distance and proximity.

This is to say that African leaders simultaneously want to increase and decrease the distance between themselves and the poor, those whom they have already ground to dust.[5] The key ambition of leaders is to create the maximum distance between them and all those below their rung on the societal ladder. But we would be mistaken to believe that the logic of the leaders only works by distancing. The reality is more sinister: there is always a distancing and domesticating of power in Africa. The big man who portrays himself as a humble lamb in front of a bigger person is at the same time very authoritarian, the lion that terrorizes his people into displaying absolute obedience, the one who traumatizes his people to extract resources for his luxurious lifestyle. African leaders simultaneously create and erase distance between them and the people. The double act is a necessary accompaniment of power and privilege in Africa. The leader wants to remain aloof from the people, but he also wants to project the image of omnipresence, omniscience, and omnipotence. The separated self is distanced, but in its omnipresent capillaries of exploitation and corruption, it is also near. There is no notion of the separateness without a sense of contiguity.

More importantly, the distancing of power between the leader and the poor is erased or reduced because of the necessity of having tactile perception of the ruled, governed, or oppressed if power is to be effectively maintained. For the leaders, there is always a tactile perception of the oppressed through beating, direct violence on the body, and especially fondling, raping, and coupling with their bodies.

The double act of distancing and domesticity is the play and display of omnipotent and omnipresent powers, all deemed to be independent of human (state) control. Achille Mbembe argues that an adequate understanding of how power works in Africa must pay attention to this double act, which forms part of the aesthetics and stylistics of power. "This double act of distancing and domesticating is not necessarily the expression of fundamental conflict between worlds of meaning that are in principle antagonistic."[6] The emphasis of the African leader, the signal of the all-powerful leader, often, if not always, involves inscribing opposites, realism, and its simulacrum within the same *episteme*.

Third, there are dual understandings of power in everyday African social existence. There is the notion of power as the imposition of one's will on others in a social relationship to get what one wants or to at least alter others' behavior to one's advantage in spite of their resistance.[7] Many of the actions of African leaders are informed by this notion of power—that is, power as "violence" or "domination." This understanding of power is particularly helpful when they are struggling to win elections, which are akin to warfare. Elections, as strategic competitions for governmental power, carry high stakes because winners get access to state power that allows them to loot public treasuries. This is not the only concept of power in the postcolony. There is also power that comes from cooperative action, from working in agreement with others. This is akin to what Hannah Arendt once taught about power: "Power corresponds to the human ability not just to act but to act in concert."[8] Many traditional communities in the African postcolony still rely on this notion of power to generate common will to execute projects.

Somewhere between these two notions of power, there is that of power as maintenance of social relationships. This is the idea that leaders have no intrinsic powers of their own and that withdrawal of followership or obedience deprives a leader of his or her power and authority to act on human beings or control human affairs.[9] The core meaning is that leaders in traditional African communities build up their power to benefit their followers or constituents, and if such leaders were to forget themselves, to become too unresponsive to the citizens, their followers would withdraw support and render them powerless. This way of thinking is not at all surprising once one grasps the importance of relations as constitutive of both society and personhood in African communities. Holding and keeping political power is not just about demanding obedience, praise and exaltation, appropriate responses to leadership, or the execution of projects but about dynamically maintaining deep, thick relations and social bonds with the people. All forms of power, be they political or spiritual, are always predicated on the strength of social bonds among persons, and the fracture or rupture of the bond or the displacement of harmony in the bond means erosion of power and authority.

At the beginning of this section of the interlude, I stated that my theorization of the postcolony will focus on three desires: epistemology, power, and recognition. We have so far dealt with the first two. We now turn to the third desire. I will draw my example from African Pentecostals. What I am calling *recognition* here pertains to their internal subjective identity. African Pentecostals hold within themselves two identities: a new internal-subjective identity of noble, divinely chosen children of God and the old external-objective identity of *part of no part*.[10]

The dual identity of African Pentecostals refers to them as both privileged persons or masters and also "degraded" human beings, a servant class. All this brings to mind Nietzsche's theory of how different classes (slaves and masters) value life differently, generating different forms of morality in the same society.[11] According to Nietzsche, the religion of the nobles is that of gratitude, the affirmation of life, and satisfaction before the gods, whereas the essence of the religion of the rabble is fear (and hope). One group feels satisfied with life, nature, and society as given and enjoys them; the other is resentful of the same.

The problem with African Pentecostalism is that these two feelings coexist in the same persons or largely in the same group of believers. Two agencies are joined in one human body. It is no surprise that preachers like Bishop David Oyedepo of Winners' Chapel, Nigeria, boldly affirm life in their prosperity gospel even as they argue that God has called them to deliver Black Africans from slave/colonial mentality.[12] In fact, they often boost their prosperity gospel by exploiting the fears and hopes of Black Africans who, as citizens of economically backward countries, are longing for financial uplift. The aristocratic class of African Pentecostals—or those African Pentecostals who have adopted the noble mode of evaluation of life—in their words and deeds let the rest of their communities know that the values of good and bad are deemed to arise from reference to themselves.

Our theorization of the postcolony will be incomplete if we ignore what animates the connections between these three dimensions of epistemology, power, and recognition. Any serious scholarly analysis of a religio-cultural situation should attempt to bring to awareness the underlying values and principles that animate the situation, reveal its inner conflict, and likely lead it to the beautiful or to the monstrous that lies within the symbols of its community's tradition. The animating power for the social practices of epistemology, power, and recognition in the postcolony is *fantasy*. Here I want to expose the "fantasy-construction which serves as support for the [postcolonial] 'reality' itself."[13] Nigerians are not the so-called dupes of ideology; they are complicit in the construction of the postcolonial reality or the ideological fantasy that sustains it. Both leaders and citizens are constitutive of the postcolonial reality: the meaning individuals attribute to it, their drives, their fantasy that all things are possible in Nigeria, their enjoyments, and their energies are all embedded in the cultural processes, the socio-symbolic universe of meaning making in the postcolony. Many Nigerians contribute to the frustratingly inescapable fantasy that interpellates them. Ideology is motivated in each person from within, via desires that are complicit with the postcolonial status quo. Nigerians use desire-driven fantasy to avoid staring into the void, abyss, and chaos that make up Nigeria. This Nigeria that many Nigerians fail to look at or recognize is not some naked reality out there but rather the fantasy that structures each of their realities. In fact, Nigeria is not separate from such fantasy. As Slavoj Žižek puts it, "Fantasy constitutes our desires, provides its coordinates; that is, it literally 'teaches us how to desire.'"[14]

So, in analyzing or conveying the experiences, dialogues, practices, and behaviors of the subjects in the postcolony, I do not resort to any view that *they know not what they do*. Their illusion or their acceptance of the hegemonic ideology is never portrayed as a matter of false knowledge but is always presented as rooted in the fantasies and ideological dreams they have constructed for themselves and then tried to live in. Žižek captures this point well when he states,

> If our concept of ideology remains the classic one in which the illusion is located in knowledge, then today's society must appear post-ideological: the prevailing ideology is that of cynicism; people no longer believe in ideological truth [no longer believe in the truth of their nation-state]; they do not take ideological proposition seriously. The fundamental level of ideology, however, is not that of an illusion masking the real state of things but that of an (unconscious) fantasy structuring our social reality. And at this level, we are of course far from being a post-ideological society. . . . [Ideology is the belief] which is radically exterior, embedded in the practical, effective procedure of people.[15]

My point is that the subjectivity in the African postcolony is structured by fantasy that circulates around the three desires of spiritualist epistemology, unbridled power, and need for recognition. In the postcolony the subjects could easily be equated with their own fantasies; they become an object of fantasy. The circulation of fantasy around any of these three desires has proved dangerous for Africans. I do not have the time and space here to elaborate on the character of each of these circulations, but it will suffice to briefly focus on one of them, that of the imbrication of power and fantasy. There is a deadly mixture of power and fantasy afoot in Africa. African leaders act with divine impunity calculated to cow the masses; they live flourishing lives with conspicuous consumption that give the impression that they have the divine right to stay above the economic mess they have created, while the people have the devilish privilege to wallow in the excrement of poverty. What the political leaders do is tantamount to defecating on the faces of the people. In fact, the state in Africa deploys the excremental in the theatrics and display of political power. On these points, Achille

Mbembe states it well when he writes, "Defecation, copulation, pomp, and extravagance are classical ingredients in the production of power, and there is nothing specifically African about this; the obsession with orifices results from the fact that, in the postcolony, the *commandement* is constantly engaged in projecting an image of itself and of the world—a fantasy it presents its subjects as a truth beyond dispute, a truth to be instilled into them so that they acquire a habit of discipline and obedience."[16]

Any attempt to understand the religious-cultural-political character of African postcolony must reckon with the dynamic constellation of deformed epistemology, violent power, recognition (split identity), and the role of fantasy in both animating and binding these desires or social practices together. What I have done in this book is lift up fragments or dimensions of social life in the African postcolony that cast light on the working of these practices. For instance, in chapter 3, "The Pentecostal Incredible," I address the issue of deformed epistemology in the Nigerian postcolony. In chapter 4, I deal with the subject matter of power as violence in the postcolony. The issue of recognition, which I have analyzed as split identity, comes up in chapter 5. The split identity or consciousness generates a tension, which in a certain sense mediates Pentecostals' interactions with the political system.[17] This tension—as a reflection of the experiences of life as Black and as Christian in one totality—presents another viable angle to enter the study of subjectivity in the postcolony. Pentecostals, in their external objective identity as African Blacks, are part of humanity marked by an excess weight of social suffering, part of the despised and marginalized in global politics, *the part of no part* in world affairs. As Blacks, they really do not have a voice, no part in the act of governing the global *commons*. As Christians—born-again, saved, and sanctified—they consider themselves chosen and noble. African Pentecostals—especially the Nigerians among them—are claiming that they have been specially chosen by God to lead the *final* evangelization of the world before the second coming of Jesus Christ and to draw the Black race into global economic and technological supremacy. Their understanding of chosenness is not limited to the view that God has cut a special deal with them to establish God's kingdom in the foreseeable future but also encompasses the idea that he has opened the structure of hope and expectation of the future to the Black race as a whole.[18]

It is germane at this junction to explain the relationship between the theory of the sacred as defined here and the concept of culture as used by anthropologists, especially Clifford Geertz in his argument "Religion as a

Cultural System," which is about the relationship between religion and culture.[19] First, as I noted above, the sacred is not a religion; religion constitutes only a certain constellation of transcripts of the sacred. Second, the sacred is not a culture. It is the set of possibilities that a culture creates, sustains, or destroys. The sacred is less than culture, and yet it is the fount of culture since culture is beholden to the sacred as the universal set of possibilities and human creativity. Third, the sacred as defined here is not a force that "tunes human actions to an envisaged cosmic order and projects images of cosmic order onto the plane of human experiences."[20] But this is what religion does according to Geertz. I have argued earlier that religion, as a configuration of possibilities, is a subset of the sacred. My notion of the sacred or the transcript of the sacred is a theorization of how a society or culture actualizes its potentialities for human flourishing. My notion of the sacred is not a conception of the general order of existence and does not affirm any "transcendent truths," as Geertz conceives religion.[21] The sacred as defined here is not a mana-like power.[22] The sacred is neither a transcendent being nor an impersonal ultimate reality at the core of existence. It is a creation of human sociality, human interactions, and the so-called social or collective brain. Furthermore, whereas religion offers *interpretability* according to Geertz, my notion of the sacred does not necessarily do that.[23] The function of interpretability is executed by religion as a specific constellation of possibilities and impossibilities within the sacred in given place. (In my conception, religion is subset of the sacred. Besides, sacred as defined here is not primarily about explanation, prediction, and control (EPC). Religion, through its instrumentality of EPC, endeavors to explain, predict, and control possibilities, however respectable, fantasmatic, consistent, or rational the effort is.

The reader who is engaging with my new conception of the sacred and only reading it through the inherited notion of the sacred might have a problem fully grasping the arguments in this book. Even if the reader reads it as a new concept but ends up transferring the form and content of his or her understanding of God (gods, spiritual beings), religion, transcendence, or culture to it, he or she might still not comprehend it in all its nuances. My notion of the sacred is not one of these familiar terms. It is a way to organize our thinking about possibilities of human existence. Broadly, the new concept of the sacred affirms that possibilities are part of human life, even if human life is in some sense more or greater than the sum of the possibilities. Possibility is not just one determinate element among the elements of life; rather, it is the element-itself that gives existence to all elements but is not itself one of those elements. This element is nothing but the human dynamic creative power. It is what gives rise to and grounds the possibilities of human sociality. In some sense of the operations of an adaptive network relationality, human beings are grasped by the power of the element-itself and driven beyond themselves into an ecstatic union with the non-yet of the accomplishment, excellence, or actualization of their potentialities.[24] This power to go beyond what is extant into an ecstatic union is the sacred—but it is not supra/supernaturalistic. The word *sacred* is a figure for this ecstatic power, the sheer depth and awe-inspiring character of possibilities and by extension the human dynamic creative power. I use the word *sacred* to capture the argument that human creativity is irreducible to the sum of their finite particular creations or creative acts. And at the end, human creativity or the possibilities and impossibilities arising from their creative acts are an incomprehensible mystery at any present moment. With a retroactive gaze, we can always explain them. This explanation itself is a human creative act and hence part of the sacred. In sum, the sacred has three parts (this is different from its axiological components of the beautiful, the monstrous, and the ridiculous). The parts of the sacred (as the dynamic creativity of human beings, not an immutable absolute substance) are (a) source—human beings; (b) the dynamic act of creation—acting; and (c) products—transcripts, the becoming of human beings as an outcome of their creative acts. The sacred becomes actual in its products, "accidents," "instantiations."[25] These three feed into one another in a perpetual loop, enriching (beautiful), destroying (monstrous), and knife-edge equilibrium (ridiculous). Being, acting, and becoming are together because they are done or created together. The name *sacred* is the phenomenological context of their mutual relevance, the human act of creativity. The transsubjective ground of the togetherness of the source, act, and becoming of human creativity is the sacred. Basically, I am using the name *sacred* for the dynamic creative human act. Collectively, human beings are the source, act, and end of their creative process.

Being, acting, and becoming are one. Human beings act (create) and become, meaning they create products that include themselves (that is, remake themselves) and their self-interpretation, artifacts, institutions, ideas, and so on. All these harbor im/possibilities for being and becoming. When being acts and creates products that promote human flourishing and are good for others, then we say the sacred is beautiful. But when the acting (activity of mind and body) goes in the opposite direction, we say it is monstrous.

When acting is at the saddle point between beauty and monstrosity, we say it is ridiculous.

To bring this section to a close, let me state that to study the sacred as a universe of possibilities in the African postcolony is to describe and explain how Africans are actualizing their potentialities across various spheres of life that are conditioned by their constellation of epistemology, power, and recognition, a constellation structured by fantasy. This is the gentle and persistent explanatory model that runs throughout this book. The architecture and actualization of potentiality in the postcolony grounds its sacred and thus explains and normalizes the particular ways of organizing possibilities for human life.

Transcripts: Sources and Methods

In this study I deploy many methods, including field observation, interviews, textual analysis, and philosophical reflections. I also use historical analysis. History helps me to engage the ethical and political, not as a philosopher positing a set of abstract principles, but as a historian embedding persons' or institutions' behaviors, actions, or utterances in their unique particularities and histories. History is pressed into very specific services to draw out shapes of a political theory that speaks to the Nigerian situation. This book "is neither a history of ideas nor an exercise in sociological history, but it uses history to propose a style of critical reflection on" the Nigerian political society.[26]

The theory of the sacred—undergirded by, filtered through, and sourced by pluriversal methods—helps me to interpret human conditions in the African postcolony. Social practices (as a constellation of ideas, doctrines, telos, affectivity, rituals, and concrete actions) constitute the "texts," the transcripts that I analyze. Possibility/impossibility is an intrinsic aspect of social practice, and social practice provides the means by which its stirrings are brought to observable, concrete (bodily) completion. A transcript is occasioned by, transpires as, and lies amid the site of the social. It is constituted within practice. To theorize the transcript this way is to locate it as rooted in, emerging from, cohering to, and constituted by what Theodore Schatzki terms a "constantly evolving nexus of arranged things and organized activities."[27]

Practices or transcripts are studied, investigated, or interrogated so one can understand how Africans actualize their potentialities, generating, deploying, and organizing the possibilities of life. As I have already argued above, the "texts" that are used to tease out the transcripts are organized to tell the story of how the dynamic constellation of certain desires for epistemology, power, and recognition undergird, create, and are in turn affected by the sacred. The book develops one principal concept, the sacred. It then studies the way in which the logic of the sacred is played out in different contexts in the postcolony, providing concrete examples of how possibilities and impossibilities interplay to condition various institutions of religion and politics.

The methods are different and complicated, as the protean subject matter of the African postcolony demands. The axiological structure and flows of the postcolony are multidimensional and as such demand any analysis to move back and forth between empirical, practical levels and theoretical considerations. Methodological parsimony would make it attractive to stick with only empirical analysis or philosophical theorization to furnish a simplistic, clear-cut path to knowledge about the postcolony. But this is not in agreement with the variegated and complex landscape of the postcolony, which is energetic, "chaotic, fecund, and emergently ordered."[28] The landscape of axiological possibilities surpasses what can be grasped once and for all. This book, which studies the valuational dimensions of the postcolony's life habitat, requires clarity of philosophical concepts to track its depth and flows. On one hand, we never simply encounter the axiological possibilities of the postcolony—the beautiful, the monstrous, and the ridiculous—standing apart from our interpretations. On the other, since the values of the beautiful, the monstrous, and the ridiculous are not rooted in some transcendental realm but in concrete, historical sites of human existence—registering and creating values—the study has to engage the empirical lifeworlds of Africans. Through that engagement, we can see how they are generating and nurturing the beautiful, birthing and deploying the monstrous, and inventing and staging the ridiculous to actualize their potentialities.[29]

Rightly or wrongly, I have found a lot of good resources in continental philosophy in my endeavors to explore the theoretical considerations and to inform my understanding of the empirical lifeworlds, to explore the intersection between the theoretical and the empirical, which is at once epistemological, political, religious, and theological at its deepest level. Continental philosophy also equips my scholarship to affirm and unsettle studies of the sacred by bringing them into conversation with the African data and experiences as I understand them.[30] Continental philosophy provides me with the method and approach to produce the kind of phenomenological analyses of the sacred or religion that are relevant to the arguments of this book. Using continental philosophic interlocutors for my analysis has enabled me not only to probe religion and politics deeper but also to extend the study of the sacred or the transcripts of the sacred in Africa into philosophy.

I have attempted to express the structural dimensions of the philosophical thought of ATR or African Christianity by making use of critical theory and political philosophy as vehicles for the transmission of some of the stabilities and instabilities of African cultural-religious consciousness. In doing this (that is, in expressing the deep structures of African spirituality in continental philosophical language), I have been careful not to collapse the distinctions between the philosophy of ATR (and African Christianity) and the critical tradition of continental philosophy/political theory. I do this in at least three ways. First, continental philosophy is a methodological tool and not the determinant of the regnant issues of African religions in my studies. It is not deployed to disparage African religions or to say their leading interests and concerns are lackluster. I *emically* deploy continental philosophy to interrogate, conceptualize, clarify, and rigorously analyze the internal regnant issues, elements, themes, concerns, and practices and to lift up their assumptions to intellectual scrutiny. Second, the knot that holds the texture of my philosophic discourses of the sacred in Africa is the African worldview that serves as their hermeneutical root note. Though the language and categories of continental philosophy are deployed to organize the data for analysis, it is the African sensibility that provides the tonic key to properly discern the ontological, epistemological, ethical, imaginative, and theological implications and senses of Pentecostal practices.[31]

Continental thought has not merely served as "receptors and conveyors of African religious and moral meanings" but also worked as an *animus* for the philosophical expression of African spirituality and helped me to penetrate the internal life (values) of African philosophical practice or way of being.[32] Consciously or unconsciously, writing under the pressures of African religious/philosophical thought and the current political situation, I might have subjected some of the taken-for-granted elements in continental thought to fresh questioning. But is it not arguable that I have creatively rearticulated and reframed traditional African religious thought, plundering its ideas and notions in the service of social ethics, political theory, or religious philosophy to generate novel insights, concepts, and assemblages in continental thought? Hopefully, all these may one day result in a slight change in the orientations of the critical theory and philosophy of African traditional religions.

Finally, I realize that this book is very multidisciplinary, and I cannot possibly address all its methodological questions at once. As is usual with this kind of study, there will still be some readers who insist that the methodological issues I have addressed are not adequate to sufficiently direct future inquiries into the intersection of the sacred and the postcolony. Let me respond as my Boston University colleague Wesley Wildman once put it: "All of these methodological issues warrant discussion at much greater length and depth than is possible here. But that is not the purpose of this book. Methodological self-awareness and reflection is, in this context, quite secondary to the material findings of inquiry."[33] The book itself demonstrates the feasibility of the methodological approach of this inquiry.

1

THE SACRED AS IM/POSSIBILITY

Introduction

Postcolonial Africa is burdened by the sacred. It is the burden of this chapter to define and describe the nature of the sacred. The burden Africa bears is imposed by two problems: the quantity of the sacred and the sacred's quality, so to speak, its ordering. The burden exists because Africans are not producing enough of sacred's quantity and quality to meet their needs and wants. The sacred is not only rooted in human agency but also fundamentally contingent. The sacred, before it becomes a being, divine power, or religion, is the supreme capacity of human beings to create and actualize potentialities; phenomenologically, it is identical to human freedom, the actions to initiate something new amid ongoing social processes, the right, the justice of existence itself.[1] In what follows, I develop this conception of the sacred by drawing from the experiences, philosophies, and theologies of Kalabari (Niger Delta, Nigeria) and African Pentecostals.

The Sacred as Sets of Possibilities

The sacred is near all human beings at all times. We encounter its omnipresence in our everyday possibilities, and we are always trying to shape it even as it shapes us. Actually, the sacred emerges from how we understand, relate to, treat, and divine im/possibilities of our everyday life. In every society there are three sets of possibilities: (a) one that is open to all individuals; (b) another that is available to only a few and from which the rest of society is excluded; and (c) the universe of possibilities that are yet to be fulfilled or not yet available to all persons and institutions. The last (c) is actually the *horizon of unfulfilled possibilities*.

And there is the law (as acts of legislature, *nomos* and *ethos*, symbolic structures that regulate practices and representations, or specific regimes of interpretations of the [oral or written] scripture/faith, and so on). The law acts to bring the range of possibilities to manageable proportion and distributes them into the three sets. There are included and excluded possibilities in every existing state of affairs. It is the law that defines the boundaries of these three sets, what is possible and what is impossible. The law is the power that regulates possibilities and access to them. It is the law that tells members of a community what works within a given framework of relations.

There is also grace or its equivalent in every society. Grace has the power of the exception (to use Carl Schmitt's language), which can act to stop, suspend, open, or reopen the enjoyment of certain possibilities. Sometimes, grace can transcend laws or boundaries from within them, such that potentialities are actualized not in spite of the restrictions of the law but through them. This is like a player mastering the rules of a game and then initiating new skills to overcome obstacles. Every invention, every innovation, every revolution, and every scientific breakthrough has always been about extending the boundaries of the possible, making what was once impossible become possible.

How does this knowledge of the three sets of possibilities lead to a conceptualization of the sacred? The person-to-person encounters of our daily lives constitute a ground for the "holy" to emerge. These encounters are often part of social practices, overlapping social practices, and generative of social practices. While a particular social practice fulfills a finite set of possibilities, the originative space of the encounter of person to person that engenders the social practice is a horizon of unfulfilled possibilities. The excluded or the unfulfilled is a primordial soup out of which can crawl the religious, the sacred. This originative site is the sphere that social practices try to exclude from view or reckoning. What is excluded and unfulfilled is believed to transcend the passage of time, and this makes it sacred. What is sacred in any society is believed to always have a purchase on eternity. As sociologist Richard Fenn has recently argued, the sacred is the embodiment of unfulfilled possibilities: "Because the sacred embodies only *unfulfilled* possibilities, it always points beyond itself to the full range of possibilities for either salvation or destruction. This set of all possibilities, both actual and hypothetical, I call the Sacred, and it is to the sociology of religion what dark matter is to astrophysicists, or 'the god above the god of theism' is to theologians."[2]

This realm of unfulfilled possibilities haunts the realm of realized possibilities and pushes it toward the not-yet. In every human-to-human encounter that both limits and enhances the power of being in each self, something develops that lies beyond such an encounter. No matter how innovative a social practice or law is, it always defines the limits of aspirations and institutionalizes the set of possibilities of human interaction that the system of society is willing to allow at a given moment or deems practicable. Yet the law or social practice is haunted by the unfulfilled possibilities. Over time, this brooding sense of the haunted will give rise to some kind of resistance; something brings the awareness of such unfulfilled possibilities into popular consciousness for a more abundant life.

Many in traditional African cultures have long taken for granted the idea that the holy emerges from social practice. Among the Kalabari of the Niger Delta in Nigeria, the holy or a god's power is an emergent phenomenon of human worship; like social systems, it realizes itself through practices. The holy emerges and is ensconced in the social practice of worship. The gods arise from such practice insofar as their power of being is in it. The gods are conceived as a source of tremendous power. But the power that the gods possess is believed to depend on the social practice of human worship. Their powers derive from human worship, and therefore humans can reduce or completely efface the power of any god by withdrawing worship.[3]

Most believe that spirits and gods do not have intrinsic powers of their own and that the withdrawal of worship from or worshipful dependence on a god deprives it of power and authority to act on humans or control human activities. Kalabari insist that a god that is not worshipped loses its power. So if a god becomes too furious or demanding, they will tell it from which tree it was carved (*"agu nsi owi baka kuma en ke o kara sin en dugo o piriba"*).[4] This means that a community can unanimously annul the power of a god by refusing to worship it.[5] Robin Horton interprets the aphorism this way:

> Literally, if a spirit's demands become too burdensome, the whole congregation can join together to destroy its cult objects, and by this unanimous act of rejection render it powerless to trouble them further. . . . Broadly, then, the more people lavish offerings, invocations, and festivals upon any spirit, the more powerful it becomes both to reward and punish them. And conversely, the less they attend to it the less powerful it becomes—up to the point at which unanimous rejection results in the complete loss of power. Generally, of course, a single man cannot reject a spirit at will; for while he is only one among a congregation of many, it will have the power to punish him.[6]

This way of thinking is not at all surprising once one grasps the importance of relations as constitutive of both society and personhood in Kalabari communities. Worship is not just reverence, obeisance, praise and exaltation, or appropriate response to a deity but the dynamic maintenance of deep, thick relations, a social bond with a deity. All forms of power, be they political or spiritual, are always predicated on the strength of social bonds among persons, and the fracture or rupture of the bond or the displacement of harmony in the bond means erosion of power and authority.

In the Western tradition, Emile Durkheim long ago pointed out to us that individuals generate some sort of divinity when they come together. In the collective occasion, they discover their connectedness with one another, deem themselves transformed and transfigured, and discern a set of possibilities that lie beyond the community. The sacred emerges in this setting of corporate identity and "collective effervescence" and claims for itself the capacity to transcend the ravages and passage of time. The *numen* is generated when the individual sense of identity is merged with that of the group or collective. Under these conditions, the sense of possibilities soars to new heights, repressed elements jostle to float to the surface, and the numen emerges. The crowd or the collective comes to embody—however temporally—the impulse of the numen. To experience the numen "is to find oneself in the grip of a passion or presence that seems to come from beyond oneself."[7] But often this feeling of being affected by a presence that seems physically absent or distant is also the experience of ecstasy, "of being beside oneself, or being captivated by the presence of another soul who seems to take precedence over one's own."[8]

To experience the primitive (numen), one may feel that it is God, a distant and invisible being, who is present and at work beneath the forms of everyday life. Alternatively, one may settle for the unseen but palpable presences of angels and saints.[9]

The Structure of the Sacred

In Kalabari (Niger Delta, Nigeria) worldview and philosophy, the notion of the sacred as a set of possibilities is encapsulated in one of the words for God, *So*. The word *So* refers to both destiny or directing destiny and the sum of possibilities available to the people. In a sense, the two meanings of the word are not different. *Destiny* in Kalabari understanding refers to the set of life possibilities allotted to a person before his or her own birth.

So in the sense of destiny refers to the dialectical outworking of the *telos* of individuals, communities, and the world. It is an unfolding world process that is not confined to follow a fixed groove. The shaping of destiny is done by or rather understood via the possibilities that *So* makes available to each person, group, or institution. (*So* when applied to individuals is called *so*, to households is *wariteme-so*, and to communities is *amateme-so*. We will refer to this application of the notion to particulars—the matter of destiny—as lowercase *so*.) The directing concept of *So* is not just about working out of preassigned telos. The concept of *So* directs the people to note their limitations, the set of possibilities opened to them or excluding them, liberatory potentials for the transformation of selves and structures of society, and the sum total of possibilities conceivable given their level of social, technological, and economic development. Let us refer to *So* as applied to the sum of possibilities as uppercase *So*. The uppercase *So* is the set of possibilities excluding individuals, cultural institutions, and social structures. More precisely, it is the universe of possibilities from which some are defined as available to persons and institutions and others either remain unfulfilled or simply exclude them at any given time.

When lowercase *so* and uppercase *So* are taken together, we get the sense that *So* is the ultimate source of possibilities and the principle of limitation or selection. This combination of infinity and limit defines the structure of the sacred as lived experience in Kalabari worldview, shedding important light on our idea of the three sets of possibilities that mark the sacred.[10]

I would like to note that the uppercase *So* and lowercase *so* are not opposites in Kalabari. Thus what is not part of uppercase *So* is not confined to extinction. The uppercase *So* is the ground of lowercase *so*. The lowercase *so* is only a set of appropriated or available possibilities at any given time. For instance, a person may have the *so* to be a good dancer from all the possibilities that are available to members of the community and even beyond. If the person dislikes being an artist, he or she can go to a diviner and ask for the *so* to be changed and thus draw another career from that unlimited urn of possibilities that the uppercase *So* can give, and it is a pool that can never be completely realized. A person can literally ask for any set of possibilities, but *So* has the right to defer or "project into the future whatever may be too much for any community or society [or the individual] fully to experience or acknowledge in the present."[11] Because an individual can be given or allotted only a part of the set of all possibilities available to the community at any given historical moment, what he or she has "always points beyond itself to the full range of possibilities for either salvation or destruction."[12] As Richard Fenn puts it, "At some level, societies know that they are based on the foreclosure and postponed fulfillment of possibilities for both life and death. Every social system ... creates an index or prohibited satisfactions. ... The sacred always offers only a very limited embodiment of unfulfilled possibility."[13]

Individuals may encode within them the possibilities allotted to them by the social system (or the gods), but they always stand to look upon the uppercase *So* as the embodiment of unfulfilled possibilities. Humans can imagine alternatives not currently available to them and can take steps to attain what is denied them. In fact, this is the whole impetus and impulse behind *bibibari*, the recanting of destiny.[14]

What does the Kalabari notion of *So* tell us about the nature of the sacred as an im/possibility, the impossible possibility? There are three principles or forms of relationship in what the Kalabari call *So*, and they will help us to address the question. Within what the Kalabari named *So*, there is an uppercase *So* as a kind of creative force, the inexhaustible ground of (impossible) possibilities that overflows into human activities. *So* in this sense is considered as *Tamuno*, the Supreme Being. Second, there is *So* as the principle of limitation—the part that gives meaning and structure to the infinite possibilities and results in modification and concretion so that there is no chaos. Third, there is a feedback mechanism that works to properly align the interaction of the first two principles in the context of a particular person's or group's life. This mechanism is called *bibibari*. This is the continuous process of retooling the actualization of potentialities, the appropriation of possibilities and their reshaping.

Bibibari is the process through which past possibilities that determine a person, institution, or group are themselves retroactively changed. The past in this process becomes something like Deleuze's pure virtual past. The Kalabari believe that a person is created to embody a certain destiny: there is a virtual self that follows each person, and in this sense one's concrete deeds do not add to one's virtual past, as they only unfold what one is, as one only becomes what one is. The fact that *bibibari* is part of this process means that ultimately the Kalabari do not take a literal teleological reading of a person's destiny. Destiny as a necessity is an outcome of a contingent process. People's deeds are not a mere acting out of their atemporal encased set of possibilities, as any of their numerous acts can retroactively reconstitute their past. They can change their eternal past, the transcendental coordinates of their existence. "We have thus a kind of reflexive 'folding back of the condition onto the given it was the condition for': while the pure past is the transcendental condition for [their] acts, [their] acts do not only create new actual reality, they also retroactively change this very condition."[15] This change in the condition for their acts now gives their lives a new necessity (destiny), but it is only a necessity they contingently created. In this process of *bibibari*, there is unfolding, folding, and enfolding of possibilities that are reversing necessity into contingency and in turn contingency into necessity.

The overall lesson the Kalabari notion of the sacred teaches us is that the realm of the im/possibility, the impossible possibility, is the sacred. Put differently, it teaches that how a society understands, treats, and manages its possibilities or sense of possibilities defines its notion of the sacred. The sacred is not understood only as a site where a society constructs and deconstructs its notion of impossibility; it is also the site where, in the open sight of everybody, the people perform the trick of making what they regard as "transcendence" (beyond, impossible, not yet possible) to be internal to the world, integral to the process of unfolding possibilities, to work in immanental ways. It appears that without these sleights of hand in society, in social life, civilization itself becomes impossible. If there are no impossible possibilities in the sacred, everything is impossible. The founding order of the sacred is that the forbidden acts or jouissance are already impossible. If the sphere of the impossible does not exist in the sacred and by extension in the society it encompasses, then one finds oneself at any moment trespassing the limit of the possible, breaking arbitrary or nonexistent boundaries. In this scenario any act or movement is already forbidden, a transgression of a nonexistent impossibility. The constant transgression of a nonexistent impossibility means anything one does is impossible. Thus every possibility is forbidden.[16] We need the limits set by the sphere of the impossible to know that our actions are within the sphere of the possible, within the acceptable bounds of our community. If we do not know where the limits of the impossible begin, then it means they begin anywhere and everywhere and are within the realm of the possible, and thus members of society would appear to be trespassing the limits of the possible all the time.

The basic paradox of impossibility is that it is both possible and unavoidable. It is never fully eliminated and is always there but, simultaneously, overcome. Every conversion of impossibility into possibility generates a possible impossibility; every conquering of impossibility generates a new horizon of impossibility, limitation, and so on. Possibility creates the impossibility it tries to subdue. So if we eliminate impossibility, we also remove possibility. This reversal provides the definition of the realm of impossibility. It is the result of itself or the outcome of possibility, which both mean the same thing. All this suggests that the sacred plays some functions in social existence. Its invention, discovery, or imposition serves to oversee the aspirations, hopes, and expectations of the members of its community. It encourages the search for alternative possibilities. The sacred becomes corrupted or works against itself and society when it discourages the search and implementation of alternative possibilities. Sooner or later it will be replaced or displaced by another (new) form or version of what members of the society consider sacred.

Purpose of the Sacred

With mindful ignorance, let me say that the purposeless purpose of impossibility is to make possibility possible.[17] The sacred forbids an act because it is trying to impose a rational order onto the prerational chaos of the universe of possibilities. The perverse core of the sacred is to encourage or nudge us toward an abyssal act of freedom, to act outside the enchainment of possibilities open at any given moment to impose a novel rational necessity on uppercase *So*, the universe of possibilities, as if through the act of freedom the fecund void of numinous impossibility directly transforms itself into phenomenal possibility. The act momentarily tears the veil that separates possibility from impossibility, forcing all obstacles into the past. The act happens *in the present* but changes *the past itself*. For without such freedom (as per Immanuel Kant or Friedrich Wilhelm Joseph von Schelling) a society and its sacred cease to promote human flourishing. In the case of *bibibari*, this kind of act can reach deep into the eternal past to re-create a person's terrestrial destiny. This is not dissimilar from the temporal event of conversion in Christianity, which rewrites the eternal past of predestination.

Connecting this view of conversion to Kant's notion of freedom, Slavoj Žižek has this to say: "The later Kant articulated the notion of the noumenal act of choice by means of which an individual chooses his eternal character and which, therefore, prior to his temporal existence, delineates in advance the contours of his terrestrial destiny. Without Divine act of Grace, our destiny would remain immovable, forever fixed by this eternal act of choice;

and the 'good news' of Christianity, however, is that, in a genuine Conversion, one can 'recreate' oneself, that is *repeat* this act, and thus *change (undo the effects of) eternity itself.*"[18]

So what does all this tell us about the so-called realm of impossibility? The sacred stands for the paradox of impossibility, which maintains its status of impossibility precisely by its stubborn attachment to the dimension of possibility, which serves as its unacknowledged vitality. Without impossible possibilities, impossibility ends up as an empty, lifeless, self-identical void. The implicit claim of the sacred is that its declaration of impossibility is none other than the assertion of not-yet possibilities, possibilities waiting for the act that will transform them from the numinous to the phenomenal.

I can almost hear you, the reader, turning in your chair. If impossibility is only not-yet possibility waiting to materialize, then there is really no true impossibility, only psychic (or "false") impossibility. This line of thinking misunderstands the sacred; it is irrelevant whether the realm of impossibility exists as long as it is effective in constructing the way our deeds, insights, or breakthroughs pass from myth to existence, serving as a reference point to make sense of the improbable character of our accomplishments. "By definition, there is something so improbable about all [*novum*] that one is in effect questioning oneself about its reality."[19]

One more point before I drop this topic. For two reasons, the distinction between psychic and true impossibility is unnecessary. First, the impossible is impossible because it does not exist, but nonetheless we attribute properties such as excessiveness to it and forbidding intercourse with it. This is why a couple of pages ago we stated that the founding order of the sacred is that the forbidden acts or jouissance are already impossible. This nonexistent thing presides over people's actual striving, and if its effects on actual persons are to disappear, then the texture of the sacred as we know it will dissolve. The sphere of the impossible is the *Real* around which the sacred as a system operates.

Second, the sacred, according to the Kalabari, who can tell a god from which wood it was carved from, is not some kind of a transcendental spirit who controls human history, nor does it ossify possibilities. It is none other than the human process of dealing with life's possibilities—reflexively shaping and reshaping potentialities in the midst of obstacles—through which the process of knowing *So* takes place and human consciousness of mega-Spirit (a kind of hyperobject) thus arises. Out of the foaming ferment of human creativity in dealing with the entangled possibilities of coexistence,

So arises fragrantly, as Hegel might be tempted to put it. (Let us not forget that the very emergence of the sacred is in itself mysterious or adds to the "sacredness" of social intercourse. An "objective order" emerges out of the interactions of individuals, and once it appears it cannot be reduced to the interactions; it stands above or is viewed by them as a substantial agency that now determines, controls, or conditions their lives. This is what Slavoj Žižek calls "the ultimate mystery of the so-called human or social sciences."[20])

Once this *So*, the sacred, arises among the people, it is not just a blind mental process of fears and hopes that regulates social life or the interactions between possibility and impossibility. There are persons, practices, rituals, dances, utterances, and institutions that proclaim its status as sacred, and it thus appears to develop self-consciousness, a life of its own.[21] Here I am using *self-consciousness* in the sense Hegel applied it to the state, as "the self-consciousness of a people."

The self-consciousness of the state has nothing mental about it, if by *mental* we understand the sorts of occurrences and qualities that are relevant to our own minds. What self-consciousness amounts to, in the state's case, is the existence of reflective practices, such as, but not limited to, educational ones. Parades displaying the state's military strength would be practices of this kind, and so would statements of principle by the legislature or sentences by the Supreme Court—and they would be that even if all individual (human) participants in a parade, all members of the legislature, or all justices of the Supreme Court were personally motivated to play whatever role they play in this affair by greed, inertia, or fear *and* even if such participants or members were thoroughly uninterested and bored through the whole event and totally lacking in any understanding of its significance.[22]

Impossibility as the Sacred

The way we have conceptualized the sacred—the set of possibilities that is cast against the background of impossibility and that imposes itself over the collective life of a community as a "being"—differs from that of religious scholar Jeffrey Kripal, who talks about impossibility as the sacred. Whereas we have focused on possibilities and im/possibility in social existence, Kripal takes the possibilities of the paranormal as the sacred. He argues that what rational thinking, modern science, and materialism consider to be impossible, enchanted events (psychical phenomena) happen in the physical, objective, material world, and it is this paranormal impossible possibility—the weird and wonderful—that is the sacred. The sacred is the reality of the paranormal within a materialistic, disenchanted worldview. Kripal maintains that the psychical is "the sacred in transit from the traditional religious register into the modern scientific one."[23] The sacred proper, he adds, is "a particular structure of human consciousness that corresponds to the palpable presence, energy, or power encountered in the environment," which modern science rules out as impossible.[24]

Another important difference between my conceptualization of the sacred as the im/possibility and Kripal's view of the sacred as the impossible is that he keys his notion of the impossibility to an underlying metaphysical reality, which a disenchanted, established modern scientific method cannot access. For us the sacred is not necessarily the supernatural or metaphysical but the social structure ("the hypertext") that arranges, distributes, blocks, and invents possibilities over time in the lived world.

Mark C. Taylor's view of the sacred also disagrees with the ontotheological stance of Kripal. To Taylor, the sacred is neither being nor nonbeing; it is "the condition of possibility and impossibility of both being and nonbeing. If the sacred were a ground, which it is not, it might be understood as the ground of the ground of being, which otherwise is 'known' as God."[25] In simple language, he views the sacred as *interstitiality*, a relation of neither/nor rather than binary opposition. It is relation "as such." The sacred as interstitiality does not mean that the sacred is an instantiation of the interstitial. Taylor argues that "the site or more precisely, the *para-site* of the sacred is the interstitial. I would not use the term 'instantiation' in the context because it suggests too much stability or fixity. Rather, the interstitial is the domain of alternation (one of the nuances of altarity) where the sacred oscillates in an approaching withdrawal and withdrawing approach. The interstitial is neither here nor there; it is not present and yet not absent."[26] In other words, the sacred is fragile, fleeting, and slippery.

Catherine Keller, in her book *Cloud of the Impossible*, represents an alternative theological position to the stance of both Taylor and Kripal.[27] While Taylor insists that the neither/nor of his a/theology is not mysticism à la negative theology, Keller takes the position that the im/possibility of existence is elucidated (but not grasped) by a mysticism-hugging negative theology. Her negative theology, she holds, is not a mere opposite of theology or a simple absence of metaphysics of being but a "denegation" of the attributes of God and contestation of the knowability of God. She, unlike Kripal, does not decipher the fleeting presence of concretions caught in the interstices of being and nonbeing or in the trail of the cloud of impossibility as the sacred. Her negative theology does not take a stance opposite that of the established scientific worldview. It is rather about the struggle over time by theologians and physicists to say the unsayable with language that is recalcitrant to the logic of neither/nor. This neither/nor, which she situates in the density of relation that constitutes the fabric of existence and creativity, holds the key to deciphering the sacred, the site of the im/possibility. Amid the noise and nonteleological entanglements of relations in and impossibility of revelation from the infinite density of our micro and macro worlds, there emerges signification—an overture, at least, to the production of a sacred order. But there is no necessity to its emergence from the network of relations. What she calls "the cloud of the impossible" and what she leaves unthought in her book hold tantalizing clues to her thinking about the sacred.

The Trails of the Cloud of Impossible

Though Keller does not directly theorize the sacred, there are hints that she understands the sacred as the set of all possibilities. Let me lay out the logic that warrants this assertion—a position based on my interpretation of her book and the implications of her line of arguments. (And this position is also condensation and clarification of what I have already said about the sacred, now filtered through the lens of the *Cloud of the Impossible*.) The position is inherent in Keller's thought, but Keller did not comprehend its implications deeply enough; she felt she was dealing with negative theology rather than a theory of sacrality. Keller explains that existence is a network of evolving relationships. Possibilities or potentialities are nothing but aspects of relationships, and those relationships define the possibilities and potentialities.[28] We live in an expanding universe of relationships. Some of the possibilities are background independent, and others are background dependent. (Being background independent means, inter alia, that an event emerges that was not in the cards by retroactively positing its own conditions of possibility.) Time seems to "evolve" with the event; time and event appear to be codependent. The sacred, the floating site of im/possibility, is where the pressure and tension of the relationships coincide, where they simultaneously push apart (pressure) and pull together (tension). Religion names the *coincidentia oppositorum* as deity and the pressure and tension as wrath and grace, respectively. Religion is articulated around the belief that something (agency, deity) external to the universe of relationships and possibilities not only imposes order on it but also ultimately makes the choice of possibilities and potentialities for us. If a religion does not admit to an outside agency, it posits that the agency is the power of the universe of relationships as a whole. Religion helps human beings to organize and conceptualize their experience of the sacred.

Let me now take the reader through some of Keller's suggestive statements on the sacred, even as I endeavor to unearth their creative impulses. My initial reading is that the closest she comes to conceptualizing the sacred is what she calls "the primordial locus of possibilities," which at the same time urges the actualization of possibilities.[29] This primordial locus is another name for the impossible that engenders the possibility itself, which is endlessly made and undone. At the core of this never-ending process, there is a lure of planetary creativity and disregard for congealed hierarchy. More precisely, the sacred is our infinite entanglement, which invokes, invites, and sustains care for its finitudes. She argues that the entanglement and creativity that sustain it are theopoetic—that is, God making, or the bodying of God. But this God, in keeping with Keller's negative theology and expansive process theology, cannot be positively determined or known. This God is not some kind of positive agent that guarantees or underlies creativity itself. The "divine element in the universe" is not a "congealed God-entity," not an idol.[30] We do not really know this God or what we designate as God. At best, God, who she argues is an outcome of creativity itself, is the lure of all other creatures. This unknowing of God, she holds, should energize an alter-knowing of the relation between God and world, or at least a rejection of the inherited classical view of the God-world relationship. Over and over again, she rejects the idea of a discrete, unentangled God (subject) acting on God's world or human bodies (object). She maintains that God is entangled in the relations of all creations and is part of non–ex nihilo creation, which unfolds, folds, and enfolds within the primordial locus of possibilities, the site of im/possibility.[31]

The divine boundlessness that enfolds and unfolds within the im/possibility of relations is not only by the Cusanus's logic of the *coincidentia oppositorum* but also by reversal of classical verticalism. Not only do transcendence and immanence coincide in relationalism, in nonabsolute Absolute, but also the experience of the Absolute is *evental*, manifesting in vulnerable flashes. In Keller's thought, the Absolute mediates creativity in a process in which the temporal, the creatable, is everlastingly *infini*.[32] And this Absolute (*Resolute*) itself is a fragile, changing concretion, the "Most-Moved Mover."[33] The logic here is that the eternal in the classical sense is unstable, changing, and that the noneternal (created, creativity) is what is everlasting. Between the ultimate category of creativity and becoming nature (becomings in process), the Absolute (Resolute) shines forth, entangling each actual occasion in new possibilities.

Keller's book invites the reader to meditate on the "possible impossibility": the reader is mindful to ponder how what is now considered impossible can generate new possibilities. Impossibility birthing new possibilities! This is an inversion of commonsense logic. In this vein, the vertical relation between the eternal (above, spirit, "uncreated") and the temporal (here and now, the flesh, created) is inverted, not in the sense of transcendence demoted to immanence but in the sense of the flesh being more lasting and continuous than the spirit.

To reiterate, for Keller the impossible is the sacred—at least according to this reading. This is not because the impossible is God or God is the impossible but because the sacred is the traces of the possible impossibility woven through all the processes of life or it is the cracks in the network of relationships that turn up possibility that had appeared to be impossible. The cracks or traces are not engendered or bolstered by an inaccessible transcendence, outside power, external entity, or independent substance but by the energy of the relation itself, the cloudy radiance and resonance of the effervescence of life that form and deform existence.

I need to quickly point out the methodology of my engagement with or critique of Keller's work. I do not here present an orthodox engagement with Keller's thought in the *Cloud of the Impossible*. I am only attempting to follow a trail of the clouds of her original thinking as it folds, enfolds, and unfolds implicitly through the book. I invite the reader to join me to regain or uncover the creative impulse that Keller missed in the actualization of her thought, to walk with me to connect to "what was already 'in [Keller] more than [Keller] herself,' more than [her] explicit system, its excessive core."[34] This is to say, join me in reading Keller to isolate the key breakthrough of her thought in this book as it relates to the notion of the sacred as a set of possibilities and impossibilities, im/possibility; then exploring how she necessarily missed this key dimension of her own discovery; and, "finally, showing how, in order to do justice to [her] key breakthrough, one has to move beyond [Keller]."[35] This going beyond means betraying the "letter" (actual) of her thought to grasp its "spirit" (virtual). So precisely what dimension of the sacred shines through in the explosion of thought on the clouds of impossibility, in her negative theology and in the concrete actualization of the creative impulse in her book but has slipped into the virtual state and haunts any close reading of the book? What is the proper embodiment of this excess betrayed by Keller's book?

Let us begin this exercise with her description of negative theology. She dwells brilliantly on its nature, arguing that it is about lack or contrariness. It is all about excess that escapes speech.[36] Contrariness designates a form of difference within classical theism or authorized space of talking about God, while the excess that escapes speech designates ways of talking about the divine that gesture to a breakdown of the preapproved linguistic and "rational" space for such discussions. Here it appears she has unknowingly stumbled onto two types of lack: there are the *lack proper* and the *hole*.[37] There is a constitutive lack that does not threaten the system of knowledge or order of being per se. A hole designates a gap in the system or order of being. In this sense, the contrariness or lack she mentions—to use Žižek's words—is only "a *void within a space*, while a hole is more radical, it designates the point at which this spatial order itself breaks down (as in the 'black hole' in physics)."[38] Her book did not explicitly name the hole, which would appear to provide the aim and goal of her brand of apophatic theology. Its goal is to circulate around the concept of God within the theological space without reifying God, claiming a certainty of knowledge, or providing a contemplative sanctuary in the face of uncertainty, and its true aim is endless circulation around its goal object. Perhaps its satisfaction is its repeated failure to pin down God or the impossible possibility that ever eludes the human reach.

She conveyed the sense of the second type of lack, the hole in ontotheological knowledge space, with her brilliant discussions of entangled particles whose mutuality is characterized by "faster-than-light relationality."[39] She transmitted the apophatic effect of the quantum world of particles and waves in her discussions. Their world of unbroken wholeness "actually appears as the discontinuous quantum jumps and jitters."[40] Here the very lack seems to be holes in the system; entangled particles dance and operate in unanalyzable, indeterminate ways. Their apophatic entanglement appears to demand that we drop the whole mechanistic order that informs scientific imagination in order to analyze it. Quantum entanglement is an impossible possibility. She missed the key dimension of hole as a form of lack in her work.

Keller's focus on ontological relationality robbed her of the idea of another hole, the "black hole" in social reality or sociality, the play of impossibility in reality. This hole gestures to the im/possible, to the terminally difficulty term God, and to God's existence or inexistence. Following the creative impulse of her thoughts, one could conclude that the new emerges, that an impossibility becomes a possibility, because there is no power in social existence that controls the preconstituted totality as possibilities. The im/possibility is the inherent immanent power of creativity in human communities, which can retroactively create the condition of possibility of the novum. She may or may not agree on what the existence of black holes in the fabric of social reality (cracks in the fixity of potentialities) represents. Perhaps for Keller the "black holes" in social reality express the One of Creativity (Becoming) or there is no underlying oneness (created or creatable).[41] Nothing or something? The notion of the sacred does not rule out one or the other. The answer depends on the community.

Žižek argues that the existence of "black holes," an impossible possibility in reality, means that God does not exist. But for African Pentecostals, their presence confirms the existence of God; there is a God, transcendent or immanent, that springs surprises on the extant configuration of things. It appears that Žižek and Pentecostals share the same sense of the sacred—at least in the sense we have interpreted it in this chapter, as a common field of potentialities and possibilities without an omega point. But Žižek and Pentecostals differ on where to place God in (*en*) the oceanic plenum of the sacred.[42] Pentecostals place God in (*en*) it and nominate the same as its anchor and guarantee.[43] Žižek rejects all these, preferring a simple sacred without father or mother and without site of privilege or reification within it.

Let no one think that Žižek's rejection puts his position absolutely at loggerheads with Pentecostalism. Pentecostalism's two-pronged position on the sacred (godly and special mundane events, or "potentiality" and "virtuality") is always mediated by the playful character of the Pentecostal spirit. Pentecostalism "profanes" the sacred without abolishing the sphere of the sacred. It *deactivates* the aura that attends to the rites and stories (myths) of the sacred sphere.[44] Pentecostalism demystifies the sacred and shows the profane as inherent to the sacred.[45] This is not done in disbelief and indifference toward the divine but is "a behavior that is free and 'distracted' . . .

released from *religio* of norms before things and their use."⁴⁶ For Pentecostals, the sacred is dispersed into multiple sites of encounter (space is cut so that the *trans-* of transcendence is not a "cross over or going beyond" but a tracing of "being-with"). Pentecostalism is the sacred in a *playful* mode.

We have gone too far ahead of ourselves in our plan to discuss the missed opportunity in Keller's second type of lack (negative). Let us now return to it by unveiling what French philosopher Quentin Meillassoux understands by *potentialities* and *possibilities*. His conceptualization of these terms will help to shed light on what we have come to consider as the set of possibilities, the play of im/possibility in reality. Meillassoux makes the distinction between virtuality and potentiality:

> *Potentialities* are the non-actualized cases of an indexed set of possibilities under the condition of a given law (whether aleatory or not). *Chance* is every actualization of a potentiality for which there is no univocal instance of determination on the basis of the initial given conditions. Therefore I will call *contingency* the property of an indexed set of cases (not of a case belonging to an indexed set) of not itself being a case of sets of cases; and *virtuality* the property of every set of cases emerging within a becoming which is not dominated by any pre-constituted totality of possible.⁴⁷

Meillassoux's definition gives us a new language to conceptualize the sacred or to reexplain what Kalabari or the Pentecostals understand by the sacred as a set of possibilities. He shows that events can happen because of their potentiality, that something comes out of a preexisting set of possibilities. If we roll a single die and any of the numbers (1–6) comes up, then that is a possibility becoming actualized. But if we throw the die and the number 7 comes up, then virtually something new has come up. Number seven has no place on the die, in the preexisting set of possibilities, but the emergence of the new retroactively creates its own condition of possibility. As Meillassoux puts it, "Time creates the possible at the very moment it makes it come to pass, it brings forth the possible as it does the real, it inserts itself in the very throw of the die, to bring forth a seventh case, in principle unforeseeable, which breaks the fixity of potentialities."⁴⁸ As if in a gesture ahead of its time, Meillassoux throws a view of the emergence of phenomenon ex nihilo before Keller's *creatio ex profundis*, not as a denial that events draw from their *situation* but as an assertion of radical contingency based on an ontology of *non-All* or radical becoming. He continues, "If we maintain that becoming is not only capable of bringing forth cases on the basis of a pre-given universe of cases, we must understand that it follows that such cases [the New] irrupt, properly speaking, *from nothing*, since no structure contains them as eternal potentialities before their emergence: *we thus make irruption ex nihilo* the very concept of a temporality delivered to its pure immanence."[49]

Here we are seeing in different registers what the Kalabari and Pentecostals consider to be the operations of the sacred. The virtuality, the emergence of the new that is not mere actualization of preexisting possibility, that Meillassoux is describing here resembles the entangled particles of the micro-quantum world that Keller describes. Meillassoux—and Žižek following him—clearly sees the potential theological or religious use of his argument of ex nihilo emergence of the new and quickly proceeds to block it by giving a materialist interpretation of it. Meillassoux states that "every 'miracle' thus becomes the manifestation of the inexistence of God, insofar as every radical rupture of the present in relation to the past becomes the manifestation of the absence of any order capable of overseeing the chaotic power of becoming."[50]

Žižek concurs: "This emergence of a phenomenon *ex nihilo*, not fully covered by the sufficient chain of reasons, is thus no longer—as in traditional metaphysics—a sign of the direct intervention of some super-natural power (God) into nature, but, on the contrary, a sign of the inexistence of God, that is, a proof that nature is not-All, not 'covered' by any transcendent Order or Power which regulates it. A 'miracle' (whose formal definition is the emergence of something not covered by the existing causal network) is thus converted into a materialist concept."[51]

This play of potentialities, possibilities, and virtuality in social existence is what I mean by the sacred. Materialist scholars like Žižek and Meillassoux obviously call it another name, and religious people like African Pentecostals view it differently. For some it is strictly profane, for others it is strictly holy and religious, and for Pentecostals and Kalabari, as we have seen, it is in *coincidentia oppositorum* with the profane.

The kind of new discourse of the sacred that is in some radical *coincidentia oppositorum* with the profane has been extracted from a trail of the clouds of Keller's original thinking as it folds, enfolds, and unfolds implicitly through the *Cloud of the Impossible*. We have attempted to uncover the creative impulse that Keller missed in the actualization of her thought, to walk in the trail of the clouds to connect what was already in Keller more than Keller herself did. We will continue to isolate the key breakthrough of her thought in the *Cloud of the Impossible* as it relates to the notion of the sacred. As stated earlier, in this kind of exercise we will betray the "letter" (actual) of her thought to grasp its "spirit" (virtual).

When reading Keller in the light of our theory of the sacred, we must bear in mind how her implicit view on the sacred differs from the argument in this chapter. This difference enables us to search for the proper embodiment of the "excessive core" in her thought betrayed or neglected by *Cloud of the Impossible*. One source of this difference relates to the orientation of her book. She focuses more on ontological relationalism than on the regulative force of sociality.[52] As a result, we have to think her thought after her to show, for instance, that the sacred is constructed out of the feelings of possibilities at the level of language, culture, and materialist affectivity. What does the fold between our unknowing of the divine and planetary inseparability mean for bodies in interactional/intra-active ritual chains? If one enfolds and unfolds her idea of the body of God, the enfleshing of infinite entanglements, and de-hierarchization of the typical divine-human relation, the thought arises: Is sacred, the lure of something, not the fleeting event over the density of entanglements of bodies? Her work, which examines the entanglement of the divine and unknowing in many facets of human and beyond-human lives, does not explore how entangled human bodies generate the sacred or the sense of the sacred. She fails to explore how her own conceptualization of the relation between unknowing and relationality itself moves her reader to ask, How do entangled bodies become surfaces for the fleeting appearances of the unknowable God? Or how does God temporarily construct Godself (or God's flesh) from and in relations of entangled bodies as *real presence*?

For a scholar intensely focused on entangled bodies and relationalism and interested in the discourse of the sacred in some radical *coincidentia oppositorum* with the profane, the neglect of real presence as a locus of the divine is somewhat surprising. In my opinion, real presence, which is experienced across (almost) all religions, provides us with an important perspective to develop a planetary ecumenical and doctrine-resistant sense of the sacred. If Keller had applied her analysis of im/possibility to how the divine manifests in the forms of affectivity of bodies, words and voices, relics and arts—that is, to real presence—she would have given body to some lines of argument that now haunt her text.[53] This is an opportunity that what was already in the *Cloud of the Impossible* more than in Keller's conscious articulation of her ideas. There are lines of argument in the book of which Keller herself is unaware, arguments that will help us understand a dimension of the sacred as experience or as enacted in co-affective worship services.

Now, to understand the African Pentecostals' logic and practice of the sacred as revealed in their co-affective worship services, we turn not directly to Keller's explicit arguments but to her logic. For some time I have been mulling over the Pentecostal logic of sense, trying to understand how Pentecostals invert the eternal-temporal order to "construct" God on their bodies and senses. They share this skill of inversion with Keller. She is patently good at inverting any transcendence-immanence schema in constructive theologies. How does one ferret out this hidden line of similarity in the *Cloud of the Impossible*? Before my active contemplation of the Pentecostal practico-ethical and enkinaesthetic theology and Keller's constructive-theoretical theology, Gilles Deleuze's *Logic of Sense* has indirectly taught me how inversion takes place in worship services. Deleuze, following the Stoics before him, inverted Plato's dualism between the eternal ideas and material things, which are only fleeting appearances of the eternal in the empirical, sensuous world. For Deleuze, this view shows that material bodies are the "substance and cause" and that the fleeting becoming of sense located at the interstices of being and nonbeing is the immaterial virtual effect.[54] In his words, "The Stoics are the first to reverse Platonism and to bring about a radical inversion. For if bodies, with their states, qualities, and quantities, assume all the characteristics of substance and cause, conversely, the characteristics of the Idea are relegated to the other side, that is to the impassive extra-Being which is sterile, inefficacious, and the surface of things of things: *the ideational or the incorporeal can no longer be anything other than an 'effect.'*"[55]

Keller missed the opportunity to examine how bodies entangled in worship display and play the sacred or how immanent sensing bodies engrossed in affective reciprocity also invert Plato's dualism in the fashion of the Stoics and Deleuze. This is because she does not connect or extend her notion of planetary entanglements, clouds of impossible clouds, and im/possibility to worship services, where literal bodies and their sweat, breath, and agitated dust create clouds of their own, folding, enfolding, and unfolding the divine. Careful observations of Pentecostal worship services after hard thought about Keller's book, Deleuze's logic, and Žižek's notion of fragile Absolute led this scholar to discover the *Pentecostal logic of sense*. Pentecostals in their worship services appear to invert the dualism of eternal and fragile material reality into the dualism of sensuous material bodies and such bodies' generation of the eternal or the Absolute as fleeting experiences, moments, or waves of divine presence, which in turn serve as the bodies' opposite. So instead of the human body being the extremely fragile, fleeting reality, it becomes the hard particle, and the Absolute appears fragile, as flashes or bursts of energies in the matrix of bodies.

Pentecostalism gives us a deep sense of how the sacred is constructed and, as Annalisa Butticci's work on the concern for the *real presence* among African Pentecostals in Italy shows, how the poor and marginalized migrants deal with what we called impossible possibility.[56] Catholic and Pentecostal aesthetics of *real presence* encounter each other in agonistic contact zones. African migrants, *parts of no-part* in the Italian society, are attempting to invert the powers relating to the generation and control of real presence. Butticci narrates the story of the encounter between African Pentecostalism and Roman Catholicism in Italy, a story in which the weak and the powerful share a common space, from the lens of the powerless. In doing this, she exhibits the sensitivity and acumen of James Scott and Michel de Certeau in highlighting the everyday practices and weapons of the weak that African Pentecostals are using to subvert overbearing authority in the Catholic stronghold of Italy. She clearly shows how the subjugated, marginalized, and racially degraded Africans are struggling to carve out a space to worship God, earn basic human dignity amid the Italian Catholic ordering of space and privileges, and create possibilities for their own human flourishing.

At the very sophisticated theoretical level that Keller performed her thought, the *Cloud of the Impossible* could not shed light on the sacred as an entanglement of the bodies pushing the boundaries of the senses and social spaces or as a concrete struggle for the distribution of the im/possibility. More importantly, the lack of examination of the "cloud" of impossibility as it might relate to the sacramentality of the (im)possible, a nonexistent thing, shows that to do justice to her book and grasp its spirit one has to move beyond her thought. The impossibility, impossible possibility, is not only the nonexistent thing that has properties and exercises effectivity but also the Real around which society or religion operates. I wish Keller worked out the way in which "false" impossibility operates as the reference point by which the system of possibilities deduces its truth and the sine qua non of the way systems in general operate. Our fantasy about possibility and alternatives is articulated around our belief in the realm of impossibility. And Hegel has taught us that this belief is "objective" as it materializes in the way a system or society functions.

Keller's brilliant analysis of the unknowing (unknowable) cloud of impossibility operates mainly in a very different epistemological register from Pentecostal thinking, like most of the mainline theologians and philosophers of religion, and she thus missed a key dimension of the application of her thought to charismatic and spiritual movements, which mark the public resurgence of religion in the twenty-first century. The mystery of impossibility that she focuses on is the mystery and mystique of unknowing, suffering, uncertainties, ecological catastrophe, and the religious other. It is not the intense, passionate attachment of an everyday mystic who struggles to inhabit the perceived tiny crack or gap between noumenal and phenomenal to erotically approach things in themselves. What would it mean for Keller's understanding of the mysticism of the impossible possibility if she were to consider an intensity of eros toward the mystery of God so strong that it shatters (however briefly) the very transcendental coordinates of knowing and unknowing, releases our perceptions from their human coordinates, and pushes them outside human reality (as per Deleuze)?

All these insights bring us to the Pentecostal notion of the noumenal, things in themselves. Often modern theologians see the noumenal in Kantian terms, opposition between phenomenal and noumenal. But this is only a limited way of interpreting what Pentecostals understand as the noumenal. The noumenal also refers to impossible phenomena, things that are excluded from taking place in the extant order of being/things. The noumenal is the impossible whose happening shatters the coordinates of our symbolically constituted common reality. "The gap that separates us from noumenal is thus primarily not epistemological, but practico-ethical and libidinal: there is no 'true reality' behind or beneath phenomena; noumenal are phenomenal things which are 'too strong,' too intense or intensive, for our perceptual apparatus, attuned as it is to constituted reality."[57]

Keller's missed opportunity is this: having rejected a transcendent, classical godly dimension to human reality, she could not reverse or transcend the Kantian logic of opposition between noumenal and phenomenal, of the inaccessibility of things in themselves.[58] What she needed to do in a Hegelian fashion was to transpose the split between noumenal and phenomenal onto a split within phenomenal itself, as the split between normal "gentrified" phenomenon within usual human coordinates and "impossible" phenomenon outside symbolically constituted human reality.[59] (Though the "impossible" phenomenon is outside human coordinates, it is still part of the human reality, nothing but a *fragment of the sacred*.)

This distinction between "gentrified" phenomenon and "impossible" phenomenon helps us to get a better conceptual grip on Pentecostals' understanding of miracles. The commonest, everyday meaning of *miracle* in Pentecostal circles is akin to what Alain Badiou calls *event*. As with an event, what composes a miracle or "impossible" phenomenon "is always extracted from a situation, always related back to a singular multiplicity, to its state, to the language that is connected to it, etc."[60]

Concluding Thoughts

The key idea of this chapter is this: the sacred could be considered the set of possibilities—opened, closed, hypothetical, or unimagined to a society. But the sacred is not a set of all sets; it is not an absolute totality of all possibilities in a given society. There cannot be a set or entity that is a collection of all possibilities, all sets of possibilities, and all there is. French philosopher Alain Badiou in *Being and Event* used the mathematical theories of Georg Cantor (1845–1918) to show that such an entity cannot exist; no set can belong to itself. The number of parts or subsets of elements in a set is larger than that of the elements themselves—there is an irremediable excess of subsets over elements such that there cannot exist a set of all sets.[61] The sacred is infinite, but it cannot be the largest, the last infinite.

We do not want to miss the opportunity of stating that the sacred in one crucial sense is about how a society understands "the concept of the new." How does the new emerge? How does it come forth as causality constrained by historical life, amid preconditions, and yet remain "underivable" from its conditions? The sacred is the most constitutive and determinative modality for liberating or chaining the "virtualizing power of time" or for creating the new.

The sacred in this sense of possibilities and the emergence of the new is common to all societies (secular, profane, or not) across time. Where societies differ is with the name they give to the sacred. They also differ on the basis of whether or not they conceive it entitatively, nonentitatively, or some combination of both. In the past the deity was referred to as the Sacred Itself, with no distinction between god(s) and the sacred. Religion is only one of the institutions deployed by societies to manage human interactions with the infinity of possibilities. Priests tell people how to approach the deity in small doses of possibilities, never presupposing that members of their societies can face the full ply of possibilities in any one moment. And once in a while an apocalyptic prophet comes around to slightly lift up the veil on the sacred, and we see in staggering detail the "monstrosity" of the sacred.[62] The veil is often so lifted to "spell" the "end of history" to those the prophet wants to see come to ruin.

Richard Fenn puts it well: "Direct exposure to all the possibilities contained in the Sacred would of course stagger the mind and the imagination. Who can stand in the presence of the deity, the Sacred itself? That is why the deity is best approached in the form of lower-case sacred, since it is crucial that the entire range of possibilities for both life and death itself remains unfulfilled if even limited access to them is to be granted. Otherwise, as the apocalyptic imagination has long known, were these possibilities for salvation or destruction to be fulfilled, the end would have come."[63]

Today, in the postmodern, postindustrial society, religion no longer has a monopoly on overseeing access to the sacred, and many people no longer equate the sacred with the god(s) or deity. But there is a lingering attitude toward the sacred that is a carry-over from the premodern time into our secular or postsecular society. Actually, distinguishing between past and present society on the basis of secular/profane and nonsecular is not an adequate way to understand attitudes toward the sacred. The correct approach is to investigate whether the predominant worldview about reality is an *All* or *non-All*. Belief in *All* (One or Being) means the world is governed by law: there is "a determinate set, finite or infinite, of possible cases—a law, deterministic or aleatory, always comes down to the specific set of indexable cases."[64] Time is what enables the actualization of these cases or eternal possibilities. But belief in a non-All reality means that reality is always incomplete and that time is not subordinated to the role of effectuating the universe of possible cases but has the power to modify the set of possibilities. Insofar as postmodern society or traditional societies of the past always find a way to circumvent the "pure power of chaos of becoming," the argument about secularity and sacredness of societies as keyed to historical periods is not very convincing.[65] Let me here quote Meillassoux, on whose work I have relied to make my arguments on the periodization of secularity:

> In the guise of a radical evolution, it seems that since the Greeks, one conception, and one only, of becoming, has always imposed itself upon us: time is only the actualization of an eternal set of possibles, the actualization of Ideal Cases, themselves inaccessible to becoming—this latter's only "power" (or rather "impotence") being that of distributing them in a disordered manner. If modernity is traditionally envisaged ... as the passage from the closed world to the infinite universe, it remains no less true that modernity does not break

with Greek metaphysics on one essential point: finite or infinite, the world remains governed by the law—that is, by the All, whose essential signification consists in the subordination of time to a set of possibles which it can only effectuate, but not modify.[66]

In this regard, whether by religion or other institutions, the conception of the sacred has been "reduced" to the effective practices and procedures directed by a society to enable the cosmos and nomos to maintain themselves against the threat of chaos by strengthening and renewing the ethos. One of the primary roles of religious imagination and the habits of other organs overseeing the forbidden aspirations of people is to explain, control, and predict the pattern of appropriate responses to the passages, damages, and surprises of time. Religion, political systems, the economy, and others often function to assure society of its mastery over passage of time. The sacred (in this constricted viewpoint or as shortened as religion) is how a society oversees life with regard to continuity between the past, the present, and the future. The key goal of the practices and procedures of the sacred as religion is to control the passage of time over life and society's institutions by subordinating the "virtualizing power of time" to a superior power or set of powers.[67] The aim of the controlling intent is to ensure that novelties, radical (or unauthorized) ruptures, do not emerge to defeat all continuity between the past, the present, and the future. For such novelties, or "miracles," to paraphrase Meillassoux, will become a manifestation of the inexistence of order, of any power capable of overseeing the chaotic power of becoming and the aspirations of the people.

One result of these attempts to subordinate time to a set of possibilities as preset by the law of an All reality is that the sacred comes to be primarily seen not only as a community's energy brought to deal with the passage of time and change but also as the ways a community experiences, understands, interprets, and strives to transcend time. Instead of thinking and doing something to overcome the subordination of time to an eternal set of possibilities, scholars should focus their scarce energies on theorizing sacred and profane times, temporal orientations, rate of time preference, and so on. The key question about the sacred today is how to liberate the sacred or the virtualizing power of time from religion or from the oversight of so-called superior power(s).

Our earlier descriptions of Pentecostals' understanding of the sacred and their penchant for miracles suggest that they are unconsciously rooting to overcome the subordination of time to an eternal set of possibilities; their effective practices and habits appears to be beckoning for the "virtualizing power of time" in the twenty-first century.[68] This is one good way to interpret the orientation of the Pentecostal movement toward miracles, radical ruptures in the continuity between the past and the present. There are also at least three problems with their understanding and approach to the sacred. The critical irony of the Pentecostal appetite for miracles is that if their wishes are fully realized, the pure power of becoming, which no power or order can control, will be delivered to the world. And as both Meillassoux and Badiou suggest, every miracle would then become a manifestation of the inexistence of God. Finally, it is uncertain whether Pentecostal theologians can think about the kind of sacred that is beyond religion and the profane, or beyond good and evil, without philosophizing about becoming, possibility, and potentiality—ideas not always celebrated by classical theism or by Pentecostal preachers. For everyday Pentecostals, at least in part, the sacred is an affectivity of space and time. It is a manifestation or interstitiality of the space of possibilities and the virtualizing power of time. There is a certain impossible possibility of theologizing the sacred in the Pentecostal movement.

In the next chapter, we will examine how African Pentecostals deploy their notion of sacred to "conjure," cajole, command, or solicit spirits (Holy Spirit, angels, and demons) to manifest in their worship services in ways that will enhance their human flourishing and enable them to achieve justice of existence. Chapter 2 demonstrates how Africans pursue the creation of possibilities or the actualization of their potentialities by shifting the central locus of sacred-human encounter to the special worship of Christian God, the type that implicates believers in a red-hot spiritual warfare with all forces and persons perceived to be thwarting their flourishment.

2

DEMONS AS GUESTS

Aesthetics of Pentecostal Prayers

Introduction

Let me start by stating that the study of the transcripts of the sacred is a report not on the sacred itself but on the aftermath of the sacred: the owl of Minerva takes flight at dusk. We can track or trace the developmental logic of the sacred only with a retrospective gaze. With our retrospective understanding, we gain insight or hindsight to enable us to correct or condition the generation of im/possibilities. Such efforts in themselves constitute our participation in the developmental logic and its refinement. In this chapter I identify prayers, especially spiritual warfare, as a transcript of the sacred. Spiritual warfare is not only an engagement with the sacred but also an outcome of previous engagements with the sacred. I will examine how African Pentecostals generate the transcripts of prayers and deploy them to restage or recreate the sacred in their communities.

The central locus of the divine-human encounter in the worship service and the primary theological activity of Nigerian Pentecostals is not the Eucharist or preaching but prayer. The prayer spirituality has as its objective the attainment of human flourishing as empowered by the Holy Spirit.[1] Prayer is, above all, concern with the power to command and prescribe the destruction and creation of possibilities and potentialities. The power is exercised to control the possibilities of life, to distribute persons and groups to places in society and to their assigned tasks. In this Rancierian sense, prayer is an aesthetics itself. This is aesthetics in the sense of the destructive and constructive staging of possibilities, the distribution of the sacred as the universal set of possibilities. The prayer form whose study can best uncover both the aesthetics of prayer and prayer as aesthetics is what Nigerian

Pentecostals call "hot prayer," spiritual-warfare prayer. In this study I will focus on one important dimension of hot prayers, the practice of inviting demons as guests to church. My preliminary investigations have revealed that it is most generative of ideas for a theory of Pentecostal aesthetics.

Simply put, this chapter attempts to construct a theory of Pentecostal aesthetics through the lens of prayers. It does not engage aesthetics from the usual route but from an interpretation of the search and enjoyment of *real presence* during prayers by Nigerian Pentecostals. To do this I begin by offering an ethnographic description of hot prayers, a special type of spiritual warfare practiced by Nigerian Pentecostals. After the description comes an analysis of what the Pentecostals consider to be the biblical and cultural justifications for their practice of hot prayers.

On the basis of the thick description and analysis of hot prayers, I will craft a theory of Pentecostal aesthetics—that is, aesthetics of real presence. This theory has four movements. In the first movement, I excavate the three existential questions driving the quest for real presence by Nigerian Pentecostals: What or who is manifesting as real presence? Who controls what manifests? What is the value of what manifests?

The second movement develops Pentecostal aesthetics in terms of finding and locating the inner teleology of the formation that holds and harmonizes the existential questions. What is the inner teleology of their quest for real presence? How does Pentecostal thinking about the questions and responses to existential questions fit together as an "artwork," so to speak? This way of approaching the subject matter engages a Kantian, Enlightenment view of aesthetics. What exactly are Pentecostals thinking about when they invite the demons as guests? How does their thinking fit together as a harmonious whole? Here, I am channeling the Enlightenment view of aesthetics that says that when things harmoniously fit together they have a certain inner teleology, their own beauty as an end in themselves. I call this second movement in the theory of Pentecostal aesthetics that I am crafting the beauty of aesthetics, the aesthetics within aesthetics. *Aesthetics* in this chapter is primarily limited to real presence, so when I proceed to consider the inner teleology of the tight formation of questions and responses as a whole object, I am at a second-order level of aesthetics, so to speak. The beauty of the inner impulses of Pentecostal aesthetics is in the harmonious relations of its existential questions. The formation of questions and answers constitutes a whole that is an end in itself. How do we judge the practice of real presence as an end itself?

The third movement considers hot prayers as part of Pentecostal worship, a bigger object that is neither a means to an end nor an end in itself. Rather, worship in Pentecostal circles occasionally turns into a *pure means*.[2] How do we rethink Pentecostal aesthetics when worship at a particular time and place is neither a means to an end nor an end in itself? The teleology of hot prayers rides on our understanding of the ends-and-means relationship. Kant believed that a true art is not a means to something outside itself. It is an end in itself. In this Kantian perspective, we have two forms of relationship. A thing could be a means to an end or an end in itself. There is, however, a third form, when the relationship is only a *pure means*, when as a means it is not directed toward an end. Once a means loses its end, it has become a pure means. The worship as pure means is open to anything, such as momentarily freeing itself from the capitalist logic of the commoditization of worship. Our understanding of worship as a pure means is crucial for mapping Pentecostal aesthetics. This perspective gestures at once to the deepest concrete, empirical dimension of Pentecostal aesthetics and also to its most abstract ideal; this is the most idealistic and the most materialistic theory of Pentecostal aesthetics.[3]

Finally, the fourth movement speaks to how Pentecostals are trying to redistribute possibilities available in the sacred given their understanding of the sacred as the universal set of possibilities.[4] The desire to distribute, redistribute, or restage possibilities is the primary reason they engage in hot prayers. This is why they are willing to traffic in the real presences. This is why they are asking the three existential questions: How can God manifest? Where can God manifest? And what is the value of the manifestation? The value is in their struggles to come to terms with the utility of real presence, with how it can help them to change their life's possibilities. Pentecostal aesthetics is about the distribution of divinely empowered life possibilities for human flourishing.

It is germane at this point to explain how I will be using the term *real presence*. This refers to how the immaterial, invisible, supernatural, or divine is made present, real, tangible, or visible in material forms through bodies, embodied prayers, sensations, sacraments, space, objects, and temporality. It investigates how real presence is enacted or performed in Pentecostal hot prayers as demons are invited to the holy grounds of prayer spaces. These so-called demons were either demonic entities mentioned in the Bible or popular Christian literature or revered gods in African traditional religions (ATR).

ATR, which has greatly influenced Nigerian Pentecostalism, also has its practices of inviting the gods as guests. In ATR the gods are invited to be feted and celebrated, but Pentecostals invite the same gods, renaming them as demons, to roast them in the fire of the Holy Ghost. How do we understand or theorize the aesthetics of Pentecostalism when Nigerian Pentecostals call down fire on the old gods who honor their invitations and often manifest their presences through *real presences* in sacred Christian prayer grounds?

I approach the task of responding to this question as a work of cartography. I map the landscape of this spirituality, "the work of providing markers and directions for" the terrain of Nigerian Pentecostal aesthetics of presence, by laying the theory (knowledge) of African traditional religions over the terrain or landscape of Pentecostal practices and beliefs "to see how the lines of theory might map the contours of" Pentecostal aesthetics.[5] This chapter does not assume religions as units or cultural wholes that can be easily compared or translated but seeks to examine a particular set of interactions between African traditional religions and Nigerian Pentecostalism, to compare their modes of relating to—what they consider—the more-than-human realm of existence. I am basing this approach on Peter van der Veer's brilliant book *The Value of Comparison*. He argues that when we want to make this kind of comparison we should focus on "fragments of social life" rather than taking everything as a whole. He believes that the fragments enable us to gain a perspective on the larger life or cultural wholes that we would not ordinarily gain if we were to focus on the whole from the start.[6]

My methodology for the study of Pentecostal aesthetics is informed not only by the work of van der Veer but also by those of anthropologists Bridget Meyer and Annalisa Butticci, whose studies of aesthetics focus on real presences.[7] Meyer has shown that Pentecostal worship is a fabric of material and sensory experiences, an aesthetics of persuasion. "One of the most salient features of Pentecostal/charismatic churches is their sensational appeal; they often operate via music and powerful oratory, through which born-again Christians are enabled to sense the presence of the Holy Spirit *with* and *in* their bodies, wherever they are, and to act on such feelings."[8] Meyer argues that aesthetics—sense and sensational forms—is central not only to the understanding of how Pentecostals and charismatic Christians sense the presence of the Holy Spirit but also to their politics. "Understanding religion as offering a particular aesthetics, which forms religious subjects by tuning their senses and enabling modes of embodying the divine through sensational forms, brings together sensation and power. Aesthetics is not outside power structures but enmeshed with them."[9]

Butticci says that the Prayer City of the Mountain of Fire and Miracles Ministries in Nigeria "was purposely created to accommodate massive crowds of prayer warriors and to shape the emotional, sensory, physical and collective experience of prayer."[10] She describes a typical public collective prayer session with these words: "Thousands of men and women fight their battle against demonic spirits and manifest miraculous touch of the Holy Spirit by throwing their bodies to the ground . . . shaking, trembling, rolling, and screaming at the top of their voices. The smell, sound, touch, and sight of so many people furiously praying is overpowering. . . . The massive movement and sound of the crowd and the multi-sensory experience of this spiritual and social catharsis are all overwhelming."[11]

Butticci's other work among African Pentecostals in Italy demonstrates how Catholic and Pentecostal aesthetics of *real presence* encounter each other in agonistic contact zones. African migrants, *parts of no-part* in the Italian society, are attempting to invert the powers relating to the generation and control of real presence. Butticci narrates the story of the encounter between African Pentecostalism and Roman Catholicism in Italy, the story of the weak and the powerful sharing a common space.

Meyer's and Butticci's approaches to the study of Pentecostal aesthetics differ from that of Steven Félix-Jäger, which grounds Pentecostal aesthetics in a theory of art. Yet his work is faithful to the idea that Pentecostalism is deeply concerned with the physical and embodied forms of life in the Spirit.[12]

Another scholar who has studied Pentecostal aesthetics is Ashon Crawley.[13] He directs his attention to the spirituality of African Americans. Crawley's is not about the arts, at least not in the sense Félix-Jäger uses the term. Crawley's focus is not on the real presence of God. His theory interrogates how scholars can draw out the aesthetics embedded in the shouts and whoops of Black folks in the church, in their speaking patterns in the church, or in their preaching styles. Crawley wants to know what all of these tell us about the aesthetics of Black Pentecostals. What does this mean for interpreting the social life of African Americans as oppressed minorities in the United States?

His 2016 book *Blackpentecostal Breath* studies aesthetics as alternative modes of existence performed by African Americans. He formulates his theory of aesthetics by drawing from their practices and interplay of breath (whooping), shouting, noisemaking, and speaking in tongues. He examines these practices not only as a critique of the violence of the exclusive and hierarchical American racial normativity but also as the sensual foundation for the emergence of social life among marginalized minorities and for the creation of "otherwise possibilities."

Of the four scholars whose works I have just reviewed, my approach to the study of aesthetics is closer to that of Meyer and Butticci than the other two. I consider aesthetics primarily in the sense of the manifestation of the divine in the physical. I consider aesthetics as a kind of divine touch. It is in play or display when the divine (what a group of people consider as their deity or god) is made real, vicariously tangible, visible in the worship space. Aesthetics is about the role of bodies as sites for the manifestation of the divine. I am interested in how the Pentecostal aesthetics of persuasion is mobilized through the staging of miracles, the healing of the bodies, and the amelioration of socioeconomic predicaments. This interest compels me to ask what is going on when Nigerian Pentecostals invite demons to show themselves, to manifest themselves in their worship services and spiritual-warfare exercises. What is going on when they invite gods and the presence of gods to be vicariously seen or tangible in their gatherings?

The Phenomenology of Hot Prayers

What are the hot prayers within which the practice of inviting demons as guests occurs? Since 1993 I have observed hundreds of this kind of prayer. I will give a short description of such prayers based on my experience and notes. They are normally conducted as part of a spiritual-warfare exercise. They are usually considered to be a very serious matter undertaken to arrest life-threatening situations or events that thwart human flourishing. The pastor (the prayer leader) and the participants are really concerned about the problems they are facing, the obstacles before them, and they believe that their problems or sufferings are caused by demonic spirits.

Hot prayers start like any regular prayer: with praise and worship, Bible reading, preaching, and the tempered solicitation of the manifestation of the power of the Holy Spirit. The changeover to hot prayers is a very delicate operation. Pentecostals believe that if the pastor or prayer warrior leading a hot prayer segment is not skilled, something could really go wrong during the session. The manifestations of both the demonic and the holy could become wild and uncontrollable. It is not uncommon to see in such chaotic sessions some worshippers trying to strip themselves naked, women falling down in the spirit and exposing underwear and undergarments, other worshippers vomiting, some exposing secrets of other members, many screaming and shouting, and others being prevented by the workers (those assisting the prayer leader) from running out of the room in their ecstatic stupor. But we are getting ahead of our story.

The pastor starts a hot prayer session by saying something like this: "Now I want all of you to invite every demon, every spirit, every foul spirit on your case to appear right now. Call them from the east, from the west, from the north, from the south. Let them show themselves. Call them to a meeting, convene a meeting, and let them actually appear." The pastor—supposedly with higher anointing and higher spiritual powers—will also command the demons to appear. Pentecostals believe that when they convene such a meeting and bark their orders like sergeants major the demons will hear their voices and appear at the site where the holy soldiers are pronouncing the summons. Pentecostals believe that in the spiritual realm there is no "space," so even if demons are busy somewhere a million miles away and they hear the voices of believers engaged in spiritual warfare, they will manifest immediately. As Pentecostals bark the commands of their invitations, some worshippers in the room will begin to have manifestations; serious spiritual possessions will begin to happen.

As they invite these demons to come into their gathering, the whole place will be charged with spiritual power and spiritual presences. Pentecostals say that when the place is charged, they are filled with the power of God, the power of the Holy Spirit. At the same time, we have a visible presence of those demons in the sense of manifestations, possessions, shouting, and screaming, because all the invited demons are believed to be in the air in that room.

As the demons are intensely gathered, the pastor will issue another command. He will now call the angels of God—the warring angels of God with the flaming swords of God—to also come into the room as guests. As the angels gather, the pastor will ask them to surround the whole room. "Now I call a hundred thousand angels with their flaming swords to gather together and secure the place. Make sure none of the demons that came escape. Block all their escape routes."

In that tense moment almost everybody is screaming, barking orders, speaking in tongues, groaning, crying, or praying fervently. The pastor goes on to say, "Angels of God, I release you to slaughter them now. Slaughter the demons! I call down the power of the Holy Ghost; fire of the Holy Ghost fall on the demons now; fire of the Holy Ghost come down and fall on them. The thunder of God explode in this room right now." In this charged moment, some people will begin to scream, crying that they feel that their skins are on fire. Such worshippers believe that they are feeling the sensation of burning skin because the demons in the room are burning, the demons are feeling the heat of God, or the demons who are in them and troubling them are being burned alive so they will exude from their bodies. These visceral cries, primordial screams, and chilling shouts are considered to be the very visible manifestations of the presence of demons.

Sometimes, the demons that are invited to the room and subsequently given to the fire of the Holy Ghost as fuel do not have to travel very far to enter the room. They already reside in the believers issuing the command. One of the popular prayer lines in a hot prayer session is this: "I bind all evil spirits *in me* or that are attacking me, in Jesus' name."[14] This short prayer line suggests that the demons are permanent guests, ever-present beings in any Pentecostal gathering. Since demons dominate the imagination of Pentecostals, especially during spiritual warfare, they are always with them, in their heads. The enemies have to be constantly kept at bay. Such demonic enemies are therefore permanently unwelcome guests; nonetheless, they are guests all the same. Demons are also guests in Pentecostal households, as Nigerian Pentecostals believe in what they call "household enemies" in the forms of the spouse, children, in-laws, and servants. They talk about demons attacking them in their dreams as sexual predators. Demons are guests in Pentecostal bedrooms. In deliverance sessions, during warfare prayers, the demons are invited to speak, to reveal how they entered into a person, only to be expelled. Often, observers in the prayer room ("war room") will gather to hear demons speaking through possessed persons, even as they are praying to defeat the demons and strenuously covering themselves with the "blood of Jesus."

The fight against demonic guests is not restricted to demons currently possessing any believers or operating in the present time. Pentecostals can presumably go into the past and summon demons that made evil decisions against them and retroactively cancel such decisions. They do this by asking the demons to reconvene their meetings. Pastor Daniel Olukoya, the general overseer of Mountain of Fire and Miracles Ministry in Lagos, is an expert in issuing this kind of invitation and many others like it as a way of settling spiritual problems. Observe the prayer point he selected for his church members in December 2015 as they prepared to enter the year 2016. He had asked his members to engage in prayers for the last seven days of the year. On the prayer schedule for December 30, there was one prayer that caught my attention as I was researching the phenomenon of demon invitation. It reads: "Committee of demons who sat on my case, I convene your meeting, I cancel your decision, and I bring the power of God against you in the name of Jesus."[15] Nigerian Pentecostals like Olukoya are saying they have the ability to reconvene past meetings of the demons that have dealt with their cases. In the prayer sessions, once the demons reconvene, the Pentecostals can cancel their decisions. Here the Pentecostal is just being nice. In other cases, Olukoya and any one of his church members would set such demons ablaze.

What is really going on when the demons are brought into the holy place of worship to be burned alive or have their past decisions canceled? At least five things are going on. First, there is an *ambiguity of the sacred space*; the unholy is invited to the holy space. This should trouble you if you are a Christian who believes that the worship space in the church is the holiest ground and that Pentecostals have turned it into a theater of demons. You were taught in your Sunday school classes that demons and God are not supposed to mix. But now you are reading about Pentecostal Christians consciously inviting the unholy to a kumbaya dance with the holy in the name of doing something for God.

Second, there is synesthesia (intertwining of the senses) in the room of the spiritual confluence. In the encounter with the demons, all the senses of the body are intertwined. Prayer is a synesthetic encounter. When the Pentecostals hear the words of a commanding prayer, they converge on sounds and their meanings, yet what they find is a sequence not of phonemes but of images, something seen; the vocal sounds trade their ears for their eyes. The eyes, ears, and other organs or channels of perception are brought together in the heat (*hit*) of prayer, in a synesthetic collaboration, "which ensures that a phenomenon apprehended by one sense is instantly transposed into the other."[16]

In that space-time of critical hot prayers, the worshippers—prayer warriors—are hearing the pastor's words, but the words are automatically transposed into images of demons being commanded, and such demons are seen by the eyes. It is not only the holy and the unholy that come together in spiritual warfare but also the senses. To fully inhabit that Pentecostal room of hot prayers, the believer needs an imagination not only to hear the words the pastor utters but also to see images. Some Pentecostals say that at the critical moment of the command to burn demons they see flashbacks of bodies burning and writhing in fire. They also say they smell burning flesh. They are reflexively in or near the fire. We also have the commingling of the senses: when they hear fire, they not only hear it but also feel it on their bodies.

I know that people cry in such moments. But I cannot tell whether their cries are traumatic. After people go through trauma, something that remains from the past event returns as a flashback to haunt the present. When the pastor issues his commands, the congregation members not only hear him but also receive various images, flashbacks of past traumatic experiences. The present is mixed with the past. This is another form of commingling, with the past and the present colliding with or interpenetrating each other. Sometimes the future, as a vista of hope and personal betterment, joins the party of the other time units. These are moments of traumatic lows and ecstatic highs.

Let us not forget that prayer itself is one huge dance or symphony of the senses. It offers a short step to the kind of synesthetic experiences I have just described. For Nigerian Pentecostals, prayer is asking and receiving. This is not only in the sense of human beings putting forward petitions and God granting requests but also in the sense that every prayer is "an open circuit that completes itself only" in converging and commingling with things, senses, and beings in the human and more-than-human world to generate and maintain its unity and coherence and thus render itself factual and efficacious.[17] Prayer is a synesthetic flowing together of matter, spirits, senses, and worlds "into a dynamic and unified experience."[18]

When a Nigerian Pentecostal prays, the prayer is not completed with the vocalization of words. The prayer goes and grabs something, touches something, be it an animal, a human being, a spirit, or whatever, and brings it into its circle of constituted and constituting powers. Prayer is set up as an open circuit that collects things or beings together so that it will be effective, so it will complete itself in the circuit of asking and receiving. Otherwise, the prayer cannot complete the part of receiving. This is so because a prayer is not just the word the believer speaks; it is an open circuit that must complete itself. It does so only by converging and commingling things, senses, and beings in the human and more-than-human world.

If this all sounds confounding to you, then take a look at what God says in Isaiah 55:11: "So shall My word be that goeth forth out of My mouth: It shall not return unto Me void, but it shall accomplish that which I please, and it shall prosper in the thing whereto I sent it." The words you hear from God actually have legs, and they are moving and achieving something. Whatever they need to commingle and do, they do. Isaiah 55:11 says God's word does not just go out but must go out, do everything in the world, change everything, and come back and report to him. For Pentecostals, the words of their fervent prayers must act as words emanating from God's mouth.

We stated above that there are five things that happen when the demons are brought into the holy place of worship to be burned alive or have their past decisions canceled. We have so far examined two of the five things that occur when the demons arrive. Third, the practice of inviting demons as guests in Pentecostal prayer meetings might have something to do with communal therapy. Let us imagine a conversation between Nigerian Pentecostals: "We have many problems, and we know that our past was not clean. We lived sinful lifestyles. In addition, we inherited ancestral curses. Yesterday, you were attacked by some wicked demons. I am in the same boat as you are. There are territorial spirits overseeing our streets, neighborhoods, and city, and they are holding us down. The solution to our problem cannot be odd individuals going off on their own and taking on these powerful demons. Let all of us bring our problems together and deal with the enemies that are troubling us, and together we can defeat them." A similar belief holds in Kalabari traditional religion. A single person cannot defeat a demon, but a group of people acting in concert can defeat any demon. As Robin Horton puts it: "Generally, of course, a single man cannot reject a spirit at will; for while he is only one among a congregation of many, it will have the power to punish him."[19] Thus, in these sessions of hot prayers, participants feel that they are doing something communal about their situations and that they can as a group generate the corporate anointing (concert of power) to invite the demons and deal mercilessly with them.

Fourth, there is also the logic of invitation: there is the play on command and strategic deception. Pentecostals believe that if they issue the command, the demons will obey. This is embedded in the whole logic of their action. Imagine for a moment a Pentecostal issuing the command to demons to gather as guests in her prayer session. She convenes a meeting and invites demons who have been troubling her in the last ten years, or those who sat in a meeting that decided evil against her, to appear in her church prayer session by "fire or by force." She must believe that she can issue that command and that whoever was in that meeting must obey her and come. In addition, she has the power to cancel their decisions. There is this sense of superiority, uncontestable authority, implicit in their practice.

Let us look more closely at the strategic deception involved in the invitation and command. She calls the gods, but she doesn't tell them what she is going to do to them. She is hoping that the demons are stupid enough to come; they can't figure out her deception. She invites them to a meeting, asks the angels of God with flaming swords to guard them, and eventually roasts them in fire or slays them. She must really believe that she is smarter than them and that they do not know as much as she does. Never mind that she will do the same thing to them next Sunday or some other time. The demons are always deemed very foolish and ready to obey the Pentecostal hangman's summons.

Finally, there is also a belief in the supreme logic of God's omnipotent will. God's will has priority over and is antecedent to and determinative of God's reason. God's will is not bound by reason; it is bound by nothing. This does not mean that God is irrational. It only means that God's creative will, his omnipotent will, is the fount for both reason and unreason. God is not self-contradictory; though having the power to do what he wills, God freely limits Godself. It is not that reason, order, or knowledge is rejected; rather, the emphasis is that order is contingent, not necessary. Pentecostalism does not reject reason but believes that God's will is unsearchable. The will of God cannot be fully comprehended. Though the will of God is not completely knowable, Pentecostals do not throw their arms into the air in despair. The will of God is readable through scripture, experience, and signs of the times—and, even then, only in part. Faith is not a search for certainty, for reason that reason cannot oppose, but belief in spite of uncertainty. (Pentecostalism affirms faith in its great ambiguity.) This is not a negative stance to *reason*, and it is not a negative faith as a matter of knowledge, but faith arises through the inability of the believer to fully comprehend God. Only when subjects realize that there is nothing they can do to fathom God, to separate faith from uncertainty, do they become open to the possibilities of the creative will of God, to the unfinishedness of all existence, which are rooted in the productive divine will, which is the groundless ground of all existence.[20]

The invitation to the demons to appear in prayer and worship services raises all sorts of questions. We have Christians, supposedly very holy, inviting the worst of the created beings, soliciting demons, to traffic with them, even if it is an unequal exchange or contest of spiritual powers. The very place that God manifests is now the site of visitation for demons. What happens to the whole concept of the worship space as the most sacred of places? In the very holiest of places, we have the coming and going of demons because they are deliberately invited as guests. What exactly is happening when Pentecostals invite the demons as guests? To respond to this question, I will resort to their use of disparate biblical verses and Christian theology to explain the logic of the invitation. I will also go into African culture to make sense of this practice of inviting demons as guests.

Biblical Precedents of Ambiguity of Place, Strategic Deception, and Authority to Dominate

I have provided a thick description of the phenomenon of hot prayers. It is time to offer an analysis of what Nigerian Pentecostals consider to be biblical and cultural justifications for their practice of inviting demons to visit prayer services as guests. They easily point to Job 2:1–10 to justify their actions. God called a meeting in heaven, and Satan was among those in the gathering. God and Satan went on to talk about how to test Job's faith in God. Is this the same God whose eyes are so holy that he cannot behold evil? How do you deal with this ambiguity? For Nigerian Pentecostals, it is simple. If God wants to achieve a purpose, he can even invite Satan to do it for him, just to demonstrate that he has power over Satan. They argue that our idea that the holy and the unholy cannot meet is not consistently affirmed by the Bible.

Another biblical precedent that helps Pentecostals to make sense of their practice comes from 2 Kings 10:18–28. Jehu, a servant of God, acted in very deceptive manner. A prophet of God prophesized to Jehu that God had anointed him to be the king of Israel. At the provocation of this prophecy, Jehu killed the reigning king and became the new king. He now turned around and said he was going to worship Baal in a big way. He asked all the prophets, priests, and servants of Baal to assemble in the temple of Baal, telling them he wanted to hold a great sacrifice for Baal. When the believers in Baal had filled the temple, he asked the priests of Baal to go around the temple and ferret out all those who were true worshippers of Baal. The priests did their job well, dragging out from the temple all those they felt were not true Baal worshippers. Next, the servants of Baal made great sacrifices and burned offerings. Jehu turned around and gave this instruction to his eighty soldiers "'If any of the men whom I have brought into your hands escapes, whoever lets him escape, it shall be his life for the life of the other. . . .' Jehu said to the guard and to the captains, 'Go in *and* kill them; let no one come out!' And they killed them with the edge of the sword" (2 Kings 10:24–25). Do we now see where the Pentecostal practices of deception or imagination can come from?

Why do Pentecostals think that they can give commands to the demons and the demons will obey? Ephesians 2:6, which they quote often, says believers are seated with Christ in heavenly places far above principalities. So Pentecostals believe that in the militarized command system of heaven they are officers above Satan and his demons. Ephesians 6:12–13 names this hierarchy in the spiritual realm for them. Ordinarily the spiritual authority of human beings is below that of principalities and rulers of darkness. But the moment persons believe in Jesus Christ, they are elevated above all principalities, demons, and other beings whose authority is less than that of Christ because they are seated with Jesus Christ at the right hand of God. Therefore, they can issue commands to demons. If a person is not with God—that is, is not born-again—then any attempt on that person's part to issue any command to Satan and his demons could result in the loss of life or severe demonic oppression.

A similar thing happened in Acts 19:11–17 when some unbelievers saw that Paul had been casting out demons and they told a man they could cast out demons from him. The man who had the evil spirit leaped on them and started beating them and tearing their clothes, and they fled naked and wounded. The demons asked them, "Jesus I know, and Paul I know; but who are you?" (Acts 19:15).

Pentecostals also base their authority to invite and punish demons on Matthew 18:18, which says, "Assuredly, I say to you, whatever you bind on earth will be bound in heaven, and whatever you loose on earth will be loosed in heaven." Nigerian Pentecostals believe that when Christians have a strong faith in God whatever they say in the physical realm automatically has an effect in the spiritual. (Never mind that the text is interpreted differently by scholars.) On the basis of their interpretation of this verse, among many others, they think that even though the demons may know about their act of deception, the demons are compelled to obey because God has given Christians supreme authority over evil spirits. The demons are not stupid; they are just powerless before the spirit-filled Christians.

The Tradition of Inviting Demons to Prayer Parties: Ongoing Internal Debates

The practice of inviting demons to prayer meetings has generated some debates within the Nigerian Pentecostal movement. Why have the Pentecostals not adopted a simple solution to their demon problems? Why don't they kill all the demons in one day and solve all their problems? Since they link almost all their problems to demons, killing all the demons in the universe will set them free forever. This is the simple solution, and they would not have to pray against them or fight them again.

Let me provide some of their stock responses to this set of questions. They are wont to draw wisdom from C. S. Lewis's *The Screwtape Letters*.[21] *The Screwtape Letters* is fictional, but Nigerian Pentecostals have elevated it to the rank of "scripture." They will say, in accordance with *The Screwtape Letters*, that when believers kill or defeat a demon, Satan will send them a more powerful demon if he is determined to bring them down. They will then add that if they killed millions of demons, Satan would supply more millions to fight them. They argue that Satan has an almost innumerable quantity of demons at his service, adding that when he revolted against God he left heaven with one-third of the angels.

If the Screwtapian explanation does not convince you, then Pentecostals will offer another one. And it goes like this: the binding of demons by Pentecostals is not final because they don't live in perpetual strict holiness as the Bible commands them to do. Believers may set a demon on fire, but as long they do not live a holy life, whatever effect their action accomplishes will eventually wear out. They can bind a demon and cast it out to the dry places, but when they fall back into sin, the results of their actions are nullified.

Ultimately it means that Pentecostals know what they are dealing with; they can't really kill the demons. They can only obstruct them for a period. The binding of demons is temporary. Pentecostals maintain that God will do the final binding with his eternal chain on Judgment Day. What they can do at this side of the eschaton is to restrain the demons for only a period. Even at that, the impacts of their brutal actions are limited, as the "bind and burning" of demons wear out because of sin or because the Christians are not God, whose actions could have an everlasting effect.

Pentecostals Are Drawing from
ATR's Practice of Inviting Gods as Guests

What are the African precedents for what the Pentecostals are doing? Horton, in his 1960 book *The Gods as Guests*, examines the practice of inviting gods as guests to human festivals among the Kalabari-Ijo of the

Niger Delta.[22] First he lays out a theory of real presence, though he does not use this term. The adherents of Kalabari traditional religion believe in the power of *real presence*, the idea that gods can manifest their presences through possession.

Second, he discusses the Kalabari system's three categories of gods: (a) community heroes, (b) water spirits, and (c) ancestors. Sitting above these categories is the supreme being, *Tamuno*. The ancestors and community heroes (the heroic figures of the community who became deified) lived within the town or its sacred forests. The water spirits live in the rivers, creeks, streams, and sea. From time to time every year, the select citizens formally go to various beaches, canoe across rivers to islands, and perform rituals to bring the gods into the towns. Once they return with the water spirits, they celebrate them, making sacrifices, holding festivals, dancing, and staging masquerade displays. And after three days or seven days, they perform certain sending-off rituals and take the gods back to their abodes inside the waters.

Third, Horton discusses how the gods present themselves during the festivals honoring them. They do so through miming: sometimes you know a god is present when somebody mimes how the god is supposed to walk or speak. Miming is not a full possession. The gods also show themselves through masquerades. When Kalabari play masquerades, the masks represent the gods in the town—the gods that they have invited in. The third form of real presence is full possession. And all three of these can move together in any one festival or any one period during a festival.

The matter of inviting spirits, gods, or ancestors into town, human abodes, or festivals is not peculiar to the Kalabari. Many West African communities have traditions of inviting ancestors and then feeding and feting them. Africans do not invite only gods and ancestors into their habitats or festivals. Hunters invite animals they want to trap or kill by imitating the specific calls of the animals to lure them within the range of their weapons. If hunters want to kill a particular male animal, they will imitate the sexual calls of its female counterpart, and the male animal will unknowingly walk into the range of the killing instruments awaiting it.

These traditions might have influenced Nigerian Pentecostals in their practice of inviting demons as guests. They don't need to be very creative in generating new ideas. They just need to rebrand old ideas and practices. We cannot really understand Nigerian Pentecostalism if we have not paid attention to African traditional religions or indigenous cultures. Nigerian

Pentecostalism is a mesh of continuity and discontinuity with or within African traditional religions.

A Pentecostal Theory of Aesthetics

What is aesthetics? Aesthetics is a matter of perception. It is about the human capacity to know, perceive, or interpret their world through the five senses. Aesthetics comes from *aisthesis*: sensation and knowledge. The question is how sensation and experience are related to the body. What kind of mass appeal do they generate in religion? Max Weber argues that when a religion puts its emphasis on experience, emotion, bodily sensation, or aesthetic media, it is making a mass appeal and engaging in emotional propaganda; he adds that this is not the way rational religiosity operates.[23] And for Kant, aesthetics is about art and the beautiful. It is what appeals to the mind, rational thinking, and the universal human faculty of judgment, not to the body and its emotion. We must situate Weber's and Kant's understandings of aesthetics within the context of the impact of the Enlightenment on Western thought. Within Enlightenment thought, the dyad of transcendent and immanent is split. Scholars came to see the immanent as the only relevant realm and the transcendent as human invention or projection. The idea that transcendence and immanence come together in objects or bodies was not of interest to them.

But in the twentieth century, the understanding of aesthetics was different. Jacques Rancière, the French philosopher who argues that aesthetics is about framing a sensory space and determining how the transcendental presents itself to sensory experience. More importantly, it is about who has the right to govern the possibility of sensation: Who can be seen or heard and who cannot be seen or heard?[24] Who assigns the rules that say you can sense this but not that? Therefore, he says, aesthetics is about the distribution of the sensible. If a group or class of ordinary citizens senses something outside the authorized order, it creates a disruption, a dissensus. It creates a new politics because it is now sensing things it was not supposed to sense.

Meyer, in her studies of Pentecostalism, looks at aesthetics as a tool of persuasion as she tries to retrieve its old meaning to demonstrate how Pentecostals deal with real presence. She interrogates how their abiding interest in real presence helps their understanding of religion, enabling them to sense the power and the presence of the Holy Spirit and to make the power of the divine tangible in the immanent. Ultimately for her, aesthetics is about sensational forms (forms of mediation); it is about form as a necessary condition for expressing content and meaning. Her theory of aesthetics avoids the dualism of spirit and matter, form and content, body and mind, and transcendence and immanence.[25]

Butticci took the theories of Meyer and Rancière and went to Rome to investigate the aesthetics of African Pentecostals in Europe. She says Protestants in general do not believe in any artwork harboring divine presence or in God showing up in any real presence. But the Catholics believe God (rather, the power of God) can be present in objects or bones of dead saints. Here Butticci is gesturing to a fundamental and historic divide between Protestants and Catholics. Then African Pentecostals came along and are retrieving the sense that God can show up in objects or persons. African Pentecostals who found common ground with Italian Catholics with regard to real presence discovered to their chagrin that differences in power between the two groups marred the building of a harmonious relationship between them. The Catholic Church says that they can control what manifests, that they know what real presence is and African Pentecostals do not. The Catholics are not debating what can manifest but who controls it. The body that has the power to control manifestation also has the authority to declare the manifestations that others cherish to be demonic and unacceptable.

Butticci demonstrates that though they all agree that God can manifest physically in objects, the Catholics say that the manifestations among the Pentecostals cannot be real, that the appearances are of African devils. The Catholics tell the Pentecostals they do not like the kinds of possessions and exorcisms that are common in the Pentecostal churches. The Africans return the compliment by saying that the Italian Catholics are actually worshipping idols (objects), which they claim harbor the power of God.

Butticci combines Meyer's and Rancière's perspectives to formulate a Pentecostal politics of aesthetics in the encounter of African Pentecostalism and Roman Catholicism in Italy. What drives her study is who has the power to mediate the presence of the divine and how claims about this power by the "part that has no part" create a dissensus.

Though Butticci works from Meyer's ideas, there are differences in their understanding of aesthetics. There is a subtle difference between Meyer's analysis of real presence and that of Butticci. Meyer's focus on aesthetics is on fulfilling the spiritual wants of worshippers. It is ultimately about a metaphysical question: What can manifest? Her interest is in how transcendence appears in the immanent. She refuses the split that Enlightenment scholarship created. Butticci focuses on the contemporary life of Pentecostals, and aesthetics is about who gets to regulate what is manifesting. Her focus is ultimately about a political question: Who controls what manifests?

The two questions (what can manifest and who controls what manifests) that Meyer and Butticci tackle are very important in understanding the aesthetics of Pentecostal hot prayer. But they are not the driving questions for me. My primary organizing question is this: What is the value of what manifests? Nigerian Pentecostals are more interested in how what manifests, the real presence, can help them deal with sickness, poverty, and other existential conditions than in the questions Meyer and Butticci are tackling. They are not debating what can manifest; it is already assumed that it is the Holy Spirit. Pentecostals already assume that everybody has a right to a democratized access to the real presence of God's Spirit. Of course, they also know that demons can also manifest, and they believe they know how to deliver believers from demonic attacks.

To recapitulate, there are three questions in this debate: What can manifest? Who controls what manifests? What is the value of what manifests? These three questions constitute an internal logic in the theory of Pentecostal aesthetics. And the three questions hang harmoniously together. Though I have separately identified these three existential questions, we cannot take away one and expect the others to stay intact and retain their full meaning. If Pentecostals doubt that the spirit they presume to be manifesting in their midst as Lord is the Spirit of God, then they can no longer focus on the third question of the ethical value of manifestation. On the other hand, if a power stronger than them is controlling what can manifest, then they cannot be sure whether the controller is giving them access only to false gods. More importantly, they lose control over how to deploy what is manifesting to enhance their human flourishing.

Together, these three conceptions of aesthetics constitute a unity in multiplicity. One approach implies another. The political is also ontological as it is a site where existence or coexistence is at stake. Ethics, as it concerns relevant states of the world and forms of commons for human flourishing, is always political and ontological. The ethical, like the political and the ontological, includes or presupposes the other two as a set of conditions for its own possibility. Thus, each one of the three parts can serve not only as an end but also as a means to the other two. Pentecostal sensibility or religiosity involves an apprehension and responsiveness to how these dimensions of (the quest for and reception of) real presence constitute a harmonious order of interests in an encounter with God.

With the last comment, Pentecostal aesthetics emerges in a surprising new sense—at least in the thought world that dwells at the intersection of Pentecostal practices and continental philosophy. Just as in a work of art beauty arises from the harmonious relation of parts, the beauty of the inner impulses of Pentecostal aesthetics is the harmonious relations of its parts, the questions. The source of order has shifted from external relations of objects to transcendence, from the external agent (God) behind real presences to internal relations among the subparts of the telos of aesthetics of prayer. The key here is to note that Pentecostal aesthetics is operating at two levels: reference and relation. The logic of real presence refers to something beyond itself: meaning and value are in terms of an external agent. But the logical structure of the telos for wanting to conjoin the divine and material seeks meaning and value in terms of relation, the logic of self-referentiality. Now someone may raise the objection that there is always the possibility of identifying a fourth question or dimension of real presence. No problem: self-reflexive systems are often characterized by "strange loops," meaning they cannot close in on themselves. They are complexly adaptive and open. This is indeed an ontological principle. So the two levels of Pentecostal aesthetics, the aesthetics of (within) aesthetics, are "both an aesthetic and an ontological principle."[26]

The particular Pentecostal sensibility toward this internal logic forces us to keep two orders of analysis in perspective. First, the real presence is about getting knowledge through embodied stuff. Second, it is about knowing how the three questions themselves harmoniously hang together. This is about the beauty of their inner teleology. These three questions, like Kant's understanding of artwork, do not need an external agent to make sense of them. In a sense, Kant collapsed the distance between ends and means. Instead of ends now being external to the means, he said ends are now inside the means itself. Ends complete themselves within themselves. The art becomes an end in itself. It becomes internal to itself; it is not referring to anything outside. Simply, it has no external reference. Meyer or Butticci only treated one of these three questions and missed the other two. Without adequately dealing with the three questions, they did not provide us with a perspective to comprehend the inner teleology of the aesthetics of real presence in African Pentecostalism. Pentecostal hot prayers have their beauty or aesthetics, just as an artwork does. When Pentecostals are engaged in hot prayers, the three questions are internal not only to the prayers but also to the worship process in which the prayers play only a part.

Which of these three questions is ultimately more important for crafting a Nigerian Pentecostal theory of aesthetics? Put differently, which of these existential questions can best guide us to an understanding of how Nigerian Pentecostals perceive their world or their abiding interest in real presence? Nigerian Pentecostals predominantly perceive and sense their God as a concatenation of real presences. They are primarily persuaded by a God who can perform miracles, heal the body, and ameliorate existential angst through the sensation and perception of real presences. Thus, my preference among these questions belongs to the ethical side: What is the value of what manifests? This stance should not be construed to mean a rejection of the other questions; the three questions are often commingled, but one must understand the telos of the Pentecostal engagement with real presences to see how the various questions properly hang together. The proper consideration of these questions as a whole set will lead us to think not only about the aesthetics of Pentecostals but also about the aesthetics of (within) aesthetics in Pentecostal worship and prayer.

We have already laid bare the aesthetics of aesthetics in the traffic of real presences in Pentecostalism. What if there is a third perspective of aesthetics of Pentecostal prayer (worship), a third level of the meaning or conceptualization of Pentecostal aesthetics? We have first dealt with the Pentecostal aesthetics in terms of real presences. Then we shifted to the beauty, the supposed harmonious order of the questions, moral queries, demands, or expectations internal to the quest for real presence. We named this second perspective the aesthetics of aesthetics. Now let us identify even a third dimension of aesthetics in Pentecostal prayer (worship).

This endeavor starts with a consideration of the means-and-end relation. Ordinarily, the end is external to the means; a person deploys a means to achieve a goal, which lies outside or is different from the means. The purpose of the means lies outside it. There are, however, instances where the means and end are not separate, where the purpose of the means is intrinsic to it and the end and means are integrated, internally related, with each acting reciprocally as both means and end. This instance is what Immanuel Kant refers to as beauty, the harmonious order of things, the aesthetics of art in his language of critical judgment.

Note what is going on here. In the first example, the end is external to the means. In the second, the end is not external to the means; the gap between them seemingly disappears. What happens next is what is called *pure means*; there is no longer an end, whether external or internal. The means is a means of itself. The means is pure bliss. Real presence is a pure means, a pure medium. Real presence, just like the worship in which it is always embedded and of which it is an integral part, is not an end in itself but a pure mediality without end.

I have argued elsewhere that Pentecostal worship, especially as it enters the "hot phase" and density of real presence, is a pure means.[27] A means is pure precisely because its *in-order-to* has not yet been decided. A decided means is no longer a pure means. For instance, worship as a pure means is a courageous openness whose *validity* defies all purposive articulation but represents the commitment of the participants, whose self-realization lies in self-transcendence. When worship tries to be useful, placed in the service of utilitarian purpose or particular ambition, it falls to the level of profitability or ritual action, abandoning its openness to surprises. *Pure means is not the opposite of means or ends but a condition of their possibility.* It is pure mediality.[28]

A pure means is without goal and also without goallessness. It is a world somewhere between end and means. Worship as a pure means gestures to the idea that God is not conditioned by means programmed to reach him. Worship as a pure means also points to this idea: God is not an end among ends, something we strive to grasp for the time being or for keeps. Somewhere between (beyond) the worlds of means and ends is God, the Unconditioned, and the spirit and truth of Pentecostal worship lies in lurching into the liminal, marginal, and "mystical" wonderland between means and end.[29]

Worship as a pure means bursts free of referents and floats in emotional currents that no longer appear to be anchored in what was once its structural foundations of problems and anxieties. Real presence now appears as a decorative surface that absorbs the existential angsts of the participants, becoming a floating sign. Real presence, which in itself is a sign of God's presence, is now further transformed into a sign of other signs, trembling signs of an originary telos of worship, signs of the participants' living spirituality; indeed, real presence becomes a sign of itself in a virtual space, with red-hot coordinates of emotional and spiritual intensities. Real presence—or hot prayer, spirit-filled worship—is an architecture of signs.

The means dominate the end. Purpose is not enough. Because the divine-human relationships are made by means more than ends, purpose in this religionscape becomes a means in worship rather than an end in worship. Purpose defines very little: the big means and the little problem is the rule in worship.[30] The means is more important than the purpose.

Is all this not another level of aesthetics—the logic of the Enlightenment notion of aesthetics pushed to its utter limits? In the beginning, the end was present to the means as an external agent; then Kant entombed ends in means, and Pentecostals came along and exorcised the ghost of end from its body of means, and now the specter of end floats above worship as a homeless apparition from Amos Tutuola's world. A specter is haunting Pentecostal worship—the specter of aesthetics. All powers of Christianity have entered into a holy alliance to exorcise this specter: Catholics and Protestants, anthropologists and philosophers, radical scholars and state spies. Where is the group that has not decried Pentecostals' excessive enjoyment of the *real*, that has not hurled the branding reproach of jouissance that appears to have abandoned the burning issues of the commonly shared world as any form of referent?[31]

Alas, this third layer of aesthetics (the third movement in my theory of aesthetics) I have just analyzed is very unstable. It is like an equilibrium at a knife's edge, ever sliding to either side of the instrument. Sooner or later— and always too soon—Pentecostals fall back to the first-order aesthetics, the pragmatic value of real presence to their quotidian existence. This is all about deploying knowledge gained from embodied stuff, information garnered through the piercing of the phenomenal veil to enhance their socioeconomic flourishing. Even their interest in the second-order level of aesthetics easily shrinks to only the third question (the economic value of what manifests), falling away from any consideration of how the three existential questions harmoniously hang together.

For them the supreme purpose of the traffic between the phenomenal and the noumenal worlds, of seriously engaging real presence, is to accomplish justice as a state of the world, not as a virtue. It is existence as such. Nigerian Pentecostals' idea of actualizing their destiny or potential is not founded on needs or on the order of possession but on the justice of the believer's existence as a child of God with a particular destiny. It is necessary to make this fine distinction if we are to fully grasp the fervency with which African Pentecostals pursue what they think is their God-given destiny. With this orientation to real presence and the attendant view of justice, I will say, following Giorgio Agamben, that there is "a striking contraction of ethics and ontology, justice is presented not as a virtue but as a 'state of the world,' as the ethical category that corresponds not to having-to-be but to existence as such."[32] This is not about the right of possession but the right of existence itself, the right of actualization of destiny itself. And it is akin to how Walter Benjamin understands justice: "Justice does not appear to refer to the good will of the subject, but, instead, constitutes a state of the world. Justice designates the ethical category of the existent, virtue the ethical category of the demanded. Virtue can be demanded; justice in the final analysis can only be as a state of the world or as a state of God."[33]

This way of perceiving prayer and real presence as tools of engaging with existence suggests a certain understanding or notion of the sacred. The notion or theory of the sacred is a powerfully integrating and structuring force for the currents of ideas about prayer, real presence, and human flourishing, as well as being their ground. For Pentecostals, the sacred is always at hand, and it is primarily conceived of in terms of possibilities and potentialities. Some of these preexist their manifestations, and others happen without a place in any preexisting set, only retroactively creating their conditions of possibility. In every society there are three sets of possibilities: (a) one that is open to all individuals, (b) another that is available to only a few and excludes the rest of society, and (c) the universe of possibilities that are yet to be fulfilled or are not yet available to all persons and institutions. This latter, (c), is actually the *horizon of unfulfilled possibilities*. The sacred is the embodiment of unfulfilled possibilities.[34] The belief in this kind of sacred is a belief in transcending limits, and the appeal to sacred is an appeal to fulfill not-yet-realized possibilities, to even actualize impossible possibility.

Prayer is, above all, concern with the power to command and prescribe the destruction and creation of possibilities and potentialities. The power is exercised to control possibilities of life, to distribute persons and groups to places in society and their assigned tasks. In this Rancierian sense, prayer is an aesthetics itself. This is an aesthetics in the sense of a destructive and constructive staging of possibilities, the distribution of the sacred as the universal set of possibilities. There is a subtle difference between what Rancière takes aesthetics to mean and the way I have just described Pentecostal prayers as an aesthetic. In my Pentecostal-inflected thinking, aesthetics is about the distribution of the sacred. Rancière thinks it is about the distribution of the sensible.

For African Pentecostals, the sacred is the infinite set of possibilities. What engages their interest is not the abstract nature of the possibilities as they endure and perdure in the sacred. They ask, How is the set of possibilities available to us? The sacred is always something bigger than them, and they are interested in tapping it for their flourishing. And they feel they can draw almost endlessly from this universal set of possibilities to get out of any constraints. As they say, with God all things are possible. So when I think of aesthetics, I think of how Pentecostals are trying to redistribute the possibilities available in the sacred. This is why they engage in hot prayers; this is why they are willing to traffic in the real presences. This is why they are asking the three existential questions: How can God manifest? Where can God manifest? And what is the value of God's manifestation to us? The value is how God's real presences help to change one's life's possibilities.

The Fourth Movement in the Pentecostal Theory of Aesthetics: Distribution of Possibilities

As we have just learned, Pentecostal aesthetics is about the distribution of the sacred, the possibilities of existence in the spatiotemporal fabric. It is the distribution of intensities of divine presence in the immanent world. Such distribution opens up a gap for possibilities to manifest. For Nigerian Pentecostals, Pentecostalism is not just a garb of spirituality they don or a system of beliefs they assent to. Pentecostalism is a mode of existing that born-again believers assume in order to access truth, strive for the new, and actualize their destiny or potential. This form of existing is always existence in the gap: the moment or reality never coincides with itself, as there is always a crack for the unexpected to happen. Nigerian Pentecostals believe that there are always cuts in the fabric of reality: there are ruptures of preexisting temporal conditions taking place not in a mythic world but in contemporary social orders, and they are created and sustained by a certain kind of agent in every generation. Put differently, Pentecostals believe that there are *time gaps* in temporality: gaps that mean that there is always a new temporality in the flux of the past, present, and future by which human beings (prayerful and spirit-filled believers) can insert themselves between the infinite past and the infinite future, thereby exercising their uniquely and supremely human capacity to begin something new and display the distinctiveness of each individual or his or her destiny.

The purpose of this insertion into temporality or living in the gap is to create or grasp possibilities of life for human flourishing. Nigerian Pentecostals insert themselves into the time gap to have or manifest the spiritual and social powers to command, order, and distribute the possibilities and pathways assigned to each person and to actualize them. Lest we forget, this view of the world is based on at least two understandings: (a) the world, in particular their lifeworld, is incomplete, unfinished, and still coming into existence, and possibility must always exceed actuality; and (b) nature, society, social structure, or existence is formed according to an imbalance in the concentrations of possibilities, differentials in potentialities, and power. Thus, aesthetics is about the distribution of possibilities—the birth, nurture, or death of possibilities.[35]

Conclusion

Let me conclude by summing up some of the lessons we have learned from this study. First, prayer is, above all, the power to command and prescribe the destruction and creation of possibilities, potentialities. Prayer is about power exercised to control how the possibilities of life distribute persons and groups to places in society and their assigned tasks. Second, in Nigerian Pentecostalism, prayer is aesthetics. It is correct to focus scholarly attention on the aesthetics of prayer, but it is more correct to consider prayer as aesthetics. This is an aesthetics in the sense of a disruptive staging of possibilities, the distribution of the sacred.

Third, in Nigerian Pentecostalism, aesthetics is ethics. Real presence is meaningful or important insofar as it can add value (especially by adding an economic and health boost) to life. Nigerian Pentecostals have engaged real presences of God in various ways. The point, however, is to deploy it for human flourishing. To deploy real presence to change the world, to seek justice of existence, presupposes a certain interpretation of world, humanity, and the supernatural. As we have learned in this study, Nigerian Pentecostals' interpretations of the world, human potentiality, and divine will are influenced by African traditional religions. In a sense, this study is also about the aesthetics of African traditional religions as they are taken up into African Pentecostalisms.

The sacred is a site not only for aesthetics (as in the distribution of the sacred, possibilities for human flourishing) but also for the manifestation of strange, deformed creatures. If in this chapter we have sought to understand how Africans deploy the sacred to enhance their human flourishing, in the next two chapters we will *demonstrate* how their fascination with the sacred and its possibilities—supported by a fantasmatic screen—has turned up monsters (from Latin *monstrare* and *monere*, meaning "to demonstrate," "to warn") in the African postcolony. In the next two chapters, we will study the monstrous dimensions of the sacred in the African postcolony. The chapters painfully indicate the political, existential, and ethical challenges that face postcolonial Africans in their quotidian encounters with the sacred. The chapters "demonstrate and warn of," in most uncomfortable ways, the monsters of the sacred in Africa.

In chapter 3, we will examine a different form of Africans' engagement with the sacred. We will study how the quest to generate and distribute life possibilities for human flourishing is leading many Africans into the rabbit holes of irrationalities and causing them to turn their backs on modernity's rationality. If this chapter has informed the reader about how the Nigerian Pentecostals stage the distribution of possibilities for human flourishing via spiritual warfare, then chapter 3 demonstrates how Pentecostalism is turning Nigerians away from rationalist epistemology and plunging them into the bottomless pit of spiritualist episteme or religious obscurantism. There is now afoot what I will call the *Pentecostal incredible*. Chapter 3 analyzes the Pentecostal incredible, demonstrating how the sacred has been distorted (bastardized, condemned, reduced) into a sensational, excessively emotional, irrational religion in Pentecostals' desperate, macabre struggles to survive the hazards, precarity, and despair of the postcolonial chaos.

3

THE PENTECOSTAL INCREDIBLE

Introduction

This book offers a theory of the sacred to demonstrate how it plays out in Africa. The theory is made concrete and becomes empirically informed as it is used as an interpretative tool to comprehend or explain social practices in the African postcolony. In the introductory chapter, I stated that in working out my theory of the sacred, I would connect it with three forms of desires (epistemology, power, and recognition) or three types of transcripts. In this chapter, I examine the social practices of epistemology as a transcript of the sacred in the Nigerian postcolony. This chapter and the next clearly demonstrate how religion has badly distorted Africans' engagement with the sacred. The stories and analyses in these two chapters exemplify the monstrosity of the sacred in the African postcolony.

Postcolonial Africa is burdened by the sacred. It is this burden that we have been studying in this book. In this chapter, I will closely examine the destructive effects of African Pentecostal Christians' pattern of thought on common life and general orientation to human flourishing. The goal is to demonstrate how distorted epistemology—more precisely, spiritualist episteme—leads Africans into the monstrous dimension of the sacred that is destroying the commons. The commons is crucial to enlivening and expanding the sacred, the universal set of possibilities available to a people.

Epistemology is the worm at the heart of the apple of African Christianity and its commons. The commons is the plumb line of the morality of African Christianity. In the commons, believers themselves—instead of doctrine and devotion—have become the display (or declaration) of Christ, not, however, as believers but as the mode of manifestation of the ethico-epistemological correlation (or constitution) of self and world (or community). This worm has many friends. Together, they are deforming the apple.

Can Christianity exist without viable commons? Will African Christianity continue to flourish if its foundations are increasingly displaced by trauma, desperation, and despair? Is Nigerian Christianity in good health when its common life in Christ is governed by deformed reason, nonreason, or emotionalism? Can Christianity thrive in a culture where there is little or no commitment to making and keeping the kinds of promises that sustain social fabrics? Responding to these questions about the commons will move us away from evaluating the success of Pentecostalism (or evangelicalism) in Nigeria by narrowly focusing on church attendance, the growth of believers, the vibrancy of deliverance ministries, or the number of churches. The narrow focus often hides the deformities that attend to the life of the commons (political, epistemological, ethical, and so on) or to the dynamics of Christ and the common life in the country.

This chapter examines the deformities of Pentecostalism in Nigeria and the ways this sickness has shaped the commons of Christian life in the country. Our thesis is that we will have a better grasp of the prospects of Pentecostalism (evangelicalism) if we focus on the kind of common life it has fashioned under the pressure of the predicament of postcoloniality. Of course, this is not the only way to decipher the future of Nigerian evangelical Christianity, but it is a good way to arrive at an unvarnished diagnosis of Nigerian Christianity. Though our examination starts with an evaluation of the diseased, crisis-ridden commons in which Nigerian Christians practice their faith, it concludes that the illness is not a sickness unto death.

Governance as trauma is the ground, the commons indeed, of Christian life in Nigeria. Governance, just like the daily existential condition, is an incredible phenomenon, a situation of perpetual crisis, or crisis as the norm. Christianity in the country is a struggle to survive the perpetual trauma of national political governance. Caught in this agonistic struggle, Christianity (especially its Pentecostal variant) has become part of what the Nigerian scholar Tejumola Olaniyan calls the *postcolonial incredible*. "The incredible is not simply a breach but an outlandish infraction of 'normality' and its limits."[1] I will transform Olaniyan's postcolonial incredible into the *Pentecostal incredible*.

There are many Pentecostals—although certainly not all of Nigerian Pentecostals—who claim to have direct insight into God's mind with the idea that this divinity demands critical resistance to the current society's knowledge systems and habitus. This God, they believe, often asks his followers to perform psychotic-delirious actions to prove their faith. The Pentecostal incredible is not simply a breach but an outlandish infraction of "reason" and Christian "normativeness" and their limits. These three "powers" bombard average Nigerian Pentecostals. First governance, a metaphor for the disaster of faith (in nationhood), attacks them; then the postcolonial incredible, a metonym for the disaster of faith (in normality); and finally, disaster of faith itself attacks as the Pentecostal incredible. In this chapter, we will analyze how Christianity/Pentecostalism participates in the reign of the incredible in Nigeria. I will conclude our discussion with a section that lays out the likely principles that might inform a radical Christian political theology that can meaningfully prepare the Nigerian citizens and state to respond to the reticulated operations of the three forms of disaster. This will include a discourse on the act of making and keeping promises to counter the uncertainties caused by these disasters. The goal is to nudge Nigerians to begin the process of healing the deformities of their variety of Christianity.

The Nature of Governance in Nigeria

Governance in Nigeria is a state of government autosuspension.[2] Government is in force only in the form of its absence, nonpresence, or suspension. Governance is a civil war within the body politic, holding the people in a life consecrated to death. In this marginal position, the traditional distinction between the past (future) and the present has disappeared. The two have contracted into one intense moment of precariousness.

The whole idea of bad governance abolishing the past and future—leaving only the present to remain—can also be accessed through the lens of trauma from the standpoint of the victims of traumatic governmentality. Trauma studies have demonstrated that the effects and memories of the past are always present in ways that suggest that the past (though not technically abolished as a temporal event) is totally displaced into the present. The now of the past is (persists in) the now of the present. The past memory, in its ongoingness and perpetual return, rebirths itself, escapes its temporal identity, and operates as the present. Traumatic events that remain, continuing with the victims, do not recognize or respect temporal segmentation between past and present. The experience of the aftermath of a traumatic event marks the future and present as unbounded, just as life and death blur into one another as death-in-life in the reliving of the event. Amid trauma or the unconcluded remains of a traumatic event, conceiving the future seems impossible. The overwhelming event that keeps returning and affecting the present continues into the future. The precipitating event that is always here with the victim in the present makes it difficult to conceive of a future life or flow of time apart from the sufferer's reality, the categories of the pain and after-living of the violence.[3]

Trauma has the capacity to unbound time segments because it is usually situated in the split between the past when the traumatic event occurred and its future repetitions. Thus, the pain and suffering of trauma are not limited to when the impact occurred but also in its subsequent violence as the subject is repeatedly reawakened to it.[4] What I am saying is this: bad governance as a traumatic affliction on the people of Nigeria has (or might have) shrunk their temporal segments into only a painful present, a traumatic middle that appears ever immobile. The suffering of bad governance does not go away. The violence of bad governance does not only reduce temporality; its immediacy also shrinks social worlds in ways that shed light on the "lotus-flower world" of most Nigerians.[5] The enormity of the pain and agony of torture and trauma often serve to focus victims' minds on the self, the contours of their bodies, cutting off connections to larger social relationships and resulting in the production of atomized individuals and the fragmentation of society.[6]

Governance in Nigeria is not the ordering of resources, human lives, social conditions, and juridical-political rules for human flourishing but the disorganization and dislocation of life within life—that is, the penetration of death into life. Governance is keeping the nation in the zone of indistinction between life and death. It is maintaining Nigeria as a camp of living dead, life-in-death.

Governance as Trauma

Nigeria is an ever-present *now* of suffering, an eternal now of perpetual curse. Governance is the site where temporality, the people, and their history come undone. This undermining of temporality, people, and their history arise from the trauma that governance has visited on the people. One of the definitions of *traumatic event* is that it is a happening that overwhelms the epistemological ballast, exceeds the conceptual-linguistic determinations, or surpasses the range of human experience such that it cannot be easily grasped or integrated into a person's or group's knowledge system or identity. Either because the event, like the primal ("original") one, occurs frequently or because images and fragments of it keep intruding into the present, the survivors of trauma tend to organize their lives around *this* present period of the pervading intrusions. Trauma alters the time of survivors, or at least their relationships to time. The past stays in the present; the present is a churning of lived and expected traumatic experiences. The past claws the future into the present. The gravitational force of the excessive weight of the traumatic event that lingers into the present bends the future into the present—the future is a reenactment of the invaded, intensified present, a kind of mathematical squaring of the primal period. Put differently, the future is only an awakening to an earlier experience. Commenting on Freud's work on trauma among World War I veterans, Shelly Rambo writes that the trauma they experienced "is not located in the past but instead is located in the gap between the occurrence of the traumatic event and a subsequent awakening to it. The suffering does not solely lie in the violence of trauma's impact (in its happening) but in the ways in which that happening, that occurrence, was not known or grasped at that time."[7]

To better grasp governance as a source of traumatic events or as the prime unyielding traumatic event for Nigerians, let us examine two basic types of trauma: historical and structural. The First World War is a historical trauma, a punctual, monumental event or series of past events that overwhelm the psyche, identity, or interpretative schema of the shell-shocked veterans. Structural trauma, according to Dominick LaCapra, "is not an event but the anxiety-producing condition of possibility related to the potential for historical traumatization."[8] We pivot to the special case of Nigeria by adding a third category that combines both historical and structural traumas into a devilish brew, *microtrauma*. This trauma does not result from a single event of magnitude and horror but follows the relentless micro daily events that produce anxiety related to the potential for the shattering cessation of existence, quite possibly from sudden devastating illness, increased poverty, terror, vulgarity of power, or death. This is daily, constant, ongoing exposure to heightened vulnerability that can disable or terminate physical, psychic, or social lives. The vulnerability—contingent, dispersed, and all-pervading—can suddenly become materialized absolute disaster "anytime, anywhere, by any means, and for any reason."[9] When daily living conditions, the encompassing environment of everyday life, become a pressure cooker of arbitrary microaggressions and microattacks, citizens begin dying by a thousand cuts that never stop bleeding.

The average Nigerian citizen is plunged into all three types of trauma, and these attacks have been going on for about sixty-two years of the postcolonial state. Under these awful conditions of constant battle with the historical, structural, and micro types of trauma, the subjective perception of the victims of bad governance is bound to change. I will describe the "present" in which the Nigerian victims of trauma-giving governance live with in this way: these words. Ordinarily, time is a flow of uninterrupted succession, a continuum, but in Nigeria it is broken in the middle, at the point where the traumatized citizens are imprisoned, at the point where their socioeconomic development is at a standstill. And this standpoint "is not the present as we usually understand it but rather a gap in time" kept in existence by constant bad governance, with its abolishing of the past and future.[10] Only because the postcolonial state inserts bad governance into the time of Nigerians, and only to the extent that the state stands its ground, does time exhaust itself into fatigued time and fatigue of time. To use Yeats's turn of phrases, the pain of the past is turning and turning in a widening vortex; the present cannot hear the past; things fall apart; the present cannot move; and mere anarchy is the center. Now a blues-dimmed, incredible-laced tide is loosed, and everywhere confusion breaks the bone of time and change. Time has lost its forward-propelling motion. This is the traumatizing truth of governance in Nigeria. It is this existential condition in which the past and the future seem to have been erased, in which categories of time are rendered inoperative, that I have named the *eternal now of perpetual curse*.

The eternal now is neither time nor eternity, and it dwells paradoxically within time and timelessness while belonging to neither. Time no longer governs the rhythm of development; it is a pure manifest and acts as an incubus. Time, having severed the nexus between human activities and the transformation of society, becomes only the tormenting pure noise of clocks, chronometers, tower bells, and aches, all sounds of the echo chamber of a gigantic torture apparatus. In this perverse state, the present deepens anomie, ensures futility, and resists redemption. Time itself is an anomic figure. Time is a prime *homo sacer* in Nigeria: it can be killed but never sacrificed to produce justice or socioeconomic transformation.

The Nature of the Postcolonial Incredible

Unbearable poverty. Excruciating suffering.[11] Unyielding trauma. Postcolonial incredible.[12] Power vulgarity. These are some of the morbid symptoms or effects of governance in Nigeria, the choking string of unutterable treason of the nation's depraved ruling class. In front, Nigerians see only immiseration; in back, they have experienced sixty-three years of deprivation; on the right, they face unending corruption; on the left, they witness the all-pervasive anomie; and at the center, Nigerians see nothing but a black hole. Governance in Nigeria is a storm blowing out of the people's patrimony, a destructive wild wind that spreads doom and gloom across the regions, piling ruin upon ruin, wreaking havoc on the ethics and morals of society.

Between 1960 and 2023, the nature of governance has drastically changed for the worse. In the mid-1960s when the five army majors struck in a coup d'état and overthrew the civilian government of Prime Minister Tafawa Belewa, governance had perhaps three possibilities. Governance could represent an uncomplicated embodiment of the citizens' hope for their socioeconomic uplift, an uncomplicated embodiment of corruption, or the uncertainty of part good and part corruption. Now we have only two options: sociopathic corruption or the uncertainty of whether corruption is going to treat the citizens with divine or demonic impunity. Chris Abani, in his novel *GraceLand*, captures something about this shift in the nation's morality in a dialogue between the protagonist, Elvis Oke, and his friend Redemption.[13] In the 1960s, when the characters were younger, the movies had three archetypes: John Wayne, the ur-character for uncomplicated goodness; the Actor, always part villain and part hero; and the Bad Guy, the embodiment of malicious evil. By the early 1980s, things had changed—the movies had changed—mirroring the changes in scale of corruption and anomie in the country. To Elvis, this was all confusing until Redemption explained: "Now dere is only Bad Guy and Actor. No more John Wayne."[14]

This novel portrays the nihilism that has settled on Nigerians as the certainties that constitute the "fence" of the ethical domain of a society have disappeared. The word *ethics* comes from *ethos*, which in its etymology means the "fence" that keeps animals within their protective pen or "dwelling," and by extension the "cement" or bonds that hold a society together.[15] Within the limits of the fence, a society seeks harmony, the harmony of ethos, the congruence between the character (way of life) of the individuals and the community's moral values. The moral institutions of the community work to translate the fence, the domain of moral values, into the bonds of the community, co-belonging. They transform the law (norms, *nomos*) into its spirit—that is, the individual internalization of the expectations and requirements of the law. In *GraceLand*'s Nigeria, there is a break in the ethos, a rupture in the specific mode of being together. The pathway between the moral principles of a people and their ensuing concrete mode of existence or way of being has been forgotten. Ethics, or the harmony of ethos, today amounts to a dissolution of the forms of practices and discourses into corruption. A new "ethics" has emerged insofar as we understand ethics as "the kind of thinking in which an identity is established between an environment, a way of being and a principle of action."[16] In *GraceLand*'s Nigeria, wracked by corruption, nihilism, and anomic repercussions of the civil war, the ethical options presented to the sixteen-year-old Elvis for self-formation and socialization as he enters adulthood are severely limited. His possible ethical turns are a series of specific conjunctions of the Colonel (the murderous agent or face of the postcolonial state), the King (a corrupt beggar who aspires to transform the system and avenge what was done to him during the civil war, 1967–1970), and Redemption (a man with an unbelievable ability to function, to survive, and to eke out a living from the deadly jaws of corrupt agents of the state). More importantly, in this novel we see Nigeria as a place in which hopes for and narratives of national economic development have been abandoned, where grotesque and obscene displays of necropower pass for the height of human civilization and existential nihilism protrudes as the wet blanket spread by what goes for governance over the citizens. Things that happen do not make sense. Ambulances do not carry sick people to hospitals but carry dead people for a fee as part of elaborate funeral processions. In one of the most moving scenes in the novel, Elvis has gone home after being tortured by the state, the Colonel, to discover that his Maroko ghetto in Lagos megacity has been razed down by the government; and in the process, his father died. He raked through the rubble where their house stood with his bare hands to find the body. A soldier discovered what he was doing and stopped him, threatening to kill him. "If you annoy me I will kill you and add you to your father." The soldier would only let him take the body for a fee, a bribe. When Elvis responded that he had no money, the soldier replied, "No what? Get out of here." He immediately "descended on Elvis and pounded him repeatedly with his rifle butt. Elvis stumbled away. The tears that wouldn't come for his father streamed freely now as he felt worthless in the face of blind, unreasonable power. He could return later, when it was dark, but he knew the body would be gone."[17] This scene broke my heart. Governance is all about humiliating the people and generating confusion all over the country.

Governance in Nigeria is the "pitiless incubus that feeds on [citizens'] most valuable possession, dreams, which it endlessly defers and derides."[18] The words between the quotation marks were actually used to describe the city of Lagos, the commercial hub of Nigeria. The disposition to see Lagos, or parts therein, as a metonym for the whole country is an old practice of the scholars and artistes of Nigeria. Fela Anikulapo-Kuti, in his song "Confusion Break Bone," compares the absolute chaos of Ojuelegba, a street in Lagos, to Nigeria.[19]

I sing about one street for Lagos	I sing about a street in Lagos
Dem call am Ojuelegba	They call it Ojuelegba
I think i compare how Nigeria be	I compare it to Nigeria
One crossroad in the center of town	
Chorus: Larudu repeke	
For Ojuelegba	At Ojuelegba
Moto dey come from east	Vehicles approach from east
Motor dey come from west	From west
Motor dey come from north	From north
Motor dey come from south	From south
And policeman no dey for centre	And no policeman to direct the traffic
Na confusion be that oh-o	The result is utter confusion!
Chorus: Pafuka na quench	It is utter confusion

Governance in Nigeria is like the traffic at Ojuelegba, a permanent state of crisis, of anomie that replaces or ruptures normality.[20] Governance is a national terrorism of power, and the exercise of this power is arbitrary. This very arbitrariness defines the present Nigerian postcolonial state. As Achille Mbembe puts it, "What distinguishes our age from the previous ages, the breach over which there is apparently no going back, the absolute split of our times that breaks up the spirit and splits it into many, is again contingent, dispersed, and powerless existence: existence that is contingent, dispersed and powerless but reveals itself in the guise of arbitrariness and the absolute power to give death any time, anywhere, by any means, and for any reason."[21]

Why do the governed accept such confusion and arbitrariness as governance, exercise of power, and sovereignty? From the perspective on Nigeria given to us by Abani's *GraceLand*, we infer that there are many forces or factors at work that we cannot fully account for in this chapter. We would like to focus on only one of them: the *postcolonial incredible*. Tejumola Olaniyan describes the reign of the incredible in these words:

> The "incredible" inscribes that which cannot be believed; that which is too improbable, astonishing, and extraordinary to be believed. The incredible is not simply a breach but an outlandish infraction of "normality" and its limits. If "belief," as faith, confidence, trust, and conviction, underwrites the certainty and tangibility of institutions and practices of social exchange, the incredible dissolves all props of stability, normality, and intelligibility (and therefore of authority) and engenders social and symbolic crisis.... A presupposed interregnum that increasingly threatens to become the norm, a norm with a rapidly consolidating hierarchy of privileges feeding on and dependent on the crisis for reproduction.[22]

The reign of the incredible is not transitional as Fela might have thought when he resisted it with his full vigor; it is a permanent state in Nigeria. It is the form the unfolding of Nigeria's history has taken at the moment. In this condition of the incredible, governance renders and heightens the vulnerability of citizens. The enormity of pain and agony of the incredible scale of social anomie, not unlike torture and trauma, often serves to focus victims' minds on the self, the survival of their bodies, and their pursuit of daily bread, cutting off connections to larger social relationships and resulting in the production of atomized individuals and the fragmentation of society.[23] It appears that instead of generating the wherewithal to challenge and defeat the incredible, most Nigerian citizens have accepted it. Elvis finds it irritating that his friends accept the condition of anomie and even thinks it funny that some feed from it or contribute to it in their own small ways. He cries, "That is the trouble with this country. Everything is accepted. No dial tones or telephones. No stamps in post offices. No electricity. No water. We just accept."[24] It is easy to see the citizens' hapless acceptance of the reign of the incredible as a case of passive nihilism, an acceptance of the dissolution of meaning or sense in the way life hangs together in Nigeria. But we should not yield to such an easy conclusion. There is a certain soteriology of ambiguity, a dialectic, a juxtaposition of opposites to it. On the one hand, there is a definite sense of loss of meaning, a sense that the country has lost something meaningful or desirable, something important for human flourishing. On the other, there is a conviction that it is important for some citizens to pursue and create alternative situations that might redeem the nation from the reign of the postcolonial incredible. The tension is between a realization that all might have been lost and the hope that there is still a meaning or credible existence that transcends the chaos and arbitrariness of the postcolonial incredible.

The weight of governance as trauma and the postcolonial incredible has a devasting effect on the common life. The disorder has created the informalization of the common life, leaving it so poorly institutionalized that much of it takes place through informal channels of relations, unable to rise above and beyond religious, ethnic, and regional cleavages. It is not public and supra-communal. The common life has not been structurally differentiated from patrimonial, ethnic, clientelistic networks and other particularistic domains. The common life is informalized to the extent that it thrives by evading the predatory state and its functions, striving to create parallel organizations for dealing with arbitrary violence. It is informalized to the extent that it is an instrumentalization of disorder. The logics, causalities, and rationalities of the informal common life resist the order that founds or sustains the common life—and benefits from disorder. The informal common life is, indeed, not a commons but a kind of national life that operates at the interstices of existing ethnic, religious, social, economic, and political networks. Its informality should not be all too surprising to scholars familiar with state, politics, and society in Africa. As Patrick Chabal and Jean-Pascal Daloz argue in their book *Africa Works*, the state in Africa is also beholden to similar networks and domains. Politics, according to them, is also informalized. The defense and promotion of the common good of the nation—the sine qua non of the common life—is all too often done through personalized and particularistic channels.[25]

An adequate understanding of informalization should be the point of departure for theorizing evangelicalism or crafting a political theology of the common life for Nigerian Christians. This point of departure is unlikely to intersect with most political theologies of the common life.[26] In the regnant political theologies, the dominant understanding of the common life is situated between a highly institutionalized state and mass society, with individuals who are separated from ethnic and infra-institutional dynamics and whose collective identification as citizens is not contingent. But what happens to the common life when the state is not strongly institutionalized, when citizens' collective identification is contingent, precarious, and uncertain, and when there is no crosscutting notion of common good?

Another implicit assumption of the regnant models of the common life is that it operates on the basis of horizontal links between citizens.

Self-defined citizens claiming political equality gather to pursue shared goals; men and women act in concert to create and sustain the power that they need to effect change in public policy. But in African nations or societies where vertical links (connections with ethnic, patrimonial, and similar groups) are relatively more important than horizontal ones, the common life has to be informalized. What is therefore more important to theologize is not the formal political configurations or visible institutions of the common life but the subterranean roots of entanglements engendered by disorder, factional struggles, and uncertainty that are at work. To further elucidate this disorder, let us now turn to the Pentecostal incredible, which has developed as a response of a segment of evangelical Christians to the postcolonial incredible and governance as trauma.

Evangelicalism as a Response to the Postcolonial Incredible

There are two types of response to the postcolonial incredible and traumatic governance that are observable in evangelical Christianity in Nigeria, especially in Pentecostal Christianity. The first is to view the church as a state, a developmental state. Big Pentecostal denominations see themselves as agents of economic development in their local communities, a miniature state providing infrastructure and acting as the owner of for-profit corporations, generating revenues for development projects.[27] Pentecostal pastors who are well connected to the state use the state security apparatus to discipline erring members.

The second is to say that "it does not make sense, but it makes spirit" to explain the unexplainable or affirm what a preexisting community fund of knowledge, justificatory system, and cultural logic will not accept. This seems like a yielding to the loss of meaningful rationality or intelligibility provoked by the daily assaults from governance as trauma. I have called this orientation the *Pentecostal hypothesis*, a conjecture to explain some surprising or wished-for facts about reality.[28] The Pentecostal hypothesis is the capacity to resist conventional wisdom in social actions. Daily Pentecostals deploy or enact this capacity through the use of the formula "it does not make sense, but it makes spirit" in their decision-making processes. The epistemological here is not about the *that* of knowing but the *how* (the performative dimension) of knowing, which is affective, emotive, and embodied practice. The resort to alternate ways of knowing and being should be interpreted not only as a resistance to modernity or a penchant for occult knowledge but as one way of coping with the trauma of governance, which has removed or is constantly displacing and desiccating the coordinates of phenomenological reality.

The formula "it does not make sense, but it makes spirit" is ambiguous—that is, it is both constructive and destructive in its operation as an epistemological guide to everyday life or adaptation to governance as trauma. In my book *Pentecostal Hypothesis*, I primarily focus on its constructive effect on Pentecostal spirituality, decision-making, and social ethics. In the next section, which I am naming *The Nature of the Pentecostal Incredible*, I will more closely examine its destructive effect on Nigerian Pentecostal Christians' ways of thinking, explaining, and talking about the world, common life, and human flourishing.

If the postcolonial incredible is the reality of the actual everyday existence of Pentecostals, then the Pentecostal incredible is the abstract spectral logic of Nigerian Pentecostals that determines their interpretation, engagement or confrontation with, and adaptation to the postcolonial incredible. The Pentecostal incredible is the mad metaphysical dance of reason in blessed indifference to common standards of justification and acceptability.[29] Solipsistic reason enthralled by the superego to enjoy is in a Dionysian revel, having rejected any master-signifier that might impose some order on its obscene dance. This reason is limitless, shattering the coordinates of our finite knowledge system with its excess. The Pentecostal incredible is reason that contains the infinite—so, at least, the limitless desire for miracles and the extraordinary lead many Pentecostal Christians to believe. All these pose a threat not only to human flourishing but also to the polity.

Our discussion below will demonstrate that we cannot adequately grasp the common life in a democratic plurality if we ignore the epistemological issues about the disconcerting matter of the Pentecostal incredible. The epistemological is political, but it does not get much traction in the scholarship on political theology. We should not dismiss the matter of the Pentecostal incredible in Christian political theology with the usual academic sleight of hand that shoos away African issues or particularity as too foreign to Western universalism. It is not enough to say all the forms of violence emanating from governance as trauma, the postcolonial incredible, and the Pentecostal incredible are too peculiar to Africa. Let us not even think that we are once again dealing with the tragic case of the otherized continent. We are not permitted to dismiss the uncomfortable triage of forms of violence as a peculiar Pentecostal mess. What if, on the contrary, the gesture of refusal of "respectable" reason, the violent rejection of a master-signifier (be it from religion within bounds of reason, orderly religion, or rationalistic theology) is the innermost logic, conviction, or stance of religion (Christianity)? Have Nigerian Pentecostals not exposed the gap between the story Christian theologians tell themselves about their faith and actions and the intimate experiences of those who sincerely hold to the (spectral) logic of Christianity as if their lives depend on it? The question that stares at us in the West is this: How do we fully assume the consequences of the three forms of violence in our Christian political theology?

What we have described as the Pentecostal incredible should not be construed as a tension between the good Pentecostal life and its bad, excretable sibling. What provokes the crisis of the Pentecostal incredible is nothing other than the intensity of Pentecostal life. Spiritual learning, an integral part of Pentecostal life, allows people to put divine powers, the numinous, to use to connect things without understanding how they fit together (hence, they can say that it does not make sense but that it makes spirit). Pentecostals do not always need to know how things, laws, or nature work. They take the complexity and unpredictability of the world into their account of the world without taking principles and physical laws as seriously as the rest of the world does. Sidestepping the principles and laws in the name of spiritual insight is one way they deal with the complexity and unpredictability of their worlds.

What is happening under the name of the Pentecostal incredible might not be a tension between superstitious belief and "good" theology. It is a tension between two aspects of Christian theology. The force of academic theology is confronted with the very nature of religion at its purest, the logic of submission to an unseen power, of ruthless intervention of the divine Real, generated by the libidinal investment and the excessive enjoyment of believers.[30] This is where I think Dostoevsky got it wrong in *The Brothers Karamazov*: "If God doesn't exist, then everything is permitted." Under the regime of the Pentecostal incredible, because God exists, everything is permitted, even psychotic-delirious acts: people lying down to eat grass like animals in the open fields, others beating innocent infants deemed witches or wizards, some spouting baleful speeches, male pastors giving women deep kisses to transfer anointing to them, male pastors placing their hands over vulvae against the thin layer of dresses to cast out the "spirits of fornication," and pastors anointing their members with minerals (sodas such as Coca-Cola or

Fanta). The only justification one needs for these unusual actions is the claim that one is acting at the behest of God's will, that one directly knows what God wants. This is so "since clearly a direct link to God justifies [their] violation of any 'merely human' constraints and considerations" and of reason.[31]

In these lights, the acts of the Pentecostally incredible Christian constitute not only a thaumaturgical suspension of the epistemological but also the religious suspension of the ethical. When faith dovetails or dissolves into "just believe or love God and do whatever you perceive God wants or what will bring you prosperity and increased anointing," without reference to any external standards as the Pentecostal incredible indicates, then the political commons is in potential danger. "In the absence of any ethical standards external to your belief in and love for God, the danger is always lurking that you will use your love of God as the legitimization of the most horrible deeds."[32]

Not to put an excellent point on the Pentecostal incredible, and to be fair to the Pentecostals twinned in its complex web, we need to bring another thought into our discourse. Is the whole matter concerning the belief system of the Pentecostally incredible Christians not a baroque, extravagant critique of Christianity (religion) itself? Is modern Christianity, Christianity in the so-called polished, varnished, and stately uppity circles, not sustained by obscene superego supplements? We all know what the Bible and the accumulated wisdom of the Christian faith say about God, supernatural magic, unscientific knowledge, talking donkeys, erotic spirits, and so on. But we have taught ourselves not to take them seriously. We say, "You want to practice Christianity in the twenty-first century? Okay, these are the injunctions and prohibitions on how not to take the Bible and God seriously." The hapless Pentecostals did not get the memo on the unwritten rules, winks, hints, suppressed amusements, and expected habit of indifference, and they take the Bible and its ideological edifice seriously and literally. Is their habit of ignoring how things actually function in the polite circles not a critique of mainstream Christianity? They have not changed the text of the Bible but have only ignored the obscene virtual supplement of the in-group, intervened in the virtual unwritten shadow of rationalism and skepticism in Enlightenment Christianity.[33]

The Nature of the Pentecostal Incredible

What do you do when you confront the common life in the nation as a *now* of perpetual curse? How do you think if you are an African Pentecostal theologian like me contemplating whether the Pentecostal brain has fallen under the claptrap of thaumaturges? Miracle workers now control the brain's neural processes among Pentecostals. And you are asking yourself, "Am I a witness to a form of collective possession that will require collective deliverance (exorcism) as the appropriate form of treatment?" to parse Cheryl Kirk-Duggan's words.[34] O wretched man that I am! Who will help me make sense of all this?

The ground, the common ground, has collapsed, shifted from ground to *Ungrund*, the groundless ground. The common ground has become chaosmos, awaiting new molding or divergences. The ground that is the common of human intelligence and the shared world of understanding has folded, crumbled, or deformed into a pathless desert. The ground of common knowledge, the world of appearances, has now shifted into the *underground* of knowledge, the "night of the world," the primordial underworld of spirits, the self-determining, self-grounding intelligence, displaced into the uncertainty that precedes the will to know arousing itself into shared knowledge, to parse Jacob Boehme.

We are witnessing the unraveling of the very structure of shared understanding that makes thought possible. The very foundationless foundation that organizes thought or defines the episteme of a people who live in a particular common has shifted. The psychic abyss that grounds thought, the modernist rationality that inheres between reason and desire, thought and unthought, known and unknown, is being eviscerated. For instance, thought and unthought, reason and nonsense, blend into ideas and actions that shatter the coordinates of preexisting knowledges. This shaking is regarded as divine. This happens as the abyss is celebrated as the spirit, or the womb of the spirit. The knowledge from this womb is an *alienated* knowledge, cut off from common structures of shared understanding, from the ground of knowledge. Hence, the knowledge is more volitional than rational. Alienation is here celebrated as divine, holy, and mind renewing. This alienated knowledge desires itself and longs for recognition; regarding itself as the glory of God, it aspires to cover the face of the earth as water covers the sea.

Is the knowledge engendered by the demotic energy of the Pentecostal incredible rational or irrational? The Pentecostal incredible is the law of *unlawing*. It is the unmooring of rationality without the burden of irrationality;[35] it is a capability to undo authoritative societal principles and regulations by faithful obedience to an authority beyond the strictures, strength, and structures of rationality and irrationality. Here knowledge is neither rational nor irrational; it folds and unfolds, swirls and staggers, with experiential, subversive possibilities made graspable or legible by the spirit. In this space of the spirit, the likelihood of discovery of shared meaning and justificatory warrants with those who do not self-identify as Pentecostals dwindles. This is so because what was formerly an agonistic religious-knowledge posture that recognizes differences and conflicts between church and world becomes an antagonistic stance that absolutizes difference, fiercely rejecting any dialogic practices of an epistemological common life. The *ecstatic reason* of the Pentecostal incredible has elevated itself to the realm of the infinite, considering itself as a manifestation of the divine or an embodiment of divine mystery. It presumably comes down from heaven. In the non-Sartrean world of Nigerian Pentecostalism, hell is not just the other person but the reason that cannot contain the infinite.

What we are witnessing in Nigeria or Africa is a chaotic liquefaction of current existing modernist patterns of knowledge and belief. If in the past the processes of capitalist modernization and the rise of Pentecostalism caused an epistemic crisis and rupture in traditional patterns of episteme (knowledge), today Pentecostalism has opened up a battlefront against the modernist, rationalistic framework for determining human flourishing or comprehending the nature and meaning in religious, economic, and political life. This is a different form of epistemic crisis and rupture. The emerging troubling Pentecostal knowledge system is occupying a territory in African modernity that renders the continental structures of knowledge production, public reasoning, and justificatory warrants vulnerable. This is not a rupture with the past but a rupture with the present, caused by impregnating the present with the seeds of the disavowed flotsam of knowledge from bygone eras. Pentecostalism, through the "work" of the Holy Spirit, opens the present time to and breathes into it the duress of the past. Shared rationality existing across the church-world distinction, across Pentecostal and non-Pentecostal cultures, has been roasted in the crucibles of divine activity that only Pentecostals can see, hear, or access.

Epistemology is the act not just of knowing but of knowing in concert with others. So epistemology always coheres or belongs to a group of people. Epistemology is consensual; it is a social practice. The Pentecostal incredible appears where epistemology is threatened in ways that signal its disappearance as a shared practice within a community, the unraveling of the old consensus that opens space for a new paradigm or consensus. The incredible may transform into a new consensual epistemology through the capacity of its "violence" to create a new concert of knowing.

It is also important to mention that the incredible is simultaneously included and excluded from consensual epistemology. Wherever it first emerges, its engagement in "violence" does not exclude it or its advocates from participating in consensual epistemology. Those given to the incredible engage daily with the extant consensual epistemology, working well within its parameters, its legitimized ends and justifications, while simultaneously practicing violence on the consensual system of rationality. This apparent disorder, this chaotic epistemology, signals the oncoming reordering of a group's consensus. With the increasing acceptance of the disorder by a rising number of community members, it is almost impossible to say where epistemology ends and the incredible begins. The Nigerian Christian community as a whole is at this inflection point.

The evaluation of the truth value of ordinary statements in the country is also at an inflection point. Under the pressure of the incredible, the evaluation of human speech undergoes deep changes. Speakers' words are judged not by whether they are correct but rather by whether they are effective. This is at the root of the axiom "it does not make sense, but it makes spirit." When the concern is over sense, the focus on an utterance is on truth and error as determined by scientific, aesthetic, or communal criteria. But there is a slight shift with the pivot to the spirit. The Pentecostals are here concerned with the difference between truth and lying (empty) words. Words lie, not because they are in error, but because they cannot accomplish what they promise; they are empty of the inner strength and truth to produce what they imply. They are empty because they did not make things happen, because they did not accomplish what they promised.[36] They are empty because words and deeds are disconnected. They are empty because words do not establish the reality they declare.

In the Pentecostal circle, there is not supposed to be much of a difference between these two statements that ordinarily bother other Christ believers: (a) in the beginning was the word, and (b) in the beginning was the deed. In the beginning was the "deed" because deeds were utterances; you declare a thing, and it is established for you (Job 22:28). "'Let there be light,' and there was light" (Genesis 1:3). Deeds are themselves words coming alive. So the criterion of speech is not necessarily whether it is true or not. A speaker can make very silly statements, but if there is the belief that those foolish statements can be transformed into beneficial deeds, then that speaker is hailed as a true man or woman of God. There is another layer to this religious obscurantism. Often the so-called men and women of God are still taken seriously after their words have repeatedly failed to translate into deeds. Why? It is because of what anthropologist Robin Horton calls "converging causal sequences."[37] Many Pentecostals will not dump a particular man or woman of God as long as they still believe in the overall efficacy of the worldview that underlines and energizes their incredible epistemology.

Is the Pentecostal incredible only a matter of epistemology? It is not so much an epistemological failure or crisis as it is an appetitive problem, a disordered seeking of emotional energy, a disordered desire for the miraculous. It is, indeed, a moral problem, the failure to properly control or regulate desire. It could be regarded as an epistemological crisis or problem of rationality only to the extent that we focus on the distinct ability of human beings to control their desires through the exercise of reason, as Aristotle taught us. But the same Aristotle regards the failure to regulate the appetitive as a moral failure and the ability to control desires as a moral virtue, a desire-regulating virtue. The Pentecostal incredible is a habitual tendency of some Pentecostals to say, act, react, or feel in ways that are inappropriate to *lawing* in order to benefit from the contingency of the expectation of a miracle.

There is also something subversive about the Pentecostal incredible. Pentecostals have developed ways of separating biblical stories, words, and practices from their conventional, orthodox, or historic meanings and putting them into quite different uses. They play with and manipulate images in the Bible. In their meetings and gatherings, they appear to publicly confirm the legitimacy of the Bible and its overwhelming influence on their lives, but they are also carving out avenues of escape from its strict, confining conventions. Under the cover of the Bible, they poach Christianity of meanings, forcefully integrating it into different kinds of imagery (which now highlights that of Christ believers grazing grass, pastors acquiring jets to soar into the sky, heartless pastors capturing spoils from the poor and hoarding the largesse of the devil), and saturating it with terminologies of power, prosperity, and profit. Above all, the Pentecostal incredible is an economy of damage. Or more precisely, it founds a site for spiritual enjoyment, exaggerated faith, and spiritual extravagance at the very moment it paves a road to the damage of Christianity, a pathway for the death of faith, a byway to the loss of limits. Many theologians claim it is silliness dressed in the mantle of religion and the loss of sense of proportion garbed in the majesty of the Holy Ghost's *kavod* (glory) and power.

Indeed, everyday Pentecostal theology is a subversive theology within Christian theology—a sort of bare, naked theology. It is a theology that does not have the protection of rationality but that is exposed to the violence of rationality, the heteronomous force of modernist all-encompassing rationality. Its pariah status is such that as a theology it can be "killed" (condemned) by anyone, dismissed, disposed, or ignored by any academy theologian as bunkum, but it can never be critiqued or engaged *as* theology. This theology is carefully considered, tracked, branded, and profiled—while being refused the academic status accorded to other theologies. The incredible theology appears not even as a polemical argument of the stately theological academy to assert its difference from it. The incredible is abjected from the universal grammars of theology.

But here I am willing to engage it and bring it into conversation with mainstream theology. In the last seventeen years, I have studied and written theologies in ways that probe its established properties, extending and stretching it from the main roads to the byways. As expected, after my doctoral degree, I wrote standard-issue stuff—still ensconced in mainstream predominant theology (for example, see my 2008 *God and Money*[38]). Later, I went into everyday theologies and microtheologies, attempting to liberate theology from its stately uppity form (for example, see my 2018 *The Split God*[39]). In this chapter, I may have gone beyond theology to what is neither theological nor untheological. It is nontheological. The nontheological does not negate a predicate but affirms a nonpredicate. The untheological negates or attempts to negate academic theology, whereas a predicate is asserted in the case of the nontheological, which undermines the distinction between academic and nonacademic theology, academic and everyday theology. The theology of the Pentecostal incredible opens a new space beyond academic theology and its negation or resistance. Stating that everyday theology is untheological means simply that it is external to academic theology and resists it, while *nontheological* means something thoroughly different—namely, that it is neither theological nor not theological "but marked by a terrifying excess which, although negating what we understand" as theology, is inherent to being theological.[40]

How do we theorize or theologize this space, this uncanny space, the site of disorder? Political theology is often about order, about God/Christ and common life. Scholarships in political philosophy, political theology, and social sciences, for that matter, are too oriented to order, to how to create order and sustain it. Now, there is nothing fatally flawed with this orientation to academic inquiry. My only concern is that it often takes our eyes away from the irruptions and disruptions that are part of every order, from the disorders that sustain orders, and from places and peoples who have only perpetual disorder, ruptures, and fragility to contend with 24-7 as their form of common life. How do we make sense of the disorder that is the common life in Africa, and how do we understand it in the light of Pentecostal Christian experiences?

Instead of talking about Christ and the common life, about Christ and order, let us talk about Christ and the *chaosmosic* life. Is Christ only God of the cosmos (common life, organized life), or is he also Lord of the life on the verge of chaos and cosmos? Please note that I am not championing disorder as the *locus classicus* of political theology but instead mean to draw our attention to places in the world where theology cannot proceed from the presupposition of preexisting order that needs to be Christically transformed. I only want us to think about those who live in disordered situations, which are the order and command of their precarious lifeworlds. I am not here to celebrate those radical theologians and philosophers who live in ordered, *manicured* societies and dream of exploding their inherited order of being and privilege to initiate something new. I am thinking of radical thoughts, new ways of relating Christ to the common life in societies that are already uprooted and always uprooting—radical in the old sense of life, lifeworld whose roots are upended. I am thinking of infusing Christian political theology with the kind of radical energy that will upend its theorized foundations.

In the next section, I will engage the works of theologian Luke Bretherton to enable us to figure out how to think of Christian political theology in the light of the Pentecostal incredible. What kinds of principles or perspectives should concern us if we are interested in crafting an *everyday theology of chaosmosic* life? If we think together of the everyday sociality of Pentecostal practices (which includes the domain of the Pentecostal incredible) and the chaos that not only define (condition) but also seem to sustain many postcolonial societies in which embodied Pentecostal praxis is embedded, then we are likely to improve our understanding of the life and growth of Pentecostalism and political theology.

The Pentecostal Incredible as a Source of Radical Political Theology

In his book *Christ and the Common Life: Political Theology and the Case for Democracy*, Luke Bretherton makes a solid, incisive case for democracy as a critical concept and veritable practice under Christian political theology. He brings together democracy (which affirms plurality, distinct identities, and traditions) and Christian theology under the rubric of what he calls a *common-life framework*, which is a methodology, a form of discipline, and a vision for life in Christ.[41] "The common-life framework is distinct from either identity politics or multicultural approaches because recognition and respect are not given simply by dint of having a different culture or identity; recognition is conditional upon contributing to and participating in shared, reciprocal, common work."[42]

Indeed, the core achievement of the book is to contest the received meaning of political theology and successfully launch an expanded, inclusive, accessible—yet rigorous—definition and meaning of Christian political theology. In this way, Bretherton's book generates a more vibrant sense of what political theology is and what good it can do to advance human flourishing. I also read his book as oriented to order. His book is an attempt to describe and analyze how the order of common life in Europe and United States of America can be sustained or understood in the light of Christian theology.

Besides, Bretherton's book is focused on societies that have rich democratic practices. This is not the case in Nigeria. Thus, as African theologian Elias Kifon Bongmba argues, the issue of recovering or founding the common political life needs a democratic base as a point of departure.[43] I am going to argue that the recovery or founding of a democratic base might not be enough to deliver the postcolonial African state from the grip of the pernicious triune powers of governance as trauma, the postcolonial incredible, and the Pentecostal incredible. But I am running ahead of myself. Let us turn to the fundamental question that is supposed to drive the conversation in this section of the chapter.

How does Bretherton's book help us think about Christian political theology in light of the Pentecostal incredible? How do we make sense of his book, given that we critiqued Christian political theology for the presupposition of preexisting order that needs to be Christically transformed?

I want us to use his book to think with and against him, to grasp for the kind of new political theology that can take as its point of departure people who live in disordered situations. I want us to follow a trail of his thought as it folds, enfolds, and unfolds implicitly through his book. This is to say, I want us to read Bretherton to isolate the key breakthrough of his thought in this book as it relates to the notion of the Pentecostal incredible interlaced with Christ and the common life.

Let me begin by stating that I know that Bretherton wrote his book for communities in North America and Europe. But I want to examine the applicability of its ideas to the Nigerian situation I have described. The great solution that Bretherton's scintillating book suggests for Nigeria amid the triumvirate of governance as trauma, the postcolonial incredible, and the Pentecostal incredible is the combination of the virtue of tolerance and the efficient administration and coordination of interests, all as undergirded by a Christian commitment to democracy.[44] Alas, something does not quite fit. Democracy is not big enough; there just is not enough material in it, in the Western capitalo-parliamentary size-five democratic dress, to fit the Nigerian body of size twenty.[45] It is only emancipatory politics that can provide ample material to sew a dress that will cover the nakedness of the current extensive necropolitical "democratic" flesh of Nigeria. Alas, Bretherton's book evades discussing emancipation—political struggle, the armed revolutionary struggle to overturn a ruling, oppressive class. Cannot the common life in Christ be engendered by emancipatory violence (*divine violence*, as per Walter Benjamin)? The reader may be bristling at this question.[46]

I agree with her that this question is the wrong one to ask because it is not within the purview of Bretherton's book. At the heart of the book is a conception of politics as a problem of intolerance and quest for human flourishing, not the problem of the absence of the egalitarian logic in the distribution of places and roles, fundamental wrong and capitalist exploitation, and the relevant quest for human flourishing. To think of politics in the way Bretherton has done is to engage in the *culturalization of political theology*—political theology as a theorization of harmonious living in different ways of life. We need a *politicization of political theology*—that is, political theology as a theorization of emancipatory politics.[47] What Nigeria needs today is a political theology that is *creatively destructive* and *constructive*. At the dimension of the creative destruction, it must accent the politics of emancipation (rupture, the radical politics of equalitarianism) as a new foundation for human flourishing. At the dimension of construction, it must show us what kind of radical social ethics can prepare ordinary citizens to disrupt the transfer of fragility from capitalist markets and other devastating social forces to them and to make themselves *antifragile*.[48]

Christian political theology needs the ethics of antifragility. Antifragility is not the opposite of fragility; it goes beyond resilience or robustness. A fragile system breaks under stress, disorder, or volatility. An antifragile system not only withstands shocks, stress, disorder, uncertainty, and volatility but also benefits from them. The ethics of antifragility is about developing the capability in the citizenry to resist the fragility of socioeconomic life imposed on them, even as they learn to deploy their resistance toward their own human flourishing. The combined weight of governance as trauma, the postcolonial incredible, and the Pentecostal incredible has rendered the life and livelihood of ordinary citizens fragile. Nigeria needs a political theology that can demonstrate how ordinary citizens can build an *antifragile* social ethics capable of resisting these triune powers to promote freedom and human flourishing. The good news is that Nigerian Christians, after years of relentless bombardment from the triumvirate of powers, have fashioned, in pragmatic terms, such a political theology.[49] How else do you think they have been surviving the bombardment?

What we need now are scholars to investigate and adequately articulate it—that is, theologize their (the citizens') experiences of coping with and evading the combined working of the three insidious powers. This is a task most suitable to those who can craft a political theology within the framework of disruptive grace, virtue as an irruptive actualization of human potentialities, and unfinishable commons.[50] Among other things, this will be a theology that thoughtfully considers the possibility of the impossible in the way life hangs together in the commons. Those Christians living in an abyss of governance as trauma require an *impossible theology* that can conceptualize a commons that allows human creativity and freedom to manifest, disrupts the hierarchical distribution of places, and makes space for persons to creatively resist obstacles to human flourishing. We need to liberate political theology from its excessive concern with order and good citizenry to serve as a liberatory principle for interrogating all extant social organizations in the name of a better future.

All these summon us to meditate on radical political theology. In this case, a theology is radical, in a certain given sense, if it focuses on how politics works in chaosmosic life rather than explaining why or how it does not. Such a radical theology involves research that seeks to uncover how

African nations marked by the Pentecostal incredible and the postcolonial incredible work, rather than showing how they differ from the logic and dynamic of so-called well-ordered ("politically developed," "spiritually matured") nations. It means we have to stop thinking that Pentecostals qua Pentecostals have an inherent character flaw that traps them in backward logic and keeps their political spiritualities from aiding Africa's political development. The so-called trap of the *incredibles* is escapable and is not destiny. The task before us now is to show how the incredibles can be turned into elements of radical politics.

The Pentecostal Incredible and Existential Anxiety

Now I want to turn to insights from Tillichian philosophical theology to deepen our understanding of the postcolonial incredible as we move closer to the kind of radical politics and theology I have in mind. Governance as trauma constitutes the structure of reality, the objective condition that Nigerians face daily. For the sake of our analysis, the postcolonial incredible could be considered as the rational structure of the mind grasping this reality. It is the attempt of subjects living in a certain reality to actualize themselves by its demands. It is the subjective condition, a response to or acceptance of the objective condition. These two factors (governance as trauma and the postcolonial incredible) have created the condition of meaninglessness. The Pentecostal incredible is the spiritual-existential distortion of both of them.[51] It is the rise of antirational forces when governance and the other incredible have destroyed the formal structures of reason. It distorts the manifestation of the depth of reason, ontological reason; this is the reason which can properly point us to the determination of the proper ends of the human sociality that is Nigeria. These are ends that should point Nigerians beyond the existing forms of their human sociality, to move their gaze further beyond themselves. It is the search for fulfillment, representing an inescapable moral call on them to deepen and widen their being, to move toward ultimate meaning and significance. Ontological reason is the longing for the source of all meaning, the driving force toward the good itself.[52] The dominance of the Pentecostal incredible distorts the manifestation of ontological reason, the rational structure of reason, in two ways. It rises and fills the vacuum created by the dual forces of traumatic governance and the postcolonial incredible with not just empty sentimentality but emotionalism that is destructive of the structure of reason, the "formal structure of the mind which enables it to grasp and transform reality."[53] It is an attack on formal reason, or whatever is left of it or reappears from its ruins.

Emotionalism is a reaction against the formalism of reason. The formalism of reason only aims to grasp reality, not shape it, and does not express any spiritual life (substance). Hence, it is seen as destructive of spiritual life.[54] Formal reason seeks neither "a truth which is present in spite of the infinity of theoretical possibilities" nor "a good which is present in spite of the infinite risk."[55] Emotionalism is a reaction against formal reason, reason that absolutizes itself. Such reason is demonic in the Tillichian sense. But the reaction to it in the form of the emotionalism of the Pentecostal incredible is similarly demonic. Emotionalism turns into destructive irrationalism when it is without rational structure, when it champions "reason" that sacrifices its formal structure and attendant critical power. As Paul Tillich is wont to put it:

> Emotion is powerless without intellectualism . . . if it remains mere emotion. But, although powerless over reason, it can have great power of destruction over the mind, personally and socially. Emotion without rational structure (in the sense, of course, of ontological reason) becomes irrationalism. And irrationalism is destructive in two respects. If it attacks formalized reason, it must have some rational content. This content, however, is not subject to rational criticism and gets its power from the strength of the emotion that carries it. It is still reason, but irrationally promoted reason, and therefore blind and fanatical. It has all the qualities of the demonic, whether it is expressed in religious or secular terms. If, on the other hand, irrationalism empties itself of any content and becomes mere subjective feeling, a vacuum is produced, into which distorted reason can break without a rational check.[56]

The Pentecostal incredible is not just faith or emotion but emotion without rational structure, a destructive irrationalism. With its "rational irrationalism," it distorts the manifestation of the depth of reason, the rational structure of reason that expresses itself in the objective-subjection condition. All this does not mean that faith itself does not include nonrational elements, but it is not identical to nonrationality. In the same vein, faith has a rational character, though it is not identical to it. It transcends both the rational and nonrational elements of believers' being.[57]

What may seem to the casual observer to be a display of faith by Pentecostal Christians is not necessarily faith per se. It is a mere traditional attitude to use God to fulfill wishful thinking for one's purposes and to manage (bandage) the wounds of existence. The faith that is borne or engendered by the Pentecostal incredible is not a movement toward something of ultimate concern, of ultimate meaning and significance. The faith acts, which are directed toward success, do not express a longing, dynamic reunion with God; they are only giving ultimacy to preliminary concerns. Paul Tillich might say that this is a faith that has not "conquered its demonic-idolatrous possibilities."[58] He goes on to add that an "idolatrous faith is by necessity fanatical. It must repress the doubt which characterizes the elevation of something preliminary to ultimacy."[59]

We cannot adequately understand the link between the Pentecostal incredible and faith if we do not grasp that the distorted faith is, at some level, a reaction to existential crisis, particularly anxiety. The Pentecostal incredible is some intriguing combination of faith (not-faith) and existential anxiety. At one level, some might interpret the incidence of the Pentecostal incredible as a careful attempt of religion to provide a meaning framework for its adherents amid the blows of the bad governance and postcolonial incredible. It is, instead, a display of the anxiety of meaninglessness, a lashing out, and a floundering in the sea of postcolonial disorder. The Nigerian postcolony (in its nightmarish mixture of governance as trauma and the postcolonial incredible) threatens citizens' ontic self-affirmation, relatively in terms of vulnerability to disaster, the sheer contingency of catastrophe, the irrationality, and the impenetrable darkness of the arbitrariness of the exercise of power, and absolutely in terms of death.[60] It threatens citizens' "spiritual self-affirmation, relatively in terms of emptiness, absolutely in terms of meaninglessness."[61] It threatens citizens' moral "self-affirmation, relatively in terms of guilt [self-implicature in societal rut], and absolutely in terms of condemnation [disgust at self and awareness of nonacceptance or seemingly insurmountable nausea]."[62] The postcolony is a symbol of nonbeing, threatening individual and social existence of the nation.

The faith that is engendering the Pentecostal incredible speaks to anxiety in the classical philosophical (existentialism) sense of the word. Anxiety is an existential response to the threat or menace of nonbeing. The forms this anxiety takes in the postcolony are devastating threats of emptiness and meaninglessness, haunting proximity, and heightened vulnerability to sudden death or disability. The threat of nonbeing—particularly contingent, dispersed, all-pervading—can become, at any time, for no apparent reason, and anywhere, materialized absolute disaster. Pentecostals, as participants in "being" within the matrix of governance as trauma and the postcolonial incredible, have distorted faith as a response to the naked terror of nonbeing. For them, faith is not the state of being ultimately concerned with God (Jesus Christ as the ground of being); faith is not the state of being grasped by the ultimate (Being itself); faith is not the state of being grasped by a seriousness that infinitely transcends the self. Nigerian Pentecostals, in a state of being grasped by the power of bad governance and the postcolonial incredible, seek to affirm themselves by surrendering the self to what they believe are sudden irruptions of the powers of Being itself that might be answers to preliminary concerns of life in the postcolony. Faith (as in chasing after miracles and disavowing reason or "reasonable faith") is a management tool as much as the distracting consumer culture or ever-rising productivity is at other climes, lands, and times.

In the polarity between self and world (world as fabricated or articulated by governance as trauma and the postcolonial incredible), Pentecostals have developed an existential response by fixating on self-formation, technologizing or weaponizing faith in a desperate and often futile attempt to take the peculiar anxiety of the Nigerian postcolony into the courage to be. The Pentecostal incredible, as compulsive self-affirmation, self-indulgence, and fanatical self-surrender, is actually an expression of "the noncreative courage to be as oneself."[63]

What kind of noncreative courage is this? It is what I would call thaumaturgical conformism. In particular, how does it deal with the anxieties in the postcolony? For thaumaturgical conformism, the essence of a person is one's miracle existence. A person is what one makes of oneself. Moreover, the courage to be oneself is the courage to make of oneself what miracle one wants.[64] Pentecostalism is existentialist, a hidden existentialism in plain sight. Without intending to turn Jean-Paul Sartre over in his grave, I can say that in Pentecostalism, "the essence of woman is her existence." In the reign of the Pentecostal incredible—under the hammer of despair and anxiety of meaninglessness—Nigerian Pentecostals do not believe that there is an essential nature, a fixed nature of a person, "except in the one point that [one] can make of [oneself] what [one] wants."[65] The Pentecostal creates what he or she is. "The essence of [one's] being—the 'should-be,' 'the ought-to-be'—is not something which [one] finds; [one] makes it."[66] Nigerian Pentecostals may talk about existence as working out destinies given by God. In reality, this mystical concept of being or existence has no real significance in the way they desperately seek to make themselves and existence into miracles. They work as if nothing is given to them (including the structures of reality) to determine their creativity. To put it differently, they pursue their existence without mystical restriction. They work to make themselves what they want and only read their "essences" from what they make of themselves.

The desperate desire to escape the suffocating, hope-dashing, and death-dealing environment of the postcolony has driven Pentecostals to consider their lives as a mere possibility they can mold as they will. They fill it with contents, orientation, and reject whatever catches their fancy to reject in traditional African culture in the hope of preserving their freedom. These contents have turned out to enslave them and drive them to the loss of the true freedom to which they aspire. The courage to be oneself, to take existence upon oneself, and to make oneself into what one wants has become, under the psychologically destructive hammer of the Pentecostal incredible, a fanatic-neurotic reaction against structures of reality and reason. Faith as an existential acceptance of an order, a potential site transcending the sordid experiences of the postcolony, has devolved into faith as an "in-spite-of" structures of rationality and reality. Faith as a desire for safety has become an infinite leap into a dogmatic certitude of miracles in which the special meaning of one's life is believed to be embodied or revealed. This faith does not really reveal the special or secret meaning of life. At best, it reveals the state of being grasped by the reality and power of the Nigerian postcolony.[67]

The Pentecostal incredible is revelation. It is an exposition of Nigerian social existence as it is. It is an honest identification of a sociality in which the structures of reality and categories of causality have lost their validity—not only in Nigeria but also in other societies.[68] The Pentecostal incredible is a silent energy coiled at the base of every common life, waiting to be awakened to threaten the social bonds and structures of reality and mind. The common life, the so-called center of intersubjective existence, is inhabited by the incredible, its truly existential double. Common life is the institutionalization of trust at the community's level, sociality. Common life flourishes when the members of the community are grasped and attuned with their *being-with*. The grasping and attunement are always penetrated by elements of doubt, the awareness of uncertainty, and elements of insecurity. When the community is regarded by its members as meaningful and powerfully relevant to their existence, the element of doubt, insecurity, or uncertainty is taken into the common life as an act of courage, the courage to belong. But when there is an anxiety of meaninglessness, when the common life as a union of power (dynamics) and meaning for its members is broken, then the incredible breaks open. The incredible belongs to the dynamics of the common life. Where there is a community, there is a tension between participation and separation. Without the element of separation, without individuals or parts, the community will be a single, simple thing, and there will be no participation by the parts in it. Out of the elements of participation is the common life, and out of the element of separation is the incredible or the paradox of chaos of common life.[69]

From the preceding, it is wrong to think that the emergence of the Pentecostal incredible is an accidental phenomenon in Nigeria's common life, something we can chalk under peculiarities of African existence. I argue that we cannot adequately understand the common life of any society if we ignore the crucial link between common life and what we are naming in this chapter the Pentecostal incredible. Nigerian Pentecostalism may embody it but is not limited to it.

A Theology of Chaosmosic Life

The task of this last section of this chapter is to develop a radical theology of the chaosmosic life as an additional address to the urgent matter of the Pentecostal incredible. First, I hope that such a theology might reunite the form and emotion of reason. This is a problematic issue to theorize or theologize. The problem of the incredible is not a standalone issue. We cannot simply solve it by "reforming" religion—that is, Pentecostalism. The problematic religion that births the cleavage in emotion is fostered by the peculiar human conditions of the postcolony. Thus, our primary focus should be on transforming the postcolony. Second, I hope to also address the anxiety of meaninglessness through an emancipatory politics that seeks to transform the postcolony. Thus, the possibility of transforming religion must be brought together with the possibility (or impossible possibility) of transforming the postcolony.

Alas, proposing solutions to address the Pentecostal incredible is wickedly difficult. To raise or transform people who take the structures of rationality seriously and have creative responses to existential anxiety, there must be good laws and ethos—societal transformation—in the postcolony. For how else can we nurture well-formed Pentecostals or Nigerians? The problem is this: Where will the good ethos be in the absence of good people, well-formed citizens? This is an enigmatic paradox. How does a religion that has been corrupted by the *incredibles*, anarchic waywardness, raise virtuous *remnants* in large numbers to transform its people and their ethos? (Is it only God that can save us? Let us leave this question or response to the paradox to the theologians and here focus on a political theoretical solution).

What are the sources of legitimation of the common life in Christ? Is it only order, the rule of law, and the reign of reason that constitute the common life in Christ, or is it irruptions, popular sovereignty, and dominance of will (enthusiasm)? Or is it all of these? Before we respond to this question, let us note one point: in seeking a solution to the plight of the Pentecostal incredible in the church and in society, we must be careful not to conclude that opposing the Pentecostal incredible with rationalism is adequate. It is also not enough to oppose the incredible with the common life, the ordered life, or trust. As already noted, the incredible, strictly speaking, is the immanent otherness of the common life. The incredible exposes the common life in order to deny and negate it. The trust, the rationality, of the common life tries to suture parts and tears in the fabric of the community, but the incredible increases the tears, lacerations, wounds, and ruptures in and of social existence. The incredible is the spasm, surplus of excitement, and violence of trust, exposing the common life for its inherent otherness.

The point of contact between the incredible (a form of nihilism) and the common life (community) is promise. Fear (of insecurity or uncertainty) with its power of nothing is the premise of nihilism. But fear, as Thomas Hobbes informs us, drives toward hope, the state of the community, and peaceful coexistence. Community is a response and safeguarding of promise—that is, the human desire and activities that provide, as Hannah Arendt teaches us, an island of certainty amid uncertainty and unpredictability. Promise is the concept or vision of "sharing with," a gift to be made, always a lack, not a possession or an expropriation. It always consists of the other—what is to come—and is inhabited by the absence of a realization, a substance, a presence. It intimates a mode of being. It is a relation that draws the individuals of a community from the abyss of incalculability, insecurity, and unpredictability with a line "which traversing them, alters them: it is the 'with,' the 'between,' and the threshold where they meet in a point of contact that brings them into relation with others."[70] In a sense, promise is the *no-thing* of the jug, the void, the emptiness that holds the contents we pour into the vessel. Just as the void does the holding for the vessel, as Martin Heidegger teaches us, promise does the community's holding. The void is the "essence" of the jug. The void is the non-thing of the thing as vessel. The nothing, the nonpresence, of the promise is the essence of the community as the void is to the holding vessel, the void of our "sharing with," "being-with." Promise constitutes not only the point of resistance against the destructive force of the incredible ("the non-thing," the power of nothing), the vortex of nullity, but also the reserve of meaningful existence ("the thing," the being-with of common life).[71] Promise, theorized in this way, is a likely solution to the disasters of faith (lack of trust, confidence). We stated earlier that the average Nigerian is encumbered and bombarded by three disasters. There is the disaster of faith in nationhood (governance as trauma), the disaster of faith in normality (the postcolonial incredible), and the disaster of faith in God (the Pentecostal incredible).

Our task now is to bring together the incredible and the common life in a unitary thought, seeing in the dynamics of the Pentecostal incredible not an insurmountable obstacle to the common life in Christ "but instead the occasion for a new way of thinking" about the common life in Christ.[72] This is to say we will attempt to think of promise as constitutive of both, the incredible and the common life. Promise is what the two have in common. Promise is their premise and protention. Christ is the premise and protention of the common life. Christ *is* promise. Christ is the grand promise. Christ is the void of the communal vessel that holds its being-with, sharing-with, but also the content that we pour or that flows into the void, and he is the jug itself. It is in this multiplicity and complexity of Christic functioning that we have the jug, the gathering together, called Christ and the common life. Alternatively, it is here that we can find a new bearing to theorize Christ and the common life as a radical theology.[73]

Christ's promises are yea and amen. If we took Friedrich Nietzsche's point that only free persons can promise, then Christ is the freest person. If the essence of personhood is promise, as Nietzsche implies, it means we cannot fully understand who Christ is if we consider him apart from his ability to keep his promises, to provide an island amid ambiguities and uncertainties, and to remain faithful to himself as the ultimate promise keeper. By keeping his promises, Jesus identifies himself as the one who is, who was, and who is to come. Jürgen Moltmann is very clear about the place of promise in Christianity. Yahweh is the God of promise, and Christianity (as well as the religion of Israel, Judaism) is a religion of promise. The promise is always in contradiction to the present, historical reality. It overflows reality with a surfeit of possibilities and points believers to the not-yet.[74]

One veritable lens through which to examine the incredibles in Nigeria is the lens of promise. The ocean of uncertainty that breeds the Pentecostal incredible cannot be divorced from decades of broken promises by the state and from the experiences of citizens growing up in communities and institutions where promises are not the islands of certainty amid oceans of unpredictability and uncertainties. Church leaders do not keep promises, the state does not even offer any guarantee in the form of promises, and communities abort promises and even dismantle the premises of promises in their own disarray. Even God, if we are to believe the Pentecostals, does not keep promises with regard to respecting the integrity of the physical laws of the universe, and the Pentecostal God certainly regards the laws of reason as abyss of uncertainty and unpredictability. Promises do sustain social fabrics—and even religion or faith. But this is one lesson Nigerians seem to have conveniently forgotten.

Thus, the first step toward tackling the issue of the incredibles is the restoration of promise, a turn to commitment to promises as the premise of political togetherness and politics. More than ever before, Nigerians need a full-blooded commitment to promise keeping as the basic covenant of their being-with and sharing-with one another. It is here that we must turn to Arendt. In her book *The Human Condition*, she associates keeping promises with political action.[75] Arendt holds that the ordinary practice of promising, of keeping promises, becomes an extraordinary act in times of transitions or exceptional circumstances.[76] The reign of the incredibles, with its deep alienation from scientific reason, certainly qualifies as a context of exception. The simple act of making and keeping promises conveys social existence as not mercurial or ruptural, but as norm governed and rational. In its simplicity, keeping promises appears as a rebuttal to the notion of a ruptural, mercurial, willful God who is deemed the agent that anchors the Pentecostal incredible, the fabulous deeds of faith. It is also a rebuttal to the *everything-scatter-scatter* logics of the postcolonial incredible.

The Pentecostal incredible, as a response to the postcolonial incredible, is complicit in the generation and sustenance of a world of lawlessness where simple promises that sustain political togetherness are not kept. Promise as a political tool suspends the "logics of rule-exception" in which both the postcolonial incredible and the Pentecostal incredible are stuck.[77] This is not the whole story. In their logics of exception, in their inclination to the perpetual suspension of reason or ordinary lawfulness of daily existence, Pentecostals and indeed Nigerians are seeking the promises that can heal their wounds of existence. They are seeking actors, institutions, and governments that can keep promises that relate to mere life and promises that attend to more life. Though Nigerians are grasping for both types of promises with passionate intensity in the *widening gyres* of postcoloniality that have unleased anarchy upon the world, they are indeed seeking the second coming of promise. Things fell apart long ago in the blood-dimmed tide of governance as trauma, and the ceremony of innocent promises that marked the birth of an independent nation on October 1, 1960, drowned in chaos soon after. Inevitably, a second hope is at hand.[78] Nigerians are thirsting for the promise of life and life more abundantly. The real revelatory power of the incredibles is the laying bare of the Nigerians' orientation to promise amid the widening gyre of the madness of postcoloniality. Where do we begin to discern the magic of the second coming of promise?

The magic of the incredibles does not lie in the grasping of their time in widening gyres but in their potentialities. Their magic is not in the despotic grip on the necks of their subjugated subjects experiencing them as *mysterium tremendum* of irrationality but in their *mysterium fascinans* of promise. The magic of the incredibles does not cohere in their disruption of reason but in their ability to make the unmasking of the extraordinary rottenness of Nigeria's constituting structures and abiding ethos into ordinary occurrences.

It is in these recognitions that we should venture to discern the emergence of the *Incredible Man or Woman* from the fashioning of the incredibles. In the very thesis of the dialectics of incredibles, there is an antithesis, which might "create" the Incredible Man or Woman as a synthesis. In the fashioning of the incredibles, there is the (unintended) crafting of a subjectivity that refuses to harmonize the plurality and multiplicity of epistemologies so as to appear enlightened; there is a disciplining that resists the urge to close off alternate ways of being by identifying with hegemonic ideas but that accepts ill-fittedness in the regnant practices of modernity. The incredibles, as we have earlier described them, are not reducible to the abnormal or the strange, "but instead are the excess, the ill-fitted, the remainder, that which escapes and resists the standard frame of" modernism's ways of knowing.[79] A person who has imbibed the subjectivity forged by the incredibles is potentially a subject with dissonant impulses. This is a person who is sensitive to excess, inconsistencies, and remainders of any structures of existence and is willing to expose the rifts and fissures of ordinary life for the sake of an agonistic common life. He or she is a kind of ideal person but is unlike those citizens of *perfect virtue* who want to stabilize social systems. He or she is the subject (looking to *virtùi* and not to virtue, looking to disruption of systems and not conformity to orders that thwart human flourishing) who wants to disrupt the systems, to overcome old relations and create new realities.[80] What can this possibly mean for politics? What does it mean for a person fashioned in an atmosphere of the incredibles to want to initiate something new in his or her society? What does it mean to consider the "antiethical" world of the incredibles to be transformable into sites of revolutionary (subversive) power? Such a person has to locate politics at sites that aspire to generate alternative practices and has to be inclined to treat the agnostic ill-fittedness of Pentecostal subjectivity as resistance to identifying politics with administration and treat juridical settlement as "the task of politics . . . [but rather] see politics as a disruptive practice that resists the consolidations and closures of administrative and juridical settlement for the sake of the perpetuity of political contest."[81]

Does this mean that all structures must be constantly contested and perpetually repoliticized? Political theorist Bonnie Honig clarifies this point for us: "To affirm the perpetuity of contest is not to celebrate a world without points of stabilization [or for that matter irrationality]; it is to affirm the reality of contest, even within ordered setting, and to identify the affirmative dimensions of contestation. It is to see that the always imperfect closure of political space tends to engender remainders and that, if those remainders are not engaged, they may return to haunt and destabilize the very closures that deny their existence."[82]

Will the Incredible Man or Woman ever emerge? I cannot believe it, but I must believe it. It is crucial at this juncture of our discussion to remind ourselves of Arendt's insight that human beings always have the capacity to act, to start something new, even in the unlikeliest of circumstances. Arendt writes:

> The life span of man running toward death would inevitably carry everything human to ruin and destruction if it were not for the faculty of interrupting it and beginning something new, a faculty which is inherent in action like an ever-present reminder that men, though they must die, are not born in order to die but in order to begin. . . . The miracle that saves the world, the realm of human affairs, from its normal, "natural" ruin is ultimately the fact of natality, in which the faculty of action is ontologically rooted. It is, in other words, the birth of new men and the new beginning, the action they are capable of by virtue of being born.[83]

This is the promise of human social existence, the potentiality of a people breaking out of the chain of events that has ensnared them. The promise of the Nigerian situation and its *plural* Pentecostals, each of whom can initiate something new and acquire new perspectives, should not be ignored. The emergence of men and women, acting in concert, who are capable of new actions will not fit a predictable model if we believe, as Arendt does, that the supreme capacity of human beings as a plurality of distinct, unique individuals is to begin. There is hope in any polity, according to her, because new people are continually added to the plurality and are capable of new beginnings. The new people coming into the world are capable of interrupting the ongoing social processes and initiating the miracle of beginnings in the apparently inexorable chain of events set in motion by the incredibles. Promise—yea, mutual promise—is not only an embodiment of human natality and the miracle of new beginnings but also a reminder of them in the haphazard contingency of the Nigerian postcolony. The incredibles are not the last words; promise is.

4

PRODUCTION OF VIOLENCE IN THE POSTCOLONY

Introduction

An adequate understanding of the religious-cultural-political character of African postcolony must reckon with its violent character of power. Early in this book I stated that we must pay attention to the dynamic constellation of three desires (deformed epistemology, violent power, and recognition) in order to grasp the working of the sacred in the African postcolony. In the last chapter we engaged the subject matter of epistemology; in this chapter I turn our attention to the issue of violent power as an integral part of the working of the sacred in Africa, the monstrosity of the sacred in the postcolony. The violent exercise of power, the social practice of dominating and altering the will of others in one's social relationships, is one of the transcripts of the sacred in Africa, one of the ways the sacred becomes actual in the lifeworlds of Africans. Simply put, this chapter deals with the subject matter of power as violence, a monstrous transcript of the sacred in the African postcolony.

Violence in postcolonial Africa defies neat categorization into secular and sacred (in the narrower, popular sense of the word) sources. We cannot discuss violence without recognizing or thinking of pain. Violence is a tale of horror and pain that resist symbolization; bodies' agony cannot be easily signified. Pain is a sensory state that makes violence private, not directly expressible or readable in words.[1] We can only feel another's pain as a matter of faith. It is in this sense that pain resists symbolization. In a different but intuitively graspable way, the scale, ubiquity, and intensity of the violence in the body politic of the postcolony are (almost) inexpressible and definitely unthinkable. Yet there are dimensions of violence in the postcolony that register as meaningful events: as humiliation, punishment, defeat, sacrifice, terror, and death. Violence (pain) is made readable through the sociopolitical conventions of telling the victims' stories. The registration of violence, the pain of violence in the symbolic realm, is not easily amenable to the divide between sacred and secular. Pain problematizes this boundary between the sacred and the secular. Pain or violence as a lived experience is a sign best read across the static, abstract academic demarcation of the sacred-secular split. Whether postcolony's ubiquitous violence shatters the coordinates of our symbolically constituted common reality or whether its intensity slips through our fine analytical net of the secular-sacred debate, we still have the imaginative commonality, which is not private, to imagine how a particular insult to our body and the psyche, precisely the pain of violence, feels.

Now imagine yourself caught in the talons of diarrhea and death:

> (1) In the camps [refugee camps in eastern Zaire during the Rwanda genocide in 1994] the living stretched out next to corpses, which no body had the strength or the means to remove. Medical workers ran from patient to patient, jabbing intravenous liquids in their arms as fast as possible, often failing to find veins. Diarrhea stained people's clothes and rags; everywhere, the smell of shit and death clogged the air. After one month, 50,000 people had died.[2]

Now imagine this happening to you as a woman:

> (2) Women had other problems, as well. The aid organizations running the camps didn't provide sanitary napkins, and women had to use rags or tear up sheets to use instead. As there was little soap, these scraps of cloth became hard and caked with blood. To their humiliation, women had no choice but to try to wash these in the same pots they used for cooking. "The blood water snaked in rivulets between the tents and little puddles of blood formed here and there."[3]

Can you feel any difference between those who died in secular or sacred space? Does it really matter if those who died in sacred space were killed by people driven by secular reason? Mahmood Mamdami gives a description of people butchered in a church during the Rwandan genocide, which was precipitated by conflicts in the secular sphere.

> (3) The church was about twenty by sixty feet. Inside, wooden planks were placed on stones. I supposed they were meant as benches. I peered inside and saw a pile of belongings—shoulder sacks, tattered clothing, a towel, and hats—the worldly goods of the poor. Then, amidst it all, I saw bones, and then entire skeletons, each caught in the posture in which it had died. Even a year after the

genocide, I thought the air smelled of blood, mixed with that of bones, clothing, earth—a human mildew.[4]

We can multiply this kind of ethnographic account, but we should respectfully move on to other forms of violence. We need to recognize the physical violence that is meted out to people, especially women, in the name of casting out demons from them. In some Pentecostal circles and Islamic deliverance rituals, the priest, deliverance ministers, or imam (*malamai*) often slap, beat, whip, and scream at "patients" or "clients" in the name of casting out demons. A Nigerian middle-class Pentecostal woman, who went to college with me, told me years ago that she once went to a Pentecostal minister for prayers so she could find a suitable man to marry. He diagnosed her as being possessed by a "spiritual husband" who was preventing her from marriage. In order to "heal" her, she said, the minister used a native Nigerian broom to repeatedly beat all over her body to expel the spirit from her. Women are more often subjected to this kind of harsh treatment than men because the ritualists believe that women are more prone to demonic invasion, more susceptible to evil spirits. Just as in many areas of life in Africa the secular and sacred are interrelated, so are they at work in the harsh treatment of women seeking divine help. Was the beating of my friend a religious cleansing exercise or a man whipping a trapped, indoctrinated woman? Susan O'Brien captures this ambiguity well in her study of exorcisms performed by *malamai* (Islamic scholars/teachers) in Kano, Nigeria. She writes:

> The spirits' insolent or evasive responses [to the malamai's intimidation and dialogue, such as shouting Quranic verses into the right ears of afflicted women] often provoke malamai to physical violence . . . which includes slapping and punching the spirit hosts on the face, head, feet, and back. These sessions can thus be disturbing scenes as two or three malamai circle around the sick woman and smack, scream at, and insult her.

In one sense, the malamai's violence can be read as a ritual inscription of prevailing gender hierarchies, in which women's negative association with tradition is reinforced.[5]

This chapter does not make many assumptions about idealized theoretical connections between the sacred and violence in explaining their mutual imbrication in Africa. It also does not tease out the intricacies of the relationship between the secular and the sacred in the production of violence in postcolonial Africa. It only aspires to describe or explain how certain problematic, troubling conflictual connections between the sacred and violence, or how some bewildering relationships between the secular and the sacred, emanate from the very pores of postcolonial

Africa. In the necropolis that is the African postcolony, not only do people kill or die for causes that they presume higher than sacred lives but also the sacred itself comes alive, assuming special dynamics of liveliness, in the very devices of the death-dealing postcolonial regime. Violence is the substance of the postcolony, and the sacred is its form. Many years after Frantz Fanon wrote about the liberating power of violence, the postcolonial African state is enslaving or impoverishing its citizens in and through "sacred" violence.

The postcolony is a veritable context for producing and sustaining the nexus between the sacred and violence. This context resists generalization or abstract theorization. When I survey the ponderous postcolony from which commingled sacred excesses and violence flow down to ordinary Africans, I realize that were the whole realm of idealized theory at my grasp, it would be inadequate to make sense of the sacred and violence in Africa. All vain theories that charm me most I sacrifice to the particular historical discourse of each connection between the sacred and violence in the African postcolony. Nothing makes sense consistently enough to engender universalizable theory on violence in the African postcolony. Inherited theoretical categories flounder and sink in the ocean of disorder that is the postcolony, which is always becoming. My plan in this chapter is to focus on the empirical.

Bjørn Enge Bertelsen has to make a similar move to overcome the binary of traditional and modern in his study of state formation in the Mozambican postcolony. Existing theories and the art of forcing empirical materials into the mold of a theoretical framework did not work for his purpose.[6] "The insistence on the empirical allows for the formation of concepts that may grasp the unending flux in a context marked by relations and constellations which are constantly forged and disassembled."[7] So his book *Violent Becomings* investigates the Mozambican state as perpetually unfolding, always in the process of becoming, not as a Leviathan that is hovering over its subjects or a bureaucratically ordered polity quietly ruling nonstate domains of the social.[8] More importantly, the book reveals the typical violent articulations of the postcolonial state with its society or traditional fields. It does this by focusing on specific contextual, historical discourses of state-society relationship in the country.

New Concepts of Sacred and Secular

Before we delve into contextual discourse, let me quickly form concepts that "may grasp the unending flux" in the historical contexts that will command our attention going forward. I want us to evade the inherited conceptualizations of the sacred and the secular so as not to "project analytical freeze frames onto what cannot be frozen" or project some old Western academic debates onto historical contexts that do not divide up neatly into secular or sacred.[9] We will develop the concepts of secular and sacred that are faithful to the manner in which the two spheres of human existence are interrelated in Black Africa. By the way, calling them two spheres is not a very precise way of talking about African spirituality. Later in this chapter, we will rethink the meanings of the "sacred" and the "secular" as played out in African spirituality.

I define African spirituality as the practices of exchanging, contesting, reducing, increasing, interacting, and renewing energies in the power of being in all spheres of life (the dead, the living, the not yet born, spirits and gods, and nature) on the basis of the dynamic relationships between all visible and invisible dimensions of being. What we call religion refers to how lives hang together in Africa, how Africans live or should live together. Religion is not a separate grouping of practices set apart from the other spheres of life as a special or institutionalized set. The academic categories of sacred and secular only make good sense if they are ultimately related to or are elucidated in terms of how people live together, organize the spheres and the interrelationships of their common existence, and seek the good life. "African spirituality is not a matter of mere belief or assent to doctrines and dogmas.... It does not primarily answer the question of what we should believe; it responds, rather, to the question of *how we should live*."[10] In the words of African theologian Laurent Magesa in his book *What Is Not Sacred? African Spirituality*:

> African spirituality does not hold as its primary objective the achievement of a specific goal among other goals, such as piety, meekness, or fear of God. If there is a goal in the perception of African spirituality, it is to totally experience the "good life" and to completely avoid the "bad life." Indeed, formal associations, societies, or sodalities similar to spiritual groups in other religious traditions can be found, but the purpose of each is to integrate the life forces for greater, better, and more abundant life in this world achieved through the constant interaction between faith, environment, and society. Consequently, there are no movements in the indigenous traditions of black Africa that distinguish the "sacred" from the "profane" or "secular." *For, indeed, just what is not sacred?*[11]

For our limited purposes in this chapter, we consider the sacred (or the religious) as an entitative ultimate concern who (that) is the embodiment of possibilities and is revered (or celebrated) as capable of taking or giving life.

In this sense, the state, church, mosque, or persons of presidents and big men and women could be regarded as sacred. Include in this list God, divinities, and community as the foundation of human, personal, and social existence. The sacred is not just about spiritual beings but also about forces or agents that can substantially alter possibilities for human flourishing in any given finite existence.[12]

The sacred is the set of possibilities opened to members of a society or excluding them, liberatory potentials for the transformation of selves and structures of society, and the sum total of possibilities conceivable given their level of social, technological, and economic development. The sacred also refers to the infinite possibilities in existence or being.[13] The sacred relates not only to the people as a whole but also to individuals, groups, institutions, and communities.

In the universe or totality of possibilities available to any society, some are defined as available to persons, institutions, and social structures and others either remain unfulfilled or exclude them at any given time. There is always a set of appropriated or available possibilities within the sacred at any given time, and there are others that society believes are too dangerous to be handled or must only be carefully managed by designated authorities. The excess of the sacred, meaning the abundant, uncontrolled release of its possibilities, is (potentially) violent. Violence is the possible outcome of the sacred that exceeds its bounds, that short-circuits the connection between what is possible and what is impossible. Amid the disorder of the African postcolony, amid the divine impunity of its leaders and "big men and women," and amid the disordered state sovereignty that manifests primarily as the limitless power to brutalize or take the lives of its citizens, the uncontrolled possibilities of the sacred easily overflow its bounds.[14] The postcolony makes impossibilities possible. It makes deadly possibilities, unthinkable possibilities, the common lot of daily phenomenal reality. Violence is numinous as a *mysterium tremendum* in its quotidian closeness to the bodies of ordinary citizens and sacrosanct in its remit as the transcendent solution to almost all disagreements in the postcolony. In ancient times or in contemporary other societies, the sacred has helped human beings to transform chaos into cosmos, but in the postcolonial world of excess possibilities and limitless violence, the sacred manifests as chaos itself. The postcolony's chaos is simultaneously old and new. It is old in its continuity and insistence (right from the slave-trade era to the colonial period) as a deadly apparatus of disciplining. It is new in its capacity to invent ways of moving human degradation and depravity forward in the postcolony, in its uncanny inventiveness in thwarting human flourishing.

The sacred and violence in postcolonial Africa are held together by chaos. The sacred deploys violence to control, manage, reduce, or increase chaos. Owing to chaos, violence is born and affronts things, values, institutions, and persons that are held "sacred" in communities. The postcolonial state, or more precisely the relationship between the state and society, is the primary source of chaos. The state in the postcolony is marked by forces of the sacred and violence. The postcolonial state is violent; its violence is sacred, and the sacred is the violent state of chaos.

Indeed, the postcolonial state in Africa inflicts a special type of violence on its citizens because of the chaotic nature of daily existence that it supervises. As already noted in chapter 3, governance, just like the daily existential condition, is an incredible phenomenon, a situation of perpetual crisis—crisis as norm. Basic life in the postcolony is a struggle to survive the perpetual trauma of national political governance. Governance in the African postcolony is not the ordering of resources, human lives, social conditions, and juridical-political rules for human flourishing but the disorganization and dislocation of life within life—that is, the penetration of death into life. Governance keeps the nation in the zone of indistinction between life and death. It maintains the postcolony as a camp of living dead, life-in-death. In this condition, governance as trauma and the postcolonial incredible, governance renders and heightens the vulnerability of citizens, the exposure of citizens to gratuitous violence.[15]

The sacred—as defined by its operations delineated above—is not a polar conception to the term *secular*. Both terms in this chapter refer to how possibilities of existence in a particular historical context are interpreted by those involved in it. If the possibilities available to a group of persons are considered to transform the world or if the group believes that their realization will make the world approximate their own word, wish, or desire, we will consider such possibilities as sacred. But if the possibilities are less forceful—meaning that they are not considered to be capable of initiating something new amid ongoing social processes—then we will consider them secular. Emerging possibilities either conform to things as they are or conform the members of the community to the existing order of things or being. Otherwise, they create new worlds. Let us name the first type of possibilities "directive" and the second type "conformative." Conformatives approximate the world as it is. Directives transform the world.

Sacred and secular are just alternative ways of talking about directives and conformatives without the troublesome polar conception or binary thinking. They are alternative ways of talking about the dimensions or features of the sacred.

Of course, it is not always apparent when a possibility available from the universal set of possibilities is a directive or conformative. Religious institutions can engender both the sacred and the secular. The political state can also do it; so can many other institutions. What we have called sacred or secular in the past are just different ways of coding possibilities. Since this chapter is not based on ethnography, wherein we ask participants to code their interpretation of possibilities, it does not make much sense for us to continue to make distinctions between sacred and secular sources of violence in the African postcolony. (Let us not forget the question Magesa asked us: What is not sacred in Africa?) We should, therefore, focus on how violence is constantly rearranging the possibilities for harmonious social existence and human flourishing in the postcolony.

Violence in Chaotic Postcolony

Many of the agents that inflict massive pain on either the postcolonial state or its citizens want to enact possibilities that will initiate something amid ongoing social processes and structures. Some of these organizations or agents name the ongoing social reality as a form of chaos that must be transformed by divine light and word. Within this perspective, the sacred and violence in postcolonial Africa are held together by chaos. Such agents argue that hardcore violence can midwife sacred possibilities from the womb of chaos into actuality. Boko Haram (BH), the extremely violent fundamentalist Islamic terrorist group operating in Nigeria, "theorizes" this perspective of the relationship between the sacred and violence in the postcolony—of course, as an excuse for its reign of mayhem. Its leader, Abubakar Shekau, argues that the Nigerian state is violent and that BH must thus use violence as an expression of sacred demand for change, arguing that a violent state of chaos is worse than killing.

After the then Nigerian president Goodluck Jonathan called Boko Haram a "cancer" in a speech in December 2011, Shekau responded, "We are not cancer. . . . The disease is unbelief, and as Allah says, 'Chaos is worse than killing' (Qur'an 2:191). . . . Everyone knows democracy is unbelief, and everyone knows the Constitution is unbelief, and everyone knows that there are things Allah has forbidden in the Qur'an, and that are forbidden in countless hadiths in the Prophet, that are going on in Western schools. . . . We ourselves haven't forbidden anything, we haven't told the Muslim community to abandon anything, we simply stand on the path of truth."[16]

Needless to say, not all Muslims interpret Quran 2:191 in the same way as Shekau. They would argue that his method of ending chaos in the Nigerian postcolony by killing thousands of innocent civilians, both Muslims and non-Muslims, is engendering greater chaos. Even those who supported the killings perpetrated by his late boss, Muhammad Yusuf, as a way to ending further chaos in Nigeria are against the type of rebellion he champions. "But for Shekau, the 'chaos' the Qur'an condemns had already come to Nigeria in the form of a heretical system: democracy, constitutionalism, Western-style education, and so on. The only suitable response was to violently oppose that system: 'Know, the people of Nigeria and other places, a person is not a Muslim unless he disavows democracy and other forms of polytheistic unbelief [*shirk*]."[17]

Here we see postcolonial violence, so-called sacred violence, masquerading as catechontic impulse in the midst of chaos, amid the postcolonial incredible. Shekau considers himself fighting to stave off disorder and impose order on what he considers chaotic. In a sense, Shekau and Boko Haram fighters believe themselves to be an arresting force (*katechon*) that can push back the chaos to save Nigeria from the chaotic powers of Christian domination, apostate Muslims, and the democratic state. Boko Haram sees itself as a withholding power to prevent *shirk* from unleashing eschatological-level disaster in Nigeria. The imposition of order that defers the eschatological paralysis of unbelief sanctifies the imperial *catechontic* sovereignty Shekau wants to establish over Nigeria and her neighbors. Yet we should not be quick to conclude that Boko Haram, even on its own terms, is strictly for the preservation of order amid the chaos it has identified and named. Chaos justifies not only Boko Haram's violence but also its state of emergency, its right to claim exception to some Islamic laws, especially the laws about not killing Muslim civilians. Alexander Thurston's brilliant 2018 study of Boko Haram clearly shows that Shekau carries himself as the sovereign who decides on the exception, the lawgiver who suspends the law, to resort to Carl Schmitt's language. Those who claim to be holier than others in their societies often quickly come to the point of self-importance where they consider themselves exceptional. Their holiness, their claim of lifestyle supremacism, is understood to represent an exception that takes them out of ordinary personhood. The etymological import of *holy* (*haglos*, set apart), the removal of a thing from circulation, now signals their exception.[18]

Catherine Keller's riff on the exception of the sovereign opens an interesting angle of view to help us understand how religious and governmental sovereign powers are fascinated with death, and in this way it helps us to link up with Achille Mbembe's conceptualization of sovereignty in the African postcolony. She writes, "Note, by the way, that 'exception' comes from *excipere*, the Latin 'to take out.' It works both ways: the sovereign exception takes itself out of the common; then the exception can 'take out' whatever impedes its ascent."[19] African political leaders and religious personalities like Shekau take out human beings that are obstructions to their domination.

As Achille Mbembe taught us, this form of exercise of power by leaders or sovereign states in the African postcolony is not about disciplining bodies to control them and increasing productivity in the economy. But it is about creating zones of death, exercising the power to take life, signifying the ultimate exercise of domination as the capability to impose death on the people.[20] While Boko Haram bases its understanding of sovereignty as control over mortality on the basis of scripture, the political leaders of postcolonial African base their understanding on their secular leadership of the secular states or governments.

The exercise of sovereignty as a form of violence over life in the African postcolony is always intimately linked with sexual violence. The exercise of sovereignty consists of sexual pleasures derived from the subordinates, from bodies violently subjugated and penetrated. Boko Haram in April 2014 captured 276 high-school girls in the dark of the night and took them away as sex slaves. What about the political leaders? They are really not different. As Mbembe argues in *On the Postcolony*:

> The actions that signal sovereignty must be carried through with style and an adequately harsh firmness, otherwise the splendor of those exercising the trappings of authority is dimmed. To exercise authority is, above all, to tire out the bodies of those under it, to disempower them not so much to increase their productivity as to ensure the maximum docility. To exercise authority is, furthermore, for the male ruler, to demonstrate publicly a certain delight in eating and drinking well, and, again in Labou Tansi's words, to pass most of his time in "pumping grease and rust into the backsides of young girls." The male ruler's pride in possessing an active penis has to be dramatized, through

sexual rights over subordinates, the keeping of concubines, and so on. The unconditional subordination of women to the principle of male pleasure remains one pillar upholding the reproduction of the phallocratic system.[21]

Before we leave this discourse of the similarities between the exercise of sovereignty by secular and religious claimers (usurpers) of authority, we need to mention that the very emergence and persistence of Boko Haram also point to the problem of violence. Here it is the failure of the Nigerian state to exercise the monopoly of violence within its territory.[22] Though the Nigerian state, starting from the colonial period, has violently dealt with its citizens, it has shown itself in the face of the challenge of Boko Haram not to command enough constituted violence to establish peace and order over vast areas of its territory. This lack of proper exercise of constituted violence is just one indicator of the incipient failure of the Nigerian state and a constant reminder of the attendant forms of violence this incompetence daily visits on the citizens.

In the postcolony the sacred is richly present in bad governance: as a child ravaged by diseases, as a criminal lynched by burning tires, as a putrefying corpse on the roadside. Governance as an unending trauma is daily reconfiguring new devilish possibilities or generating impossible possibilities in the postcolony, always diabolically initiating new ways of supplanting human flourishing in Black Africa. The sacred is also the horror of the phenomenal failure of governance in the here and now. The sacred is not necessarily in some transcendent realm but rather in the terror of existence. The failure of the state causes the death of children, the jungle justice that flaming "tire necklaces" put on mob-sentenced criminals represent, and the inability of municipalities to pick up dead bodies on the street. The failure of the state produces violence as it becomes increasingly unable to defend its citizens.

As Jason Stearns puts it, "The Congo does not have a Leviathan, a state that can protect its citizens or even impose a monopoly of violence. . . . The story of the Congo wars is one of state weakness and failure, which has made possible the ceaseless proliferation of insurgent groups. . . . These armed groups fight brutal insurgencies and counterinsurgencies that, as the United States discovered in Vietnam and Iraq, are not so much about controlling territory as about controlling civilians, who are brutalized in order to obtain resources and as retaliation for attacks by their rivals."[23]

Violence is the sacred itself. The sacred reveals itself by hiding in the midst of violence as it is made to exist by the failed (failing) postcolonial states in Africa. There is little that is original in this statement. Let us not forget that the sacred, as German philosopher Rudolf Otto informs us, is both fascinating and terrifying. It terrifies because of its overwhelming power to inflict harm. In the postcolony, the part of the sacred that is deemed to be fascinating, to be gracious and merciful, seems to have atrophied, and we are left with its singular ability to inflict pain and terror. The state in Africa definitely represents this kind of one-hand slugger of a sacred.

The postcolonial state is a system of violence and sacredness. Every day in its process of becoming, it summarizes and sharpens in itself its past and present world of violence. Its relationship with its society is a process of enfolding and unfolding dangerous possibilities for those under its domination. The state in Africa is the face of primordial violence and the preeminent taker of life. It weighs down on the people as a mass of perdition, as a mischievous incubus, an elephant, a forbidding *potestas* sitting on the rib cages of helpless masses. The state is sacred by virtue of its economy of weights and obstructed breathings. Such an economy of violence, supervised by the one-hand slugger of a sacred, blocks possibilities for the good life for its citizens.

I promised earlier that I would tell the story of the relationship between the sacred and the violence not by weaving a grand theory but by structuring our discourse of the connection around historical contexts or case studies of violence. The relationship between the sacred and violence in postcolonial Africa is discernible in the haunting sound of crushing and cracking brittle human bones under the soles of tourists walking through a church in Rwanda. But we are getting ahead of ourselves. Between April and July 1994, eight hundred thousand Tutsi were murdered in what has come to be called the Rwanda genocide; this murder spree wiped out an estimated 80 percent of the minority Tutsi population. Murambi, a tall hill in one of Rwanda's poorest provinces, was one of the sites where Hutu's dead squads or militia groups killed thousands of Tutsi. The massacre site, Murambi Technical School, has become a museum to honor the dead. On April 7, 1996, a special commemorative service was held at the site by the Tutsi-led government of Rwanda. The government had even exhumed some of the bodies and laid them out in the exhibition building. The idea is that visitors can file past the bodies and bear witness to the atrocities done to the Tutsi. Political scientist Timothy Longman reported this:

> My colleagues and I joined the line filling past the narrow cement classroom buildings. Inside each of the rooms, bodies were laid out, covered with

powdered lime to preserve them. Even so, the stench of decaying flesh was still so strong that most people covered their noses and mouths as they passed. The display of bodies was meant to resemble one of the other memorial sites in the country, like the Catholic parish of Nyamata, where bodies had been left as they had fallen when the swift RPF [Rwandan Patriotic Front] advance drove out the local population before they could dispose of the evidence of their crimes. But there at Murambi the bodies were laid out carefully on display, each room with a theme serving a didactic purpose.[24]

With this shocking display of bodies, the Rwandan authorities were not just asking people to bear witness to the crimes committed in 1994; they were also creating the memory that will hold the lives that were lost as sacred. The horrific, macabre display of bodies was carefully staged to provoke a sense of transcendence or to intimate a touch of the numinous, to make visitors feel that they are encountering something bigger than them, something that exceeds their capacity to comprehend. And to sacralize any decision the government would make to promote national security, to protect lives. Sacred lives got caught up in the sacred politics of a secular government.

The violence—in this case, genocide—happened, and the reaction to it in terms of the politics of memory reconfigured the sacred. The bodies on display restaged the sacred in Rwanda. The sacred is grisly, as exhibited by the extraordinary moral and political failure of previous Hutu-led government and international organizations to adequately respond to the murder of thousands of Tutsi. The shock effect of the bodies urges us to recognize the horror and terror of the sacred as dangerous, uncontrolled possibilities of human coexistence. The sacred is not some external deity visiting the earth with fire and brimstone but ordinary people and secular governments unleashing the dangerous possibilities of their existence, the set of possibilities normally excluded from fulfillment by civilization or a society's regime of law and order. And secular political authority that can tame such excesses, that can restrain dangerous possibilities from fully manifesting, may claim for itself some of the awe of the sacred as overwhelming power, if not become the missing fascinating half of the sacred in the African postcolony. Definitely, the Tutsi-led Rwandan government portrayed itself as some kind of *katechon* (restraining power against lawlessness, 2 Thess. 2:6).

The sacred and secular easily blend into each other in the African postcolony. This was obvious in another way, as a must-visit tourist site in Rwanda demonstrates. Dollars from the secular tourist business sustain the sacred politics of memory—a memory made necessary and inevitable by postcolonial violence. Alas, the two spheres of the secular and sacred do not always mix very well. In this case the secular appears to be stepping on the sacred, literally crushing the "bones" of the sacred. To flesh this assertion out, let us turn to a church at Ntarama, another memorial site for over five thousand people killed during the period of the genocide. An American ethnographer visited the site in 2002 when the chapel was being reconstructed, and this is his disturbing report:

> The chapel at Ntarama was initially left as it was found, with bodies grotesquely scattered around the building and grounds. Around 2001, the bodies were cleared from the church, but improvements had not yet been undertaken to create . . . a sleek memorial. . . . As a result, Ntarama was much more disturbing. When I first visited the church in 2002, several burlap bags in the back of the sanctuary were filled with bones. . . . The floor of the chapel was cluttered with the detritus of the people who had sought refuge in the place but instead found death—scraps of clothing, notebooks, and bones, some identifiable as ribs and finger-bones, others were broken fragments. . . . It was still impossible to walk through the building without stepping on bones, creating a horrifying crunch under foot.[25]

Violence as Loss of Community

Postcolonial violence is not merely about the loss of lives or loved ones but also about the uprooting of community as the foundation of personal and group identity and thus the exacerbation of the postcolonial incredible and the contribution to an ever-increasing "elemental sense of dislocation" and "cosmological disorientation."[26] In many of the instances of violence, the perpetrators targeted chiefs, priests, and other communal leaders. Jason K. Stearns, in his emotion-gripping book *Dancing in the Glory of Monsters*, paints a disturbing picture of the loss of community and humanity during the Congo civil war.[27] In a conflict at Kasika, the soldiers of Congolese Rally for Democracy (RCD) killed the priest of a Catholic church and also the village chief, Francois Naluindu, in a calculated attempt to disorganize the village. What was the reason? Some persons in a nearby village attacked RCD soldiers in defense of their own safety. In revenge, the soldiers decided to cut off the "head" of the village. Theologian Emmanuel Katongole tells us what this means: "The significance of the chiefs goes beyond their function: they embody the community and provide a vital link, a relationship like a glue between the land, ancestors, and community. Those relationships ensure a sense of both communal and individual identity, as well as a sense of belonging and stability. In a society defined by communitarian relationships and communal belonging, the chief is the community. Killing the chief is like killing the community and everything the community stands for."[28]

The radical import of what RCD did was not lost on the villagers as they lamented the death of the chief in these words: "In our tradition, the *mwami* [chief] is sacred. You don't kill the *mwami* during the war. Killing him is like killing all of us."[29] Stearns's description of the macabre killing not only demonstrates the "killing" of the sacred but also the unleashing of possibilities or forces that "killed" the humanity of the marauding soldiers and their civilian victims. The killers became "animals" as described by the groundskeeper of the Kasika parish where the priest was shot in the back of the head after they asked him to kneel down and pray.[30] Stearns's description of the massacre at Kasika leaves no other impression than the one that says RCD soldiers lost their humanity in the brutal civil war that claimed over four million lives:

> The way the victims were killed said as much as the number of dead; they displayed a macabre fascination with human anatomy. The survivors said the chief's heart had been cut out and his wife's genitals were gone. . . . It wasn't enough to kill their victims; they disfigured them and played with their bodies. They disemboweled one woman by cutting her open between her anus and vagina, then propped up the dead body on all fours and left her with her buttocks facing upward. Another corpse was given two slits on either side of his belly, where his hands were inserted. . . . They would kill the priests, rape the nuns, rip babies from their mother's womb, and even twist the corpses into origami figures.[31]

In the reign of the postcolonial incredible, what is normal must make way for the abnormal, fear, threat, the unimaginable, and the loss of safety that brooks no distinction between what is sacred and what is secular. To borrow the words of Marx and Engels in the *Communist Manifesto*, "all that is solid melts into air, all that is sacred is profaned," and Africans are daily compelled to face with sober senses homes that have become unheimlich.[32] Where home has become hell, where inside is now outside, the sacred, secular, and profane (as in front of the temple or house) lose their definition and the identity of the self as tied to land, community, or established social relationships collapses. Self, identity, home, and community, in the face of unsettling violence amid the complete unpredictability of life, dimmed into a blood-soaked zone of indistinction. "What was assumed, taken for granted as 'normal' on a daily basis, has disappeared, and as a result people suspend or completely lose the capacity to feel at home: 'Violence destroys this feeling and the capacity to be oneself without mistrust or pretension; it destroys a sense of at-homeness.'"[33] Neither the sacred nor the secular in the zone of indistinction has the power to generate hope in the community, to form any expectation about the future. As the community's members were enervated and perpetually tired of living in a topsy-turvy, upside-down world, and as time, space, and community all became dislocated, it appeared that the sacred or the secular had too little background "cosmic" energy to even take basic forms, to enable people to form any expectation about their future well-being. Yet there were numerous examples of how Congolese looked for ways of disrupting the violent history and their embeddedness in the trauma of violence. It is this spirit to hope beyond hope—the courage to be, to go on in spite of all the forms of nonbeing that threaten existence—that keeps Africans going in the face of the monstrous violence that relentlessly besets their continent.

It often occurs to this writer that whatever praxis of hope Africans are able to muster is not enough to save their children from the disaster of bad governance and inept political leadership that is the lot of sub-Saharan Africa. I believe that African leaders have lost their souls and hence the *future* of the continent, especially when I think about what is happening to African children, the violent dismantling of their future under the tropical sun.

Every morning the sun rises, and African leaders behave as if nothing has happened the previous day. To them bad things must always happen to Africa. But the sun that rises every morning is not neutral. It relentlessly shines its light on the decadence, poverty, and deprivations of the race. The leaders hope the sun will drown their oppressions and injustice in its eternal light. They hope that as men and women hail the wonderful light of the world with joy every dawn, they will celebrate their poor nonachievements. No, no hope for them.[34]

We must not fold this grave obscenity into ourselves, into our being. Not in this century, not in this throe of death. Every day thousands of African children die because of malnutrition and common diseases. No sane leader would ever have his or her country's future carried out in wrapped mats. But our insane leaders see it happen and say nothing about it. In this century, in this poverty, we (the citizens) should recover our future. If we are in power, we will never let thousands of our children be carried to their comfort of nothingness. In this century—in this horror!—we should never let the world give only a passing glance at our dead children within its exuberant and indifferent celebration of the abundance of life. We are worried that our "Blackness" will die tomorrow and our unborn will have nothing to say to the world. This is true because they are not equipped to speak! In this century, in this poverty, in this throe of death, we must arise like the sun and stop pretending that the helpless children being parceled out to their lonely spots are "sheltered by God's hands," sleeping as if in their "mother's house."[35] Frightened to death in the African storm of poverty, they depart without even speaking to us. In this storm, in this horror, we will no longer let them be carried out. For Africa's sake, we will no longer hold our peace.

Conclusion

In this chapter, we have examined the roles that the relationship between the sacred and the secular play in the production of violence in the African postcolony. There are seven dimensions to the relationship between sacred-secular and violence:

(a) The imbrication of the relationship between the sacred and the secular in the production of violence. African religion or way of being does not really differentiate between these separate spheres of life. Definitely, forces of both the secular and the sacred sphere are often simultaneously at play in any particular regime of violence in the postcolony.

(b and c) Each of them acting separately to produce violence. We may be able to trace the beginning of any particular violence to secular or sacred origins, but it does not mean that we can adequately understand its history or dynamics if we limit our analytical lenses to only one of the spheres. It is true that Boko Haram leaders have opined that they were fighting the Nigerian state because of *shirk*, unbelief, but it is truer to say that the failure of socioeconomic development and bad governance in the country explain more about the insurgence than differences in Quranic interpretation.

(d) Violence conditioning the relationship between the secular and the sacred. Amid the postcolonial incredible, heretofore impossible possibilities become regular occurrences, and what was possible becomes impossible. Secular and sacred authorities compete to heighten the sense of insecurity, precarity, and fragility felt by the masses.

(e and f) Violence in its multiplicity of forms reproducing or conditioning either the secular or the sacred, especially in terms of the universal set of possibilities available to Africans to appropriate for their human flourishing. Indeed, violence produces a mode of intoxication (impunity, chaos) that conditions the dynamics of the secular and the sacred in the postcolony.

(g) A mutual context of violence grounding the sacred and the secular in relation to each other. Chaos is the context of mutual relevance that enables each of them to relate to or influence the other in postcolonial Africa.

This chapter has mapped these seven dimensions across historical and political terrains to tell a story that reveals how constituted or constituting violence affects Africa's condition of life.

In the postcolony, violence is not an expression of secular pathology (the destructive drive of states to maintain law and order; it is not law founding or law sustaining, not any effort to reestablish the equilibrium of justice) or a punishment for sin (the crime of offending the gods; it is not an effort to reestablish cosmic harmony) or a sacred sacrifice (those killed are not offered to any higher cause). Those Africans annihilated by the postcolony's violence are simply guilty. They are guilty of being subjects in postcolonial Africa, guilty of leading innocent natural (mere) life. They are citizens that must be extinguished in the biopolitical disposal of bare lives. The postcolony's violence is an expression of the pure drive of the sacred as the universal set of possibilities of human existence, the excess of power of being, which strikes at African lives subjugated by banality of evil.[36]

Violence in the postcolony is useless in its "too-muchness."[37] Violence in the African postcolony "is just the sign of the injustice of the world, of the world being ethically 'out of joint.' This, however, does not imply that [the postcolony's violence] has a meaning."[38] It does not belong to any order of reason, only an arbitrary explosion of the postcolonial incredible. It is the sacred madness of existence caught on the wings of everyday structures of injustice.[39]

5

CHOSENNESS, SPIRITUALITY, AND THE WEIGHT OF BLACKNESS

Introduction

Before we enter into the thicket of conversations and arguments of this chapter, let me state clearly how its subject matter functions as a transcript of the sacred. A transcript is basically a partial manifestation of the sacred. Transcripts are "sectoral" bound expressions of the sacred, different self-consistent ways of life within the universe of possibilities. Transcript is a structured field of activity (practices) in human dynamic creativity or the universe of possibilities. The practices (activities of persons mediated by common structures of intelligibility) united in a common matrix must at the minimum have a common past and possibly common future and in the present have mutual relations with one another and with other practices in the universe of possibilities. In a simplified language, transcript is a social practice. How does this transcript intersect with one of the three major desires of postcolonial African subjects? We stated earlier that African Pentecostals—as a stand-in for Africans—suffer from split identity. The split consciousness of being Black (in this chapter, I used this term to mean Black sub-Saharan Africans) arises from Africans engaging with two antagonistic forces at the same time: (1) a world that views them as degraded human beings and (2) their self-interpretation as a special and dignified people set to conquer the world that looks askance at them. The desire for bold recognition in the world and the other desires of spiritualist epistemology and dominating power are knitted by fantasy. In this chapter we will pay attention to the desire of recognition and its associated fantasy of "global dominance." This chapter focuses on the transcript of the sacred as it is made actual in social practices of Nigeria Pentecostals who have assigned to themselves the burden of taking African Blacks to the stage of world domination.

Postcolonial Africa is burdened by the sacred. We have been studying how different groups of people or spheres of human activities are bearing this burden. In this chapter we are going to examine how Nigerian Pentecostals interpret and bear this cross. Most Nigerian Pentecostals believe they have been called by God to bear the burden of Blackness in a world where Blacks are the *part-of-no-part* and to redefine Blackness in the twenty-first century. They argue that God has chosen Nigeria not only to spiritually uplift Africa but also to trigger the continent's economic and technological takeoff. In a sense, the invention of the tradition of chosenness is meant to buoy up their sense of dignity in the midst of the terror of the postcolony that eviscerates possibilities for human flourishing. They hope in this way to reverse the negativity of monstrous possibilities that has settled not only in their own nation but in most sub-Saharan African countries.

The concept of chosenness is a key part of the Abrahamic religions. It is at the heart of Judaism; Christians and Moslems also claim to have been chosen by God. Nonetheless, it is open to constant reinvention, encouraging new sects or wings of these religions to reinterpret it in new ways in new contexts, to weave it afresh from the very fabric of faith. Nigerian Pentecostals are claiming that their nation has been specially chosen by God to lead the *final* evangelization of the world before the Second Coming of Jesus Christ and to draw the Black race into global economic and technological supremacy. Their understanding of chosenness is not limited to the view that God has cut a special deal with them to establish God's kingdom in the foreseeable future but encompasses the idea that he has also opened the structure of hope and expectation of the future to the Black race as a whole.

The belief in chosenness amid increasing race consciousness and national poverty is driving Nigerian Pentecostals to redefine what it means to be Black and how Blacks should bear the weight of Blackness in a world of historical disregard for Black people. It is the aim of this chapter to investigate and analyze these claims and the thinking behind them, in their depths and complexity, through a focused study of concrete spiritual practices. It will explore how Nigerian Pentecostals are reinventing the ancient concept and tradition of chosenness in new contexts.

Let me now state how the rest of this chapter will proceed. There are five sections in this chapter. The first section, "The Invention of Chosenness," is an exploration of the production of chosenness as a tradition in Nigerian Pentecostalism. How is the notion of chosenness being crafted in the world's most populous Black nation? This section provides some insights into how it is done. With the tradition of chosenness, Nigerian Pentecostals are claiming moral ownership of their country's problems. Under "The Weight of Citizenship," I examine how this form of citizenship participation is pushing them to produce multiple "systematic accounts" of the historical origin of the sufferings of the Black race. They have not stopped at giving the world some history lessons; they are also providing economic ideas on how to solve the problems their historical analyses have dredged up. Thus, under "Economic Paradigms" I examine how Nigerian Pentecostals are bearing the weight of citizenship by articulating paradigms of national economic development. One of these paradigms is of particular interest given our limited purpose in this chapter. It is the most-*favored-nation status paradigm*, which places Nigeria at the center of the earth and God's plan for humanity before the Second Coming of Jesus Christ.

In the remaining two sections, I offer theoretical insights into the data and arguments we have accumulated in the earlier portions of the chapter. First, I argue that all theologies of chosenness are theologies of the body. They are theorizations of a particular historical body. So to better understand the Nigerian Pentecostal theology of chosenness, I situate it within the wider theology of the human body, particularly the identity of Black bodies in particular Pentecostal spiritual practices. In the concluding section, I ask a question: Is the theology of chosenness Pentecostal at all? I offer various possible responses within the context of Christians who are Black and Pentecostal and are grappling with an ancient notion of chosenness. In this discussion, I offer parousiastic whispers of *chosenness to come*.

The Invention of Chosenness

In this section I want to explore the process of invention of chosenness as a way of dealing with the place and destiny of the Black race in the world. There are many Pentecostal preachers who are inventing the tradition of chosenness to inculcate certain behaviors, standards of holiness, and practices they hope will usher Nigerians and the whole of the Black race into spiritual and technological superiority or at least world respectability. To give the impression that this tradition is ancient and that they are only establishing continuity with the past, they reach back to events in the Old and

New Testaments to argue that the chosenness of the Nigerians has all along been a backstory of the Bible. But what the invention of chosenness is all about is actually a novel response to the weight of Blackness in the twentieth and twenty-first centuries and an attempt to forge a collective identity to make easy the bearing of this load. They have managed to transform the weight of suffering and racism into the weight of God-given destiny. Nonetheless, it is still a weight, and it calls for a different response. We will examine below how chosenness is imbricated in this new responsibility.

I will start the story of the invention by presenting portions of two sermons. Pastor Enoch Adeboye, the leader of the largest Pentecostal denomination in the country, the Redeemed Christian Church of God, on September 30, 2011, in Floyd (Dallas), Texas, delivered a very moving narrative sermon that borders on race and faith. In the narrative, he gave a prominent place to his own sensitivity toward race issues:

> There was a time after I became a Christian, particularly after I have been to Kenneth Hagin's camp meeting [Tulsa, Oklahoma, United States, in the late 1970s], I saw him laying hands on people and people were falling under the power of the Holy Spirit. I said, "God, I want this one too." I, in fact, challenged God on my way back home: "If you don't do what I saw you do in America, when I get back to Nigeria I am going to say you are racist." . . .
>
> So when I got home I told my father in the Lord—first Sunday after that one—"Please give me an opportunity, I want to lay hands on the sick." (You know we weren't doing that in the Redeemed before. Everybody was encouraged to pray on his own.) "Let me lay hands now—it is in the Bible." He said: "Okay." (You know I am his favorite boy, so he gave me some concessions.) So that Sunday people lined up and I began to lay hands upon them. Believe it or not, they began to fall. Oh, glory be to God. "And God you are not a racist."

In a slightly different version of this narrative, there were a few more details. He said that as he saw all the anointing on Hagin and the miracles that were wrought by the Holy Spirit through Hagin, he cried: "God is not fair to Black people. Why is there so much anointing given to a white man here in the United States and nothing like this is happening in Nigeria?" God replied, according to him, in this way: "If you pay the price of holiness you will also see the same level or more in your own country." He went back home determined to live a life of holiness.

The second sermon ("Nigeria: A Nation Chosen by God"[1]) was delivered by Evangelist Elishama Ideh at This Present Church, Lekki, Victoria Island, Lagos, in 2010, months before Nigeria's fiftieth independence anniversary.[2]

Ideh is the pastor in charge of Ever Present Ministries. She was born in 1962 and attended Bowie State College, Maryland, United States, where she studied mass communication. She is a widow and mother of three who often dresses in Nigeria's national colors in bands of green, white, and green and also decorates her forums for speeches and sermons in the same colors. She hails from Edo State (in the Niger Delta), the South-South region of Nigeria. Her sermon shows one of the creative ways Nigerian Pentecostals are mining the Bible to interpret the burden of Blackness.[3]

>Today I'm going to share from a message I have been passing around called "Nigeria: A Nation Chosen by God." Hallelujah. How many people know that God has chosen Nigeria for a peculiar purpose? All these things that are happening are not just happening for nothing. There is a spiritual battle for the soul of Nigeria. Hello, because of the prophetic mandate upon this nation....
>
>I'm going to trace the blessing of our nation from the scriptures. So that we begin to understand that this thing that they are killing themselves for high up there, it didn't come from anywhere but from the presence of God. Hello? The book of Genesis 2 from verse 10 it says, "*And a river went out of Eden to water the garden; and from thence it was parted, and became into four heads. The name of the first is Pison: that is it which compasseth the whole land of Havilah, where there is gold; And the gold of that land is good: there is bdellium and the onyx stone. And the name of the second river is Gihon: the same is it that compasseth the whole land of Ethiopia. And the name of the third river is Hiddekel: that is it which goeth toward the east of Assyria. And the fourth river is Euphrates.*" These are rivers with different natural and mineral resources that went out of the presence of God. The Bible says the first river, as I wrote it down after studying, went out to the nation of Israel; the river that went out into the land of Havilah went out into the nation of Israel. The second river, which is the river Gihon, went out to the land of Africa. The Gihon is the one that concerns us as a race, as a nation, and a people but I will come back to that. The third river is the river Hiddekel which went into Europe, Amen, and in the river Gihon which is the one that came forth, you know, into our nation Ethiopia.
>
>Ethiopia, as you see it, in Bible times, is not the way you see now in the physical. Ethiopia is a symbolic name for the black race in Bible times, Amen. When they want to talk about the black people in those days they call us Ethiopia. *Ethia* means black; *Pia* means face, so the Bible is telling us that it went into the land of the black faces. Another translation will say it went into the land of the Kush. Hello, another translation will say he went into the land of the niggers. How many people know that nigger is not a derogatory word? It's a word that means just black, Amen....
>
>Then if you begin to trace where did this river go into in Africa.... If you begin to study how to pronounce the right pronunciation of Nigeria, it is not *niger*. The right diction, the way to pronounce Nigeria, it is not *niger*,

it is *ni-gay-ria*. So we are *niggers*, the *ni-gay-rians*. I am not forming this o, hallelujah. We are *niggers*, the Nigerians. So this third river came out of the presence of God, carrying natural powerful mineral recourses with it, and if you want to begin to trace mineral resources in every nation that came out of the presence of God, the only way you can trace these mineral resources is to begin to search through the rivers of those nations. Hello? So you begin to wonder where did this particular river enter into. Then you begin to trace it into a river in our nation called River Nigger, that we all know as River Niger. . . .

Carry the map of Nigeria; look at where River Benue and River Niger connect. You will see a symbol like this [she makes a symbol of the cross]; you will see a symbol like this, which is the cross of our Lord Jesus Christ. Listen, this is the symbol of our Lord Jesus Christ that we all know; over the centuries, over the ages this is how we know the symbol of the cross to be like. . . . Excuse me, what am I getting here now? When you connect River Niger and River Benue you see this sign on that river. There is no nation on the face of this earth that carries that symbol. There is no country, no continent that carries that symbol. Only Nigeria has that symbolic presence of the cross of our Lord Jesus Christ upon our nation. There is a reason to that. . . .

Nigeria has been chosen as the nation that will introduce Jesus Christ to the world in his Second Coming. Oh, it's a secret I'm telling you, maybe you don't know. Hello. Just like in the days of the Israel, the Israelites were the one that introduced the name of God to the world. They were the ones that introduced him as Jehovah Shammah, Jehovah Roi, Rapha, El Elyon Elohim, Sabaoth, Shammah, Tsidkenu, Adonai, but in this time Nigeria has been chosen as a nation that will be in the forefront to usher in our king in his Second Coming. That is why those resources have been put there, it's a secret, some people might not agree with me, but I am just a prophet to deliver a message. . . .

Over the centuries, over the ages, the mark of blackness has been termed as a derogatory color. A color people look down upon. A color people despise. A color people do not want to associate with. A color that people called the slaves, the rejects, the outcast, oh the abandoned. Those ones are the Third World people. They are a nobody, but I have come to announce it to somebody here today that we are a color that has been set apart by God himself. A color that Jesus Christ himself had to wait for, on the cross on the way to Calvary. I will show it to you right now in the scriptures. . . .

Christ was waiting for that black priest [Simon, a Cyrenian], that man of color, the only one that can hear him, the only one that is sensitive to him, the only one that burns with zeal, the one called the descendent of Ham. Christ was waiting and he was pretending in the flesh as if he was tired but he was waiting for destiny to hear him. He was waiting for destiny to come forth. He was waiting for destiny to meet him at the place of purpose.

Hallelujah God bless Nigeria. . . . Our nation will fulfill its prophetic mandate, in Jesus' name.[4]

What do these two sermon fragments have in common? It appears that asking God race-based questions is not strange to Nigerian Pentecostals. Adeboye and Ideh are both putting forth knowledge, revelation received from the invisible God, as they deal with the weight of Blackness, consciously carrying the burden of Blackness into their spirituality. What they also have in common is that they both use race as a lens to interpret their experiences, to examine the work of the Holy Spirit, or to examine the burden of their skin pigmentation within the context of Pentecostal hermeneutics. These are the questions they are trying to correlate with their faith resources: How is God/Holy Spirit helping them to address the problems that relate to them? Why has God given "many advantages and privileges" to the white race?

I want to also highlight a key difference between the two preachers, separated in age by twenty years and in evolution of idea by over thirty years. Adeboye, who was sixty-nine in 2011, asked God way back in the late 1970s why white preachers were more anointed than Black preachers in Nigeria. Ideh, who was forty-eight in 2010, saw the ongoing Pentecostal revival as providential and her nation as chosen. By this assertion, she echoed the sentiments of Nigerian Pentecostals who were keen to differentiate themselves from other Pentecostals in Africa and elsewhere and also to consolidate their own identities. The respective positions of Adeboye and Ideh symbolize the genesis of the race consciousness and its transformation into the tradition of chosenness. The trajectory of consciousness here provides us with a rough guide to the invention of chosenness in Nigerian Pentecostalism. What are some of the forces that made this invention necessary?

In Nigeria there is a certain heaviness born of the sufferings, misfortunes, poverty, and misery of African Blacks. Nigerian Pentecostals have to acknowledge it, bear and shoulder it, discuss it, entreat God about it, and resist it. There is a sense of closed boundary, a sense of the weightedness of race, made palpable by the intensification of surplus suffering imposed by the external forces of racialized power and by corrupt local leaders. Black is heavy. "But the heaviness is layered, volume piled upon mass, the layers of strata composed of varying substances and differentially born. . . . Bodies beaten and broken, spirits sagged, life-span artificially and dramatically limited, whatever prospect for whatever slither of prosperity sliding from grasp because of the racial weights [and inept, depraved leadership] pulling them back."[5]

The weight that Africans, and particularly Nigerian Pentecostals, bear is constantly shifting from site to site; the weight of race and racism is constantly shifting. If yesterday it was slavery and colonialism, today it is different. The racially weighted world is felt acutely as the burden of poor economies and racism that feeds on levels of gross national product (GNP). Africans not only directly bear the brunt of low levels of economic development but also endure the devaluation and degradation of their racial identity as the world increasingly links racial respect to the performance of national or regional economies.

There is a wicked theory of GNP afoot in the world, and it assaults Africans.

Low levels of economic development in Africa have come to be interpreted as the result of Black persons' greater vulnerability to death and shame and have indeed marked them as surplus population, unworthy lives, to be excluded from the global centers of power. The logic of this hermeneutics of GNP is part of the axiomatics of the current global formation, which before any engagement and dialogue determine which race or people is to be taken seriously beyond the point of politically correct tolerance in world economic-political affairs. Today, the connection between GNP and racism is an important and particular site of the destructive weight of the world on Africans.

How do Nigerian Pentecostals respond to the socially imposed pain and trauma of Blackness? How do they explain the Black person's differentiated vulnerability to excess suffering, indignity, and death when they say God reigns and is fair to all races? How are Pentecostals weighing in to redress the sufferings socially imposed on Black Africans? What questions are they asking God about the plight of the Black race?

The Weight of Citizenship

Apart from responding to these questions through sermons, Pentecostals are beginning to create a "systematic theology" of the historical and future trajectories of the Black race. They are mutually correlating the world history and existential experiences of Blacks, as they know them, with the Bible and Christian tradition. This is a theology that not only scrutinizes the Bible and searches the ways of the Holy Spirit to answer existential questions about the Black race but also points to a glorious, hopeful future for the Black race. The way Pastor Matthew Ashimolowo deals with weight of his Blackness and the burden of citizenship as a Nigerian is exemplary in this respect. He is the senior pastor of London's Kingsway International Christian Center, the largest church in western Europe. Ashimolowo is also the author of a popular book among African Christians, *What Is Wrong with Being Black?*⁶ His thesis is that Africans (Blacks) are poor and technologically backward because of their *ur*-idolatry. God punished them for turning away from him, the true deity, and following false gods and for originating revolt against him.⁷ His book is simultaneously an expression of desire for the greatness of Blacks and a disgust at what he calls the idolatry and superstition of the Black race.

The pathos of his burden is exemplified by the opening sentence of his book: "In the past years the state of the black person globally has become paramount on my mind. I have observed that wherever black people are, whether it is Australia—among the Aborigines, Africa, Europe, Latin America, the Caribbean, or North America, we seem to belong at the bottom of the pile, or the bottom of the pyramid, economically, socially, physically, mentally, etc."⁸

His book is arguably the most systematic account of popular African Pentecostal pastors addressing the challenges facing Blacks in the world. He comes across as someone conscious of the systemic injustice Blacks face in the United Kingdom, the United States, and other parts of the world. At the same time, he is not afraid of highlighting some of the dysfunctionalities in the lifestyles of Blacks and the corrupt leadership that also explain the present socioeconomic predicament of Blacks in the world. One major problem of the book is that for solutions he focuses only on self-help projects and Christian lifestyles, ignoring how national and international structures of injustice can be transformed or dismantled to engender a flourishing life for Blacks.

This way of thinking that ties Africa's relative economic poverty to idolatry or divine retribution is also echoed by Atei Beredugo, a senior banker and politician based in Port Harcourt (Niger Delta), Nigeria. "I believe the relative poverty of the black race is rooted in idolatry. The black race started well as evidenced by the beginning of several aspects of civilization in Africa and among blacks. The sphinx of Egypt and several other artifacts are obviously [created by] Negros. But blacks forgot God, and as God has always done with those who reject Him, God rejected them and blacks declined. (See Isaiah 9:1–18 for the roots of the problems)."⁹ When asked how the Black race can solve its problems and reach higher levels of economic and technological achievement, he replied:

> Through a massive return to Christ as the first step, which the Pentecostal churches can champion. This will ignite the engine. Then a lot of sustained prayers, as the second step. This will provide the fuel. Next a large dose of

sustained strategic socio-economic actions [is needed]. This will pump the fuel/gas and roll the engines of progress and technological advancement. Any without the other will have more tedious results or limited effect. The foundation of the socio-economic sphere has to be drastically improved quality of education and progressive improvement in infrastructure. Blacks can surpass them [other races] and the time has come for this (see Isaiah 19:19–25; and Proverbs 24:3).[10]

Beredugo says that because he believes Africa is very important to God and God has not neglected the continent, he has personally directed his professional skills and competencies toward uplifting the continent. He believes God has equipped many Black professionals like him to contribute to kingdom resources and African emancipation. "Africa has more natural resources than anywhere else. This is not by chance but because of Africa's strategic place in God's programs."[11]

When asked how God plans to raise the profile of Africans and how this strategic role will be played out in today's global setting, he responded in this way:

> Through the ages, God has been bringing His children from other continents to control Africa's resources and apply it to major dispensational purposes for the expansion of His kingdom (Abraham, Joseph, Jacob and all Israel, Britain, USA, etc., each at the fore of God's unfolding agenda at the time of their control of or privileged access to Africa's wealth). In these last days, God at last has His own children in Africa, and He is set to do the ultimate in the control and deployment of Africa's resources for kingdom purposes. God is going to raise Josephs to control the resources and expand His kingdom (Zechariah 1:17). Just as Joseph's role made Israel expand and enlarge to occupy the Promise Land, the ministry of the latter Josephs out of Africa will expand the kingdom ready for the ultimate Promise Land and the coming of the Ultimate Messiah (see Isaiah 19:24–25).[12]

Not every Pentecostal pastor or layperson sees the problem of Nigeria or the Black race in terms of the kind of grand idolatry-redemption narrative put forth by Ashimolowo and Beredugo. Pastor Paul Adefarasin of the House on the Rock in Lagos, who leads a church of seven thousand worshippers, simply questions the development paradigm of Nigeria and blames Christians for joining others to ruin the country. "The Christian church is arguably 60–70 percent of the population. If she [Nigeria] is going to make a change, it requires a small group. Some of the people who have ruined this country are Christians."[13]

Pastor Lawrence Olufemi Obisakin, a diplomat and former interpreter for former Nigerian president Olusegun Obasanjo, also focuses his analysis at the local level. Having just come back from a diplomatic posting in New

York City, he was asked to lead a prayer session at the Redeemed Christian Church of God, Central Parish, Abuja (Nigeria's capital city), on Sunday, August 28, 2011, when I worshipped there. He lamented that Nigeria is not playing its historic role of lifting up Africa and the Black race because of its internal problems. He added: "In 1998 the Lord showed me that Nigeria is the giant to help Africa, but it has internal bleeding. The internal bleeding is the ethnic rancor and rivalry. As long as there is internal bleeding, it cannot help Africa; it risks collapsing."

Much earlier than Ashimolowo, Adefarasin, Obisakin, or Beredugo, Rev. Michael Ojewale in 1990 predicted that the burgeoning Christian revival was going to affect all spheres of national life. For this to happen, he called on Christians to effectively carry the burden of citizenship by praying for

> the healing of our land from all defects: social, moral, economic and political ailments lies in our prayers. . . . Nigeria is indeed poised for a revival of an unprecedented dimension. You and I are active participants of what God is about to do. Militant, strategic, unceasing and aggressive prayers will hasten the heavenly visitation. The early showers of the revival which many of God's servants have prophesied have begun already. Join the Lord's army to bring about rapid changes that we desperately need in all areas of our national life. We are at the dawn of a new era. I can see it in my spirit.[14]

We see here the call for change being linked to a vision of citizenship, techniques of the self on the self, and the political mission of healing the land. Ruth Marshall, in her analysis of what she calls Nigeria's "Pentecostal Revolution," has shown that the movement from its inception was concerned about creating a socioeconomic environment for the political and economic takeoff of the country. From their early beginnings in the 1970s, the Pentecostals interpreted their missions as "healing" Nigeria. As Marshall puts it:

> Born-again Christianity [in Nigeria] is a force not merely as a result of successful competition within the religious field, by providing spiritual and material benefits others did not. Its radical success in conversion has much to do with its reconceptualization of the moral and political order, representing a vision of citizenship in which the moral government of the self is linked to the power to influence the conduct of others. Through its project of rupture and renewal, it sets itself the political mission of healing the land, quoting Isaiah 58:12: "And they that shall be of thee shall build the old waste places; thou shalt raise up the foundations of many generations, and thou shalt be called the repairer of the breach."[15]

In this so-called revolution, what was being taught or preached was not simply a means of making heaven but a peculiar ethics. Deviation from its rules, expectations, and focus was treated not as moral failure or incompetence but as sinfulness or forgetfulness of duty. That was the core of the message. It was not a message of the mere surpassing of worldly morality; that sort of attitude was prevalent enough among Christians. It was an ethos. This is the historical phenomenon that interests us. It is the belief in the power of Pentecostalism—the move of the Holy Spirit and the power to initiate something new—to transform and elevate African society and the dignity of the Black race. Within a certain segment of Nigerian Pentecostalism, the only way of living acceptably to God included not merely a life of holiness, personal salvation, and wealth but also the fulfillment of an obligation to be God's battle-axe to uproot and destroy economic backwardness and the Black race's indignity. This was their calling. They saw themselves as an instrument of the divine in the history of Africa.

This is the weight of Christian citizenship that weighs heavily on Nigerian Pentecostals, to use the apt phrase of Kevin Lewis O'Neil in his study of Pentecostals in Guatemala.[16] He uses the word *weight* to approximate the Pentecostals' feeling of moral ownership of the problems of Guatemala.

> I develop the metaphor of weight throughout this book, relying on the experience of something pressing down on someone to communicate the felt reality of responsibility. It is the bruteness of Christian citizenship that the metaphor glimpses. Yet moral weight, in this context, should not be confused with guilt. The two terms differ at the levels of temporality and scope, at least. Guilt is a lament for what one should (or should not) have done in the past, whereas weight refers to the shouldering of a burden in the present moment on behalf of the future.[17]

Economic Paradigms

We have seen how Pentecostals are bearing the weight of Blackness by articulating ideas of Christian citizenship and expressing their desire for greatness for the Black race. They are also active on the economic front, believing that chosenness comes with the necessary economic resources to execute God's destiny for the Black race. There is a popular saying in Nigerian Pentecostal circles: "A vision without provision is television." As good Christian citizens, they consider themselves charged with the responsibility to reduce the gap between the potentiality/promise of Nigeria and its actuality/fulfillment by laying an adequate foundation for the necessary provision. There is not just one form of expressing the route to this haven of treasures, as there are multiple interpretations of the root cause of economic poverty in Nigeria. As a result, they have crafted multiple paradigms of solution to foster economic development. Elsewhere I have identified five basic theological paradigms that frame the discourse on Africa's (Nigeria's) economic development among Pentecostals.[18] Even though each of them considers poverty to be the primary economic problem, each also traces its basic causes to different sources. While the proponents of these paradigms differ in the solutions they seek, all believe that the conquering of poverty and acceleration of economic development will be important for the flourishing of humanity in Nigeria and the execution of God's plan for the Black race. Here I want to focus on a different paradigm I did not treat earlier. This paradigm is most relevant to the issues we are discussing in this chapter. I will it call the *most-favored-nation status* paradigm.

Most-Favored-Nation Status Paradigm

In international economic relations, one nation can grant another nation a most-favored-nation status in trade and exchange. Such a favored nation will enjoy preferential treatment and privilege compared to others. At the minimum, the favored country will not be treated less advantageously than any other trading and investment partner. Many Nigerian Pentecostals believe that their country has a most-favored status in the divine-human relationship. They argue that God has set it apart for a specific purpose and greatness. Around this issue, they are gradually building a *geographical theology*, thinking creatively about national space/location and theology.[19] In this theology, Nigeria is to play the crucial role in the economic and technological takeoff of the Black race. For instance, we have seen how Pastor Elishama Ideh "theorized" this with her recourse to Nigeria and its two major rivers as being uniquely branded by the cross of Jesus Christ. This kind of geographical theology is increasingly providing the underpinning for a national economic theology among Pentecostals.

Banker and financial expert Atei Beredugo (born June 8, 1965) has gone further than most Nigerian Pentecostals to develop this emerging concept of geographical theology and the key arguments of the most-favored-nation status paradigm. He even contested the presidential primaries of one of the minor political parties (the National Conscience Party, founded by the late social activist and radical lawyer Gani Fawehinmi) in fall 2010, espousing these ideas as a key plank of his economic vision for the country. In one of his campaign brochures (*The Mandate, the Man and the Message*), he stated that his passion is "to see Nigeria realize its huge potentials for the good of its citizens; see Africa return to glory; and see the lowly lot of black humanity improved."

I met with him in June 2010 in a hotel in Port Harcourt to discuss these ideas, and he whipped out a PowerPoint presentation, with maps, diagrams, graphs, statistics, and well-crafted economic arguments, to drive home his point to me. He came across as a man on a divine mission who was a bit disappointed because Nigerians were not paying the necessary attention to his "unique" message and divine mandate. "Nigeria is Africa's trigger. See where she is geographically positioned, plus her size and endowments. As Myles Munroe once put it: design depicts purpose. Nigeria needs to get focused and strategic in both prayers and socio-political management to fulfill its role."[20]

This view of Nigeria as the trigger point of the gun that is Africa is widespread in Nigeria's Pentecostalism. Hitherto, many Pentecostal Christians have interpreted it in terms of the evangelization of the world. The Holy Spirit is going to reevangelize or claim the world for Jesus Christ by "shooting" Africans into every country to spread the gospel, and the trigger point is located in Nigeria. This means Nigeria, the most populous Black nation in the world, will spearhead the effort with its human and economic resources. Ogbu Kalu captured this sentiment well when he wrote: "Africa is like a gun that God will use to deal with His enemies and Nigeria is located in the position of the trigger. Nigeria has a special place in God's redemptive will for Africa. Its huge human and mineral resources must be redeemed and made available for this noble use. Therefore, the poverty in the midst of plenty; disorganization in the midst of vast resources must be rejected. This is the generation to pray Nigeria into its proper place! Such rhetoric has captured imagination."[21]

What Beredugo has done is to shift the interpretative emphasis from evangelism to the technological takeoff of the Black race and economic development of Nigeria. He does not reject evangelism, but he thinks a viable economic and technological basis will best facilitate the work of evangelism as well as bring much-needed respect to the Black race.

From the notion of gun trigger, Beredugo goes into how God has specifically located Nigeria and indeed the whole of Africa as the geographical navel of the earth. What this means according to him (he pointed to a map during his PowerPoint presentation) is that Nigeria has both spatial and temporal centrality, almost equidistant with respect to time and space, going by the measures of latitude and longitude. According to him, this kind of location is a vantage point for the production, distribution, and coordination of global economic activities.

Beredugo added: "Nigeria is at the center of our planet, with over 150 million population, vast fertile land, oil, gas, diverse solid minerals, etc. Nigeria's global centrality, the size of the domestic market, and good access to the sea confer huge advantages that are enough to build a great economy, even without oil and gas. It is obvious that God placed something that should be great and glorious at the center of the planet."[22]

Theology of Chosenness as the Fallout of Extreme Attention to Bodies in Spirituality

The theology of chosenness of Nigerian Pentecostals would not be complete if we failed to place it within the context of the complex ways bodies are imbricated in Nigerian Pentecostal spiritualities. Nigerian Pentecostals pay serious attention to what goes on, in, or out of the human body. To them the human body, its output, and its coverings (especially feminine articles of clothing) are "signs of transcendent forms or essences that stand above them" and indices for "gauging identitarian belonging."[23] For the body to have continued access to the invisible realm for the truth of social existence, its desires and disgusts have to be carefully delineated and managed through the techniques of the self on the self. In a certain sense, it is Pentecostals' concern with bodies (their care and habits, intakes and outputs) and their vested interest in the collective destiny of the Nigerian body politic that has produced the counter-racist theology of chosenness.

Ordinarily when a religion pays an obsessive attention to the body, it ultimately makes bodies "disappear" into heaven or a similar transcendent realm. "The body is all-important and, at the same time, vanishes."[24] The point is that the extraordinary importance given to the bodies results in the "ultimate dissolution of the bodies into the transcendent realm."[25] So political philosophers Michael Hardt and Antonio Negri argue that such a form of religiosity "does not allow for the productivity of bodies that is central to biopolitics: the construction of being from below, through bodies in action."[26] But as we seen in this chapter, this view is not exactly correct when it comes to Nigerian Pentecostalism.

The shift of attention to the race-oriented (or counter-racist) theology of chosenness is not only moving Pentecostals and their bodies into action and the reconstruction of what it means to be Black but also helping them to construct human bodies and human collectives via disciplines, regulations, and normalizations that are central to sovereignty as a biopolitical project. Pentecostal thought in Nigeria is beginning to move from the spirituality that focuses on the techniques of the self on the self and the purity of the body to incorporate spirituality that focuses on the purity of the social body. Pentecostal spirituality first took over possession of the body, and now it is taking care of the life (destiny) of the population (race). Pentecostal spirituality is now being articulated at the intersection of body and population, individual and race, the organism and the species. It is now concerned not only with "bodies and what bodies do" but also with the land and the *gross collective product* and fortune of the land (social body). But then there is also the concern with how to unify the many, the congeries of multiplicity of powers and sects, into one political body or coordinating mechanism. This is the next disciplinary mode of regulation and normalization that is at an incipient stage with the rise of the theology of chosenness. Needless to say that, as Michel Foucault taught us, this kind of disciplinary mode is usually supportive of sovereignty. All this is happening in such a way that with some Foucauldian patience we can trace a line from the ways the body is disciplined (the techniques of the self on the self) to the protocols of race and discourse of sovereignty. There is a convergence of the plotlines of body, sovereignty, and race taking place around the dynamics and meaning of spirituality.[27]

Let us return to Hardt and Negri's argument that when religions, especially the fundamentalist types, pay extraordinary attention to the human bodies they dissolve them in a transcendent realm. The evidence from Nigeria does not support this claim. Nigerian Pentecostals believe that they have been chosen to perform a specific and privileged task for God, that their Black bodies must be sanctified, strong, healthy, and distinguishable to engage the worldly task of evangelism. In Nigerian Pentecostalism, the Black body is all-important, and, at the same time, it refuses to disappear or be eclipsed by a generic body of the children of God. The Black Pentecostal body, long deprived, degraded, neglected, and aware of the discourse of prosperity gospel, does not easily equate the affirmation of the body in its stark materiality with its metaphysical fungibility, indifferentiation, or "annihilation."

Nigerian Pentecostals' engagement with the body is under the aegis of a spiritual-materialist teleology: there is a belief in God's invisible hands pulling the history and progress of Nigeria forward as well as a recognition of the capability of Pentecostals' desires and struggles to also push it forward. They see the operations of both visible and invisible hands working for the actualization of the potentials of the Black race and national transformation. Indeed, in Nigerian Pentecostalism we are beginning to see identity struggles engaging with a process of liberation.

This orientation or advantage of the Nigerian Pentecostal version of the theology of chosenness is also its problem or weakness. It exposes the vulnerability of the notion of chosenness itself. The notion of divine chosenness is always about a particular historical body and about a particular people. By privileging and focusing attention on one kind of body or people, it must necessarily refuse the melting-pot (or salad-bowl) notion of all of God's children. The usual ground of chosenness necessarily leads to an exclusionary type of belonging. Even if chosenness is not based on bloodlines or on acceptance of a particular line of belief, fraternity, or affinity, it is still hostile to or rejects those outside it. It is never universal and all-inclusive. Is there a groundless ground for chosenness? Can it be grounded on contingency and uncertainty so that we are open to whoever may claim it? I am interested in the chosenness of the future, the *chosenness to come*, the *messianicity* of chosenness, which requires a new mode of speech, identity, equality, and openness to all.

Conclusion: Is the Theology of Chosenness Pentecostal?

By way of reaching a conclusion, let me restate some of the key points of this study of the weight of Blackness and Pentecostal spirituality. We have shown that Blackness has become the discursive site of assessing, negotiating, and appropriating the meaning of spirituality as severe economic dislocations of Nigeria (having lasted for over four decades) mingle with an increasing awareness of the "lowly lot of Black humanity." As a central materialist component in constructing African Pentecostal identity as we have seen it, the weight and quest for a dignified recognition in the world and for economic flourishing as a problematic are nurtured inside the discourse of spirituality (theology). What we are seeing is the mutual encoding of the theological and the racial to birth a new way of thinking, a pneumatically powered imagination and hermeneutics, that reads against the existing social order. This is one way Pentecostals are making sense of their lives as Blacks and responding to the burden and realities of their skin.

The Bible is the lens through which race is socially imagined and racial consciousness is aided to emerge within Nigerian Pentecostalism. This trajectory of imagination stands to both help and compromise faithful Christian identity. On the one hand, it plays into the imbrication of race and theology that has come to define "white theology" (to use the language of J. Cameron Carter and Willie James Jennings).[28] On the other hand, it promotes racial pride on the basis of the equality of all peoples before God and accentuates a sense of privileged divine purpose. All this might be Christian but not necessarily Pentecostal.

What makes the racial turn on hermeneutics un-Pentecostal? Without minimizing the heartfelt pains of those who have turned to the Bible to redefine their identity, it is still apropos to aver that they have not worked out their "theology" Pentecostally. To follow African American theologian Carter, they have not done it "from within the distinctively Jewish-Christian horizon of the miracle of speech, the overturning of nationalism, the theological refounding of identity within the person of Jesus of Nazareth."[29] The analysis of racism and racial burden being undertaken by Nigerian Pentecostals—though well intended and sincere—does not necessarily disrupt "the linguistics of cultural and political nationalism, including the nationalism at work in how identity is conceived and performed." To be in Christ, as Carter argues, is to have an orientation to disrupt the "faulty performance of language and therefore of identity." Christ through his life has drawn creation into a reperformance of language and identity. Drawing the world into this reperformance or true performance of the linguistics of the cultural and political is what Carter calls "the 'pentecostalization' of the world, its being drawn into his incarnate or 'passionate' way of existence into a new mode of speech and identity."[30]

How is it that Carter is basing his theological assessment of the performance of linguistics of cultural and political nationalism via the platform of the incarnation and the passion—Jewish identity of Jesus?

> Christ's life, which culminates in the "hour" of his passion, is the pneumatological foil of Genesis 11, the foil that reverses creation's self-enclosure, first and ultimately, against God, and, second and no less important, within itself. Being instrumental in effecting this reversal is and remains the destiny of Israel. Its election, in this respect, is to mediate creation's re-creation. Through Christ, the seed of Abraham, the world in its entirety is conscripted into Israel's destiny, which turns out to be the world's destiny. From this it

becomes clear that Israel's destiny is not solipsistic; its election is to be itself precisely by being more than itself: that is, by being for the world. It is to be a nonnationalistic nation, a different kind of people—the people of YHWH. This nonsolipsistic destiny is brought to fruition in Christ, who is at once child of Israel and Son of God/Son of man. He is most truly the former as he is the latter.[31]

If we turn to Brian Bantum's 2010 book, *Redeeming Mulatto: A Theology of Race and Christian Hybridity*, we may be able to expand Carter's perspective on what it means to Pentecostally speak about race. From his perspective, acting Pentecostally or even broadly Christianly would not only be about hearing, speaking, or not jettisoning the Jewishness of Jesus of Nazareth or about avoiding supersessionist thinking alone. It must surely involve joining in a new reality of kinship.[32] Or in Willie Jennings's perspective, it involves creating a genuine communion among disparate groups and nations that gives some place to identity calibrated through possession by, not possession of, specific land.[33]

There is no doubt that Nigerian Pentecostals' analysis of racial burden and destiny that accentuates blood and land and uses supersessionist language is problematic; any critique of it as we have offered raises its own problem. The question that immediately arises is this: Does the universalism of Pentecostalism dissolve all particularities? Is it not possible to see new possibilities of existence, the belief in the not-yet flourishment of a people, as Pentecostalistic in the sense of the capacity of beginning something new?[34] Is it not conceivable that the turn to racialized (counter-racist) theology is an attempt (even if desperate) to carve a new space of equality for a new reality of kinship? There is even something more.

The turn to racial understanding is in a sense a turn to philosophy and historical discourse (an attempt to forge or determine the "basic elements of historical intelligibility").[35] Nigerian Pentecostalism, history, and philosophy are asking the same question—and this is fundamentally new. Nigerian Pentecostalism is asking a question that arises from its interior, inside its African worldview—a question that history and philosophy have always asked: "What is it, in the present, that is the agent of the universal? What is it, in the present, that is the truth of the universal?"[36] The answer of Nigerian Pentecostals is that the agent of the universal is the evangelizing Black race and that the truth the Black race bears is the vigor and commitment to Pentecostalism, to the Pentecostal principle, which is considered the truth of the universal.

Let us not forget that this inclination to the universal is also a way of staging and distributing possibilities of existence—distributing the sacred—for human flourishing, While this chapter has narrated the story of Nigerian Pentecostals hoping to project the soft power of spirituality to combat or circumvent the hard reality of the monstrous sacred and to redistribute the sacred, there is another narrative of Pentecostals who are seeking a different way to redistribute the sacred, and their story is waiting to be told. It is the story of Nigerian Pentecostals whose hope of liberation starts from home, from the Pentecostal churches themselves in the nation. There are Pentecostals who are working to undermine the very structures and theologies of Pentecostalism that are contributing to the disasters of thought and order that make up the postcolony. This group represents forms of internal resistance within Nigerian Pentecostalism and by extension offers a resistance to the monstrous sacred of the postcolony. Chapter 6 narrates this emerging story; admittedly, it is a narrative of the "weapons of the weak," yet I will boldly state that its weak force might one day disrupt the present dominant scholarly narrative of apolitical, triumphant, social-justice-averse African Pentecostalism.

6

DISRUPTION AND PROMISE

The Religious Powers of Development

Introduction

This chapter engages the concept of transcript in a special way. Economic development is akin to a movement from potentiality to actuality, from a state of privation to a state of human flourishing. This movement is attributable to an underlying activity common to the contraries. There is a necessary context for the existence of the states and a presupposition for the movement between states. The context of mutual relevance is the dynamic human creativity, the sacred, the universe of im/possibilities available to a given community. Economic development is a transcript of the sacred. In economic development, we see the universal that underlies human creative activity given shape or structure. Economic development is a desirable manifest form and matter of the underlying reality, which in this state promotes (does not hinder) human flourishing. Economic development is also part of the process of the sacred gaining a new form, of human potentiality undergoing successive stages of actualization. Economic development itself "recreates" the sacred as it expands the horizon of possibilities for a people. Let us not forget that the sacred never exists in itself apart from the transcripts. The sacred is the cause of the transcripts insofar as it is the internal principle for the existence and activity of the transcripts. If the sacred "existed apart from the [transcripts, entitative and nonentitative] as their external cause, then it would be itself another kind of [transcript] and one would have to ask what causes it to exist. The search for an ultimate first cause principle of activity [in human sociality] only comes to an end when one locates that first cause in an immanent principle of activity within all [transcripts] rather than in some transcendent entity."[1] In this chapter I demonstrate that the transcript of economic development in Africa carries within itself some of the tendencies of the transcript of religion.

The thesis of this chapter is simple: I argue that development has religious powers. The forces of disruption and promise are the sacred powers of every socioeconomic development. The system of interactions between disruption and promise "embodies the *unfulfilled possibilities* [of any society]. It always points beyond itself to the full range of possibilities for either salvation or destruction."[2] For social transformation to occur, certain structures, institutions, norms, and habits must be disrupted, displaced, reorganized, or transfigured. Societies endure the pain of these changes and re-formations because of the promise of better human flourishing, because of the glory that is set before them.

Karl Marx made this clear in his analysis of capitalism. At least, the opening chapter of the *Communist Manifesto* embeds this thesis.[3] Max Weber's *Protestant Ethic and the Spirit of Capitalism* is another example of this thesis, if we read it between the lines.[4] Joseph Schumpeter's famous notion of creative destruction is a precursor of my thesis.[5] Hannah Arendt, in a different context, called the forces of uncertainty and promise the structuring forces of the human condition.[6] In our time, Jean-Marie Dru, in his book *Thank You for Disrupting*, examines the history of disruptors in the business world and their influence in bringing the promises of entrepreneurship to societies.[7]

Influenced by these thinkers, I decided to make explicit what is implicit in their thoughts so I can do the following three things in this chapter: First, highlight the process of disruption and promise as a way of thinking about development and the relations between religion and development. Second, destabilize the regnant approach to the study of religion and development. Instead of following the usual path of investigating how religion, as a separate phenomenon, intersects with development, I dig deep into the religious contents of development. Along the way of fleshing out this method of studying our subject matter, I will endeavor to examine the development powers of religion. Religion not only disrupts but also comes with promise. What I am saying is this: religion is in development, and development is in religion. Third, I view the powers of disruption and promise as the alpha and omega, the beginning and the end, of the development enterprise. Pardon me for that little exaggeration, but I hope you get my drift. The godliness of these powers will gradually emerge as we proceed.

Disruption and promise, as the constitutive components of economic development, appear to Africans as "God," phenomenologically speaking. Here I deploy Rudolf Otto's concept of the numinous, the idea of the holy, to translate or represent development as a "deity."[8] Economic development in Africa is a mystery that is simultaneously terrifying and fascinating. African nations have a deadly fascination with economic development. They, or more precisely their leaders, also view the righteous requirement of its law with terror.

There is a gap between the fascination and the terror, between the rhetoric/ideology of development and the reality of development, wherein the wrath of the *Development God*, with flaying nostrils, roasts Africans into burnt barbecue tenderloins. In a less colorful language, let me say that the gap is the site of the radical self-withdrawal of this unforgiving deity, of the erasing of the very movement of economic development to a vanishing illusion. This translation or, if you like, mistranslation of Otto's notion raises the question of what the religion of development is.

By the term *religion of development*, I do not mean the moral resources, ethical orientation, evangelical zeal, legitimacy, and authority of development agents who couch their paradigms and programs as good news and liturgies of progress, who organize and pursue the task of economic development with passionate intensity, and who swear allegiance to the neoliberal market and state. My terminology is restricted to the process of development itself, to a dimension of its deep logic. In the next section, I begin the process of unpacking this term.

Religion and Development: A Theoretical Reframing

Religion in most cases, especially in Africa, presupposes the existence of, at least, a god. Behind our scholarly interest in connecting religion to development, there is a presupposition that this *god of religion*, through her devotees—their narratives, beliefs, and practices—fosters or inhibits economic development. The commonplace scholarly orientation toward the study of religion and development is to scrutinize this god. We want to weigh her on a scale, ascertain whether her days are numbered, and if so, declare that her reign will soon be brought to an end when we divide her kingdom and give it to secularists and technocrats. What if we turn this orientation around and start by declaring that *development is a god in Africa?* Development is the "ultimate concern" in Africa.

The most existential task facing Africa is economic development. This concern preoccupies both leaders and masses, even though they are constantly thwarting efforts toward realizing the supreme goals of this task. This preoccupation establishes the conditions for Africans to decipher whether their governments are working or even existing. Economic development, or more precisely the quest for it, is *transcendental* in the sense that the concern with domesticating it is the universal structure of how the reality of nationhood, patriotism, and goods of co-belonging appears to Africans. Since the jubilant years of the 1960s when most African countries gained their independence from their colonial masters, Africans have made sumptuous offerings to the *Development God*, but he has refused to incarnate, to take flesh and dwell among them. He has rather wickedly taken hold of their imagination, often shaming them to reject their inherited cultural practices and forcing them to bend their knees to bow and scrape before foreign donors and grovel before his "priests" of development. He is a stranger to them, and his incarnation as a concrete development is even stranger to them. He is a *Wholly Other*. He is an absent-presence in Africa. But in his absence, he penetrates all spheres of their societies and their everyday consciousness of making provision for the future—that is, constructing economies.[9]

Two powerful and interrelated forces mark Africa's economic development: disruption and promise. As the representations of economic development as a *Wholly Other*, they represent the elusive powers of that slippery, recalcitrant postcolonial development project that simultaneously attracts and repels Africans. Economies develop largely by disrupting, even creatively destroying, existing ideas and structures. This power of disruption calls for and must be balanced by the forces of promise, the capacity to provide islands of certainty and hope amid the turbulence of unpredictability and sheer uncertainty of everyday living.

With the increasing chaos, unhinged spirituality, and fatigue of state structures and sovereignty in the African postcolony, the deity of economic development is merely destroying established orders without creating new orders of human flourishing—there is no promise of genuine development. The currents of disruption and promise are conjoined and animated by religion (Christianity, Islam, and African traditional religions). Religion is increasingly becoming a handmaiden of the deity of disruption and promise that has acquired sovereign powers over poor Africans. Religion is fast becoming the Angel of Destruction or the Grim Reaper consuming rationality and trust crucial for Africa's sociopolitical emancipation.

Disruption and promise are the *mysterium tremendum et fascinans*, the terror and awe of development in late capitalism. They are the numinous powers (experiences before which economic actors both tremble and are fascinated, repelled, and attracted) of the key social practices of making provision for the future. It is pertinent that we examine how religions in Africa are integral to the logic and dynamics of the bundle of disruption and promise, even as they inform its contextual manifestation. The goal is to point us toward the religion *within* development that can either sanction or sanctify, betray or bolster it. Can this religion as an internal disturbance of an economy, the grain of aggravating sand within the capitalist oyster that has enveloped Africa, be converted into a pearl?

Religion within Development: The Contours of a New Analysis

In the foregoing paragraph, I stated that the goal of this chapter is to point us to the religion within development. There are two sides to this endeavor. I have already executed the preliminary task of this aspiration: I have laid out the powers of development and the ways they operate or are received in Africa. The other side is to show how religion within development fights against itself and how its powers of disruption and promise are currently penetrating African religions. To demonstrate how the religion of development is internally split, I will turn to the politics or political theorization of African development. Later I will shift my gaze to Pentecostalism, to highlight the logic of disruption and promise that is afoot in religion itself.

This involves an examination of African Pentecostals' new orientation to their leaders: they are challenging and contesting pastoral authority in ways that we have not seen before. Has African Pentecostalism entered into a new age of disruption and promise? In its beginnings, it was certainly on the terrain of disruption and promise. But as it matured, it became sclerotic, hardening into a conservative force that supports the antidevelopment agents of the postcolonial state and celebrating spiritualist obscurantism and noncritical mindsets that are in certain respects antagonistic to economic development. Now, it appears the tide has turned, if one is not too optimistic in the reading of the sheep entrails.

The shift to dissent within Pentecostalism will enable us to explore how the god of development talks to the god of religion. How do the two gods, which hold the imagination of Africans in thralldom, communicate with each other? Do they laugh at Africa's predicament, hold long conversations about Africans' overcommitment to them, or quarrel among themselves on how to "bless" Africans? Do they cheat one another, like the god of religion frustrating the work of the god of development or the god of development "selling" African economies into foreign servitude? Let us now turn to the second part of our dual task: to the political.

Politics as an Internal Obstacle of the Religion of Development

African politics is a veritable site to examine how the "religiosity" of development itself or "religion" within development itself fights against development. Political theorist Claude Ake taught us that after independence African political leaders portrayed economic development as the *ultimate concern* of the postcolonial state. African leaders preoccupied themselves with the pursuit of development, doing so with single-mindedness and the conviction that to question their policies, dedication, and orientation to development was considered sacrilegious. The domestic bourgeois class, the political leaders, posited development as an ideology that enables them to exploit the masses. This fervent commitment and passionate attention to economic development turned out to be an obstacle to such development. The political conditions in the postcolonial state obstructed development even as political leaders pursued it.

What Ake does best in his scholarship is to point us toward how the politics that is integral to Africa's effort to grapple with the forces of disruption and promise of development inhibits or betrays national economic development. His principal argument is that political conditions constitute the greatest impediment to development. African leaders talked about how fragile their nations' independence was and how quickly they wanted self-reliant development. They capitalized on the objective need for development to fan the embers of patriotism and to serve as a strategy for power and survival. According to Ake, African leaders argued that now

> that independence had been won, the overriding task was development, without which political independence could not be consolidated and African countries would not be able to eradicate the humiliation of colonization. Against the pressure of redistribution, they argued that what was needed was hard work to further development, because the surplus had to be produced before it could be shared. . . . The hard work was to be done literally in silence; the overriding necessity of development was coupled with the overriding necessity of obedience and conformity. African leaders insisted that development

needs unity of purpose and the utmost discipline, that the common interest is not served by oppositional attitudes. It was easy to move from there to the criminalization of political opposition.[10]

This single-minded attention to development, this elevation of development as a civil religion, produced only meager success. The leaders were not ready to disrupt the colonial power structures, exploitative practices, and authoritarianism, all of which they needed for survival in the intra-elite political competition that assumed the character of warfare and depended on the raw calculus of power.[11] The more they played this game of warfare and resisted the very god of development who counseled disruption and promise, the more they could not address the problem of development and bring to their citizens the anticipated fruits of economic development. The kingdom of abundance the political leaders promised never came. The promise assumed the character of Christian eschatology, always in blessed postponement. As their failures mounted, they made more elaborate national shows of worshipping at the altar of development, while in reality they were only making token gestures to development. Yet they could not walk away from this god; they were in his thralldom. Because of the promise he held for their class survival, they dared not disrupt the grip of this god.

Once again let us hear from Ake why they could not abandon development and its unforgiving god: "For one thing development was an attractive idea for forging a sense of common cause and for bringing some coherence to the fragmented political system. More important, it could not be abandoned because it was the ideology by which the political elite hoped to survive and to reproduce its domination. Since development was the justification for rallying behind the current leadership, for criminalizing political dissent . . . to abandon it would undermine the power strategy of the elite."[12]

Politics is not only an internal disturbance of the religion of development but also a pathogen for the health of African economies and societies. How do we convert this grain of aggravating sand within the African capitalist oyster into a pearl? What will overcome the scission between politics and the god of development? It will not be the fusion of politics with the absolute requirements of the powers of disruption and promise, or the amalgamation of politics with development per se, but the recognition that politics is already the medium of the synthesis of the two opposing stances. The synthesis occurs in politics but neither in the god of development nor elsewhere. Politics is the field of mediation between the sacred powers of disruption and promise, on the one hand, and the key *social practices of making provision for the future*—that is, building and sustaining an economy—on the other hand.

Now that we have examined the political institutional framework—its fitness for midwifing disruption and promise for economic development—let us turn to the religion of Pentecostalism and investigate its readiness as a site for the possible operations of the powers of the god of development. Some African Pentecostals are initiating something new amid their ongoing social traditions, a move that is creating dissent in their churches and denominations, highlighting contradictions, and giving hope for a reformation. Their actions, though still embryonic, afford this writer an opportunity to bring the god of religion and the god of development into conversation in ways that before now were almost unimaginable. The protocol of translation is, of course, constituted around the platform of disruption and promise.

For a long time, many scholars considered religion or African Pentecostalism as one of the grains of sand preventing the smooth functioning of the god of development. Indeed, many social scientists argued that the encounter between the God of Pentecostalism, who sanctioned the prosperity gospel, and the god of development has been traumatic for the African economy. I want to disrupt this way of thinking and point us to the promise of a new thinking. Is it likely that Pentecostalism could be that grit in the oyster that eventually becomes a pearl? I cannot answer in the affirmative yet. To explore this matter, let us cast aside every theoretical weight and long-standing prejudice that besets us and let us listen with patience to the story I am about to set before us. I offer this story of dissent across three registers: tithe, sex, and pastoral accountability.

African Pentecostalism: Dissent, Contradiction, and Prospects

In the scholarship on African Pentecostalism, there are two major theoretical argumentations, broadly speaking. There is a group of scholars who present and celebrate African Pentecostals as venerable saints, as the forces behind the gravitational shift of Christianity to the Southern Hemisphere. The other group portrays African Pentecostals as the contaminating, transgressive devotees excreted by African traditional religions into the pure body of Christ and as a people whose rationality and orientation to modernity ought to be questioned. These two forms of discourse dominate the conference, seminar, and colloquia circles. But there is an emerging discourse that we ought to reckon with, if not embrace, if we are to adequately engage with the subject matter of religion and development in Africa. There is an emerging pattern of internal dissent, contradiction, and prospects within African Pentecostalism that is likely going to change the way we theorize it or evaluate its relevance to economic development.

TO PAY TITHE OR NOT TO PAY TITHE: THAT IS THE QUESTION

While many scholars have written off African Pentecostals as gullible in the sense that they were willing to pay tithes, the giving of 10 percent of their income to pastors who buy jets or live glamorous lifestyles, they have overlooked the emerging dissent among African Pentecostals about paying tithes. A cultural war has erupted in Nigerian Pentecostalism owing to the work of Ifedayo Olarinde (known as Daddy Freeze), an active online presenter. He founded a movement, "Free the Sheeple," which encourages church members to stop paying tithes to their pastors. He argued that the paying of tithes cannot automatically enrich the givers as pastors promise, and besides, no Nigerian pastor qualifies as a Levite to receive tithe. In one interview, Daddy Freeze stated, "Let me see them stop collecting tithes. Let them stop for one year. Let's see who will still be a pastor. . . . Stop collecting tithes. Preach the word that Jesus preached. At least Jesus did not collect tithes, Jesus fed the 5,000. In Nigeria, the 5,000 feed these thieves. I try to wake people up."[13]

Many of the pastors responded to Daddy Freeze by cursing him and also stating that all those who do not pay tithes are cursed and condemned to hellfire. But one of the biggest pastors in the country, Bishop Mike Okonkwo of the Redeemed Evangelical Mission, TREM, a former president of the Pentecostal Fellowship of Nigeria, admonished his fellow pastors by stating that it was not acceptable to frighten Christians into paying tithes and that the payment of tithes should be based on a desire to give to God.[14] He admitted to being in error in the past and said he has now seen the light, so he does not need to frighten people to pay tithes, he does not need to curse them if they refuse to pay, and he does not need to use what he calls "semantics" to trick them into paying tithes out of fear.

THE LOGIC OF TITHE AND SEX: A REFRAMING OF SPIRITO-SEXUAL ORIENTATION

The tithe campaign may have somewhat succeeded in terms of pastors reporting reductions in church-revenue intakes and in the new powers of congregants to challenge the unbridled powers of pastors to accumulate wealth or their authority as the master interpreters of scriptures. The picture is actually much more complicated. Tithe, both in its unchallenged reign and in its contested terrain, has triggered another form of dissent or contradiction. On Sunday, February 2, 2020, I had a conversation with a female Nigerian Pentecostal in her late twenties. She is college educated and running her own small business in Port Harcourt. In the course of our discussions, she mentioned that she has a boyfriend and revealed that she goes to an extraordinary length to correctly calculate her tithes on income from all sources (gifts, business earnings, and so on). This is a fragment of the conversation between us:

> ME: Are you saying that you keep records of all your inflows, incomes so that you correctly pay all your tithes to the last kobo?
>
> WOMAN: Yes, I do that meticulously. It is the proper thing to do. It is the way to live holy and to avoid spiritual curses. The blessings and anointing that come with regular payment of correct tithes cover and cleanse me in all areas of my life.
>
> ME: Wait a minute, didn't you tell me that you have a boyfriend and you sleep with him? I thought Pentecostals reject the idea of sex outside marriage. How come you are meticulous about paying tithes but could not care less about fornication or adultery?
>
> WOMAN: Tithing is a law of giving and receiving that even a nonbeliever can enjoy its benefits by applying it. It is a spiritual law, and anyone can key into it. It works automatically. The one who does not pay tithe will remain poor. But sex is a sin, and it can be forgiven if I go to God and ask for forgiveness. Holiness is not dependent on having sexual pleasure, which is a natural desire and you are not hurting anyone. Sex is not a source of curse o.
>
> ME: What if sex leads to pregnancy and you decide to abort? Will that not count as a serious sin or something that affects your holiness status? Besides, when you sleep with a married man are you not hurting his wife?
>
> WOMAN: I am not stupid. I use protection so I do not get pregnant. I am also not taking the married man from his wife. I am just having fun, enjoying sexual pleasure with him, satisfying my sexual desires with someone that I am attracted to. Sex is not the sin that pastors in the past made it out to be.
>
> ME: You are a member of your church choir, right? Are you saying you will not have any problem if your pastor sleeps with members of your church?
>
> WOMAN: My pastor is a woman and as such she does not sleep with anyone in the church.
>
> ME: Let's assume your pastor is a man. Will you have any concern if he sleeps with members of the choir, or with other women in the church?

WOMAN: Yeah, I will have problem with that. But if he sleeps with women who are not members of our church, it is not my business.

This conversation explains a lot about the current Pentecostal understanding of spirituality in Nigeria. The promise of quick wealth accumulation has disrupted long-established sexual mores. In their greed for money, Nigerian pastors have managed to elevate tithe payment into an iron-clad spiritual or natural law, the only law that really matters in Pentecostal spirituality. They have, perhaps, undermined the observance of any other laws and commandments from the Bible. Since they encouraged prostitutes, corrupt politicians, and sharp-dealing businesspersons to pay their tithes, they sowed the greed for wealth acquisition at all costs and by all means in their churches. Their congregants watched how tithes washed away sins and bloods of ill-gotten monies. From all these, it is a little step to the elevation of tithe payment as the axis on which Pentecostal spirituality as a whole revolves. *Pay tithe and prosper! Pay tithe and sin boldly! Going, going, gone!*

THE EMERGING ETHIC OF HOLDING PASTORS ACCOUNTABLE

In summer 2019, sad news broke out in Nigeria. Busola Dakolo, thirty-four years old, made an allegation against Pastor Biodun Fatoyinbo, the celebrity senior pastor of the Commonwealth of Zion Assembly (COZA) Church.[15] She alleged that he raped her twice when she was a teenager, nearly two decades before. In the months of June and July 2019, Pentecostals and others protested on the streets and in the camp of the Redeemed Christian Church of God along the Lagos-Ibadan Expressway. They demanded that Pastor Enoch A. Adeboye and other Christian leaders speak out against national issues affecting the populace, against sexual immoralities perpetuated by men of God, and to openly advocate for the release of Leah, a young Christian girl in the custody of Boko Haram. In the protest of July 8, some of the placards bore these words: "Adeboye, speak up for those who cannot speak for themselves"; "Adeboye, would you have kept quiet if Leah was your biological daughter?"[16] Two days before this protest at his headquarters, Pastor Adeboye spoke about male pastors' sexual immoralities in general without directly mentioning the rape of Dakolo. His admonition, delivered in the course of a sermon, drew the ire of many Pentecostals. He said, "You may say I'm old fashioned, I agree. I'll never have a private secretary who's a woman. When a woman accuses you of something, nobody will listen to you whether you're right or wrong; be wise!"[17] "When you see a sister smiling at you in a 'koi koi' way, run; run as in terror. Don't say, 'Nah, I'm a great man of God. I'm highly anointed.'"[18] These comments stirred a lot of criticism in social media.

Nigerian Pentecostal pastors are seeing their charismatic authority being attacked, challenged, or seriously contested. Some of their members, at least on social media or the internet, are demanding accountability. They often do not know how best to respond to the challenge of their pastoral hegemony, which they are discovering increasingly cannot be taken for granted. In desperation, Bishop Emmah Ison, the assistant national deputy president of Pentecostal Fellowship of Nigeria, South-South region of Nigeria, cried out, saying there are "the anti-church elements that have been in the internet. They live inside the internet. If a pastor steals yam, it goes viral."[19] Never mind that in a bid to shore up dwindling pastoral authority he was calling his fellow Pentecostals who were protesting against pastoral excesses "anti-church elements."

Note that I described the lay Pentecostals as protesting against pastoral excesses. This is far from the predominant view of the lead pastors. These big men and women of God think that they are dealing with the madness of the internet, insouciance of social media, and uncouth Pentecostals/*Penterascals*. To curb these, they are attempting to control or contain the madness, the excess madness of challenging God's anointed. They are struggling to renormalize the madness, to reinscribe the excess in the normal flow of Pentecostal spirituality. Some have even gone further to shake off a bit of their staid, stately image and inoculated their vast personal empires with the "poison" the protesters are spreading on the streets and in cyberspace, adopting the practices of the so-called "anti-church elements." The inoculation is a strategy of power and survival, an ideology of relevance. Perhaps it is in this light that we should interpret Pastor E. A. Adeboye's recent proclivity toward street protest against the failure of governance in Nigeria, the high level of insecurity in the country.[20] Are we not dealing with a (potentially) reformative event in the sense of "a traumatic intrusion of something New which remains unacceptable"[21] for the hegemonic *pentecocapitalism*? By the term *pentecocapitalism* I mean an "alliance between late capitalism and Pentecostalism that creates a Pentecostal-capitalist resonance machine, to adapt the words of William Connolly who charted the path of evangelical-capitalist resonance machine."[22] Whether this interpretation is absolutely correct or not, we are seeing Pentecostal masses reframing the narratives that have defined them for a long time.²³

Time will not allow me to give more examples of internal dissent and contradiction and renormalization/reinscription techniques within Nigerian Pentecostalism. There is no time to tell you about how Pentecostals now wage a vigorous campaign of mockery in social media against their leaders. They protest against the authority of their pastors by reducing attendance at the numerous programs their churches put up to collect their money, renew their brainwashing, and keep them from straying into rival ministries. I wish I had the time to tell you how they snicker at their pastors and make fun of them while services are going, when holy men and women of God are making holy sales pitches for tithes and financial donations in their holy sanctuaries. Lay Pentecostals are increasingly seeing that their emperors have no clothes, and they are eager to announce it. The regimes of unbridled pastoral authority are losing their legitimacy. Today, not a few Pentecostals perceive pastors' fire-spitting criticisms, curses, self-serving scriptural exegesis, and dramas over the unprecedented challenge of their hegemony as impotent panic reaction.

Are we not witnessing something that happens when a brutal regime is about to collapse? The regime discovers that its citizens are no longer afraid of it. The reality beneath its rule is gone. Yet like the cat in *Tom and Jerry*, who walks off a cliff and keeps walking in the air until he is reminded to look down, notices the abyss, and falls, many Nigerian Pentecostal pastors are right now walking on thin air. Soon they will be reminded that their Shiva dance is over, that the sheep are simply no longer afraid of them, and they will notice the abyss and fall. Or should we say that their mystical dance has entered the phase of destruction of their vast personal economico-spiritual empires and soon it will be time for the release and emancipation of their captives? When "an authoritarian regime approaches its final crisis, its dissolution as a rule follows two steps. Before its actual collapse, a mysterious rupture takes place: all of a sudden people know that the game is over—they are simply no longer afraid. It is not only that the regime loses its legitimacy, its exercise of its power itself is perceived as an impotent panic reaction."²⁴ Street fights can go on, and the government will make arrests, issue draconian decrees, and proceed with its usual elaborate parades and ceremonies, but somehow everyone knows that its jig is over. Are we there yet with African Pentecostalism?

In these examples of the contestation of tithe payment, the redefinition of the religious status of nonmarital sex, and the protestations against leaders for not speaking up against the alleged rape of Dakolo, we are seeing forms of internal resistance within Pentecostalism. We are witnessing the so-called weapons of the weak in action, with their subtle ways of resisting authorities in the movement, and are seeing some unexpected push toward social justice.[25] These events are disrupting the dominant narrative about African Pentecostalism in the West and in the academy. They call us to develop a contrarian perspective against the dominant view of Pentecostals as sitting ducks for greedy pastors to exploit or as religious roadkill to be run over on our way to forming rationality-driven development projects in Africa. The emerging story of Pentecostalism disrupts the present dominant narrative of apolitical, social-justice-averse African Pentecostals. All this is not to say that the new developments I have narrated are capable of dislodging the regnant narrative of African Pentecostals as being politically lethargic. But it brings me to the one question that I'd really love to ask, resorting to Bob Marley in the song *One Love*: Can this new political and reformative impulse galvanize the disruption-promise bundle of development by losing the grip of rabid spirituality that constitutes such a drag on Africa's economic development?

The latent optimism of this question should not make us lose sight of the fact that religion is often a force hostile to economic development and peace in Africa. The promise of human flourishing that religions in Africa possess has not materialized for the masses. Rather, Islam, Christianity (Pentecostalism), and African traditional religions are Grim Reapers of the rationality, trust, and freedom crucial for socioeconomic emancipation, especially as they are co-opted into the deadly intra-bourgeois class struggles for access to state power as the primary means of production.[26] In chapter 3, I analyzed a different set of the negativities of the religion of Pentecostalism and named them the *Pentecostal incredible*. Sociologist Ebenezer Obadare, in his 2018 book *Pentecostal Republic*, also draws our attention to some of the negativities and antidevelopment tendencies of the Pentecostal movement in Africa.[27]

The Study of Religion and Development in Africa: Methodological Issues

In academic discussions about religion and development, one of the usual approaches is to examine how either religion or development promotes or hinders the good of the other. Scholars often make this judgment over a trajectory of practices, events, or stories that connect religion and development. The other methodology is to focus on contemporary dealings, the immediacy of current events, and ongoing contacts between the two. I have taken a slightly different approach, a road less traveled. I sought a common platform of translation so I could lift up the religious powers of development. I identified these powers as disruption and promise. I then proceeded to interpret the conversation between religion and development through the economic-philosophical language of disruption and promise. The goal is to find the site where development and religion might coincide, where we can tap into the similar phenomenological reality of their numinous powers, the *mysterium tremendum et fascinans*.

If we can find this site of coincidence, a place of *coincidentia oppositorum*, coincidence of opposites, then we can possibly escape or transcend the radical split between religion and development in Africa in the extant literature. There are four ways the conjunction between the two is disavowed in the academic and popular/pastoral literatures: (1) the celebration of antidevelopment religion, as if the practice of rationality demonstrates religion's inauthenticity; (2) the opposite assertion of pure rationality as the only path to development, which reduces development to mere technical achievements, ignoring institutional framework and social-justice issues; (3) the division of religion and development, their allocation to two different segments of citizens, one of which loves religion as an idealized institution while the other pursues "vulgar" development, increments in national income that are situated outside the historicity and specificity of the realities on the ground; and (4) the false merger of religion and development in which religion's intense pursuit of rationality, "modernity," and avowal of development paradigms and programs is supposed to demonstrate that it truly loves development. However, the true miracle occurs when development and religion coincide, when development is "transubstantiated" into religion.[28] This is the residual, fifth, option I searched for in this chapter.

Let me end by drawing our attention to the radical pushbacks against the Pentecostal ecclesiastic class. The pastors themselves are also now aggressively fighting against this trend, and in their defense, they are developing bigger and more sophisticated media departments to push alternate, weaponized or aggressive narratives into the public. There is too much at stake for them not to fight back as the bases of their legitimacy, authority, and financial empires are being threatened or eroded. All these raise the issue of what kind of radical possibilities will emerge from these contestations, from these "revolutionary moments," and how they will spill over to other aspects of the African society or feed into the logic and dynamics of disruption and promise that undergird development.

I foresee five possible scenarios, which will have a huge impact on how we study the connection between religion and development in Africa. First, Pentecostalism becomes democratized and becomes a force for democracy. The struggle between the Pentecostal big pastors and Pentecostal resisters could lead to the democratization of African Pentecostalism and eventually contribute toward a vigorous development of democratic spirit and ethos of social justice in the political sphere. A set of preachers emerge who embrace the ethos of the *Pentecostal principle* and recast the gospel in a new anticlerical, antiauthoritarian, populist form—best suited to the traditions of self-rule and ideals of democracy, religious populism, and radical equality that inaugural Pentecostalism stood for.[29] Here, one is hoping that the protesters' logic eventually wins the fight.

It might also fail, and this brings us to our second point. The trend of the *Pentecostal incredible*, with its unbelievable inclination toward religious obscurantism and will-to-exclusivist spirituality, snuffs out the democratic and secularizing impulses, and the movement shrinks, becomes even more backward and fundamentalist, and retreats from the public political realm into the Niebuhrian mode of "Christ against culture."

I name the third option *alliance spirituality*. It combines the insights from the two preceding paradigms. Under this paradigm, Pentecostals do not have to choose between pluralistic democracy and sectarianism (in the Troeltschian sense). They use the best elements of democracy and the church's spiritualistic mindset to achieve what either of the two paradigms cannot achieve on its own. (Let us not forget that magico-spiritual powers or activities have always been part of the politics of postcolonial Africa.) In this combination, there is collaboration between pastors and politicians, and this can transform the intrinsic nature of the postcolonial state: the Pentecostalization of civil society and state. Obadare's book *The Pentecostal Republic* has given us a glimpse into the operation of this paradigm, under which Pentecostals view the Pentecostal ethos as the fulfillment of African culture and see themselves as the converters of African culture and society to Christ.

The fourth option relates to the *messianic vocation*.[30] It is a diagonal cut through the first two options even as it cuts into the time between the time of the now and the time that remains. Its character of diagonal cut does not mean that it is situated between both options. The two options contract into each other but do not coincide. This option signifies the caesura that divides the two options and introduces a messianic remnant in which the authoritarian impulse is dislocated into the democratic ethos and the democratic impulse is extended into the authoritarian impulse. Authoritarianism is not (*hos me*) authoritarianism; democratic ethos is not (*hos me*) democratic.

"But this I say, brethren, the time has been shortened, so that from now on those who have wives should be as though they had none; and those who weep, as though they did not weep; and those who rejoice, as though they did not rejoice; and those who buy, as though they did not possess; and those who use the world, as though they did not make full use of it; for the form of this world is passing away. But I want you to be free from concern" (1 Cor. 7:29–32, New American Standard Bible). Paul is describing a way of living in or relating to the world: Christians are to relate to the world, its institutions and events, with openness but never to regard any one of them as being of ultimate importance.

As Giorgio Agamben argues, this is the formula concerning messianic life. Messianic vocation

> calls for nothing and to no place. For this reason it may coincide with the factical condition in which each person finds himself called, but for this very reason, it also revokes the condition from top to bottom. The messianic vocation is the revocation of every vocation. In this way, it defines what to me seems to be the only acceptable vocation. What is a vocation, but the revocation of each and every concrete factical vocation? This obviously does not entail substituting a less authentic vocation with a truer vocation. According to what norm would one be chosen over the other? No, the vocation calls the vocation itself, as though it were an urgency that works it from within and hollows it out, nullifying it in the very gesture of maintaining and dwelling in it. This, and nothing less than this, is what it means to have a vocation, what it means to live in messianic *klesis*.[31]

The messianic vocation is an actual transformation of the experience of authoritarianism and democracy that interrupts Pentecostalism (as we know it today) itself. As a messianic vocation, Pentecostalism wants to be neither a form of medieval Christendom (*Pentecostal Republic*)—be the *all*, be the all-transforming and converting of society—nor a part of the all. It only wants to situate itself as a remnant, as not-all.[32] Please note that the remnant is not a numeric remainder, some kind of holy men and women set apart, but a *figure* that some Pentecostals assume because they are called to the messianic life and live as Paul advises in 1 Cor. 7:29–32.

In the remnant Pentecostalism, both authoritarianism and democracy are retained. While they remain, both are divided because their other is introduced into them. Through the remnant, the authoritarian leadership is divided and its potential for its fulfillment as an effective executive apparatus is implanted in it. On the other hand, the democratic ethos is also divided in that the particularity of appropriate respect for God's anointed (or society's institutions) is retained in it.[33] The division of position (space of protest or reaction to it) is itself divided. The messianic vocation lies at the threshold of the two positions. It is not an exclusivist salvific stance "in which all particulars are annulled."[34]

Finally, Pentecostalism, under the hammer of continuous ATR-induced Africanization of Pentecostalism and Pentecostalization of mainline churches, becomes an empty signifier for religions in Africa, the exoskeleton of the sacred presence. Pentecostalism, as an incarnation of "otherness" of extant Christianity, dies. The existence of the other Christianities (and, if you like, other African religions) becomes the only site of African Pentecostalism, the site where African Pentecostalism achieves its actuality. Pentecostalism will become the form of African religions, and African religions will be the substance of Pentecostalism. The disruption of preexisting forms of Christianity and African traditional religions that Pentecostalism engendered ends up in the promise of African traditional religions as the "spirit" of the community of believers. The disrupter is disrupted.

The five options or paradigms may not necessarily offer us the chance to cleanly choose one or the other. They are likely to exist together and overlap, as often happens with Christian churches' historical responses to the matter of Christ and culture. Thus, the paradigms may well be considered to be five possible ways of conceptualizing Pentecostalism and culture in Africa. Obviously, there is much that still awaits the labor and intellect of scholars of religion and development to adequately map out in these developments of religion within the movements of the religious powers of economic development.

Concluding Thought: Modeling the Change Maker within the Sacred

In the last section we talked about a figure or figures (institutions) of change. This was not the first time we have touched on change makers in this book. There is a certain understanding of the sacred that has implicitly propelled this thought about agents of change. I want to explicitly explore the connections between them, demonstrating how the figure of change maker inevitably arises from the interpretation of the sacred that I have provided in this book.

In chapter 3, I suggested that, perhaps, an *Incredible Man or Woman* might paradoxically emerge from the operations of the postcolonial incredible and the Pentecostal incredible to "save" Nigeria. This person fashioned in an atmosphere of the incredibles may initiate something new in his or her society to usher in the era of beautiful sacred. I am returning to this idea of *Incredible Man or Woman* to complement or impregnate option four, relating to a *messianic vocation* and the *figure*, with a different perspective. The resulting offspring bears the "heroism" of the *Incredible Man or Woman* and *communal-remnant Pentecostalism*. What founds this *event* of the *Incredible Man or Woman* and makes it of universal significance is not the singularity of person as a subject (as the idea of the *Incredible Man or Woman* suggests) but rather the message his or her accomplishments (working in concert with others) convey about the possibility of a new relationship with the sacred in the postcolony that founds the singularity of a person as the subject, as *the community hero*.

The Kalabari notion of *community hero* may speak to this person. The community hero is a person who is believed by members of the community to have fully realized his or her particular divine (sacred) aim with little or no distortion or to be in search of the maximum potential in his or her historical circumstances. The particular divine aims have been decisively realized in the lives of few individuals in history, and they became *gods* or *community heroes (amaoru)*. The heroes, human-gods, became the embodiments of divine creative purposes, the specific divine addresses (speeches, *bibi*) to the community at a specific time, and a sort of transparent medium through which the people could read (comprehend and prehend) *So*'s (sacred's) aim for the community. The men and women who had so realized themselves became effective concrete lures for both individual and collective actions. They served also for personal and corporate self-understanding at a given historical juncture and for what stood beyond them. Such men and women, in actualizing *So*'s particular ideals for themselves, expressed *So*'s general aim for their entire community, and it was received by all members of the community.

The interpretation of the work of *community heroes* and their reception is not timeless. When the historical situations that brought their works into collective consciousness and sustained them changed, their valuation also altered. Thus, with the coming of Christianity and the expansion of the communicative reaches of the community, new heroes embedded in religiously relevant historical situations were sought. Kalabari-English anthropologist Robin Horton argues that as the Kalabari horizon expanded owing to increasing spheres of commerce, transportation and communication networks, and long-distance trade, the heroes they kept also changed or tended to change.[35] In the cosmological adjustment that ensued, many of the symbols and understandings of the old worldview were carried over.

When one looks at the conception of Jesus of Nazareth as the Christ and as the second person of the Trinity, one discerns some resemblance with the Kalabari conception of *So* and community heroes. Now I am not saying the Kalabari community in the nineteenth century, when they began to convert to Christianity in good numbers, consciously worked out the similarities between their conception of *So* and the Christian conception of Jesus as the *logos*. But for our limited task in this study, they are worth noting for the purpose of enriching the Christian theology of excellence being developed in this work.

According to Christian theologian Lewis S. Ford, the logos is the totality of possibilities God envisages for the world or the totality of creative possibilities inherent in the nature of God. Jesus Christ is seen as an incarnation of the logos, the creative Word addressed to humankind.[36] In Paul Tillich's thought, the Christ event is taken to be the emergence of a new humanity, a *New Being* who represents the closing of the chasm between potentialities and actualization. In the man Jesus of Nazareth, the New Being has been realized, and thus there are radically new and creative possibilities for the transformation of humankind and history. Such "unique" actualization of potentialities is of universal significance and must lead to the creative transformation of historical existence, according to Tillich.[37] The indigenous Kalabari understanding of *So* and *community heroes* is remarkably anticipatory of these received Christian theologians' conceptions of *logos* and *New Being*.

The notion of community heroes is speaking to something profoundly human or common in cultures and religions. In many cultures and religions, there is a discussion of disremption between potentialities and actualities, between what the "true human being is," what he or she is "essentially," and what he or she actually is or what he or she is existentially. The pursuit of or belief in the extraordinary actualization of human potentiality holds out the possibility of permanently closing the gap, a search whose goal is elusive, and yet as in Kalabari and Christian communities, there are figures who have been identified to have closed the gap between essence and existence and who hence stand as models and lures for others' becoming. Such figures are believed to be capable of ushering in a new age of healing, wholeness, and salvation.

We have sought to understand our *Incredible Man or Woman* in the light of Kalabari *community heroes*. This is all the more important because it enables the reader to understand how the idea of the *Incredible Man or Woman* is deeply rooted in the notion of sacred as a universal set of possibilities and is decisive for comprehending what human life in Africa should be in the presence of earnest commitment to harnessing the beauty of the sacred. This connection to the expanded notion of the sacred that I have been crafting in this book strongly encourages me to reformulate the *Incredible Man or Woman* not as a person (at best, only figuratively so) but as the community itself. The *Incredible Man or Woman* is not just about individual heroism or the unique actualization of potentialities but also about communal healing or transformation and about the community. A community can become the community of the *Incredible Man or Woman* if it deliberately and self-consciously orders its life, activities, and creativity in accord with the basic, restorative principle of the *Incredible Man or Woman*. In becoming the community of the *Incredible Man or Woman*, it becomes the place where the beauty of the sacred is actual, and from there it overflows into future generations and into the world.

All this tells us that any study of the beauty of the sacred must become (include) a political theory that speaks to the transformation of the coordinates that organize our existence, eliciting an interruption of the flow of social life. This is to say such a study must not be restricted to the creation and maintenance of "a reasonable, just, and stable social order" but must be a theory of rapture.[38] "Rupture is the occurrence of the impossible, when the very ground under our feet shifts in order to transform the point from which we see" our socioeconomic reality.[39] This calls for a subject that emerges as "a break within time and because of this break, the subject has the capacity to form values that make life worth living."[40] This break within time can only be gestured to and cannot be offered as a traditional promise of the future. Hannah Arendt writes: "This small non-time-space in the very heart of time [i.e., the break within time], unlike the world and the culture into which we are born, can only be indicated, but cannot be inherited and handed down from the past; each new generation, indeed every new human being as he inserts himself between an infinite past and infinite future, must discover and ploddingly pave it anew."[41]

CONCLUSION

I HAVE TOLD THE STORY OF THE AFRICAN postcolony, which has diverse forms that cannot be easily harmonized. I did not tell the story as a way of offering an account of how African postcolonial culture achieved its current ("coherent") form out of contradictions, dialectics, and emergent spirituality. And it is not advisable for us to seek to harmonize the various fragments in order to present a hegemonic narrative. I avoided specifying the *what-is* of the African postcolony and instead focused on the *how*: the interactions of fragments of social life by which African culture (polity) is always becoming what it is. The *how* is the animating power of the *which-is*, *which-was*, and *which-is-to-come* of the *what-is*. I laid out a series of fragments and developments with differing narrative tensions to convey something about the genius (spirit) of adaptation and unfinished responses to problems or challenges of the African postcolony. These responses and adaptations put the emphasis on African agency, indigenous philosophies, and local practices as a way of organizing structures of meaning.

Indeed, this study has also directed readers' attention to the fragmentary nature of the African postcolony. The postcolony is full of fragments, and I endeavored to tell its story by thinking in "parts" and not in unified cultural wholes. And it is in its fragments that I have sought to understand it deeply. To this end, I have attempted to affirm the "spirit" of the African postcolony. *Spirit* here does not mean a distilled essence, changeless core, irreducible substrate, or perfection of being. It was deployed for the sake of highlighting specific observations, contemplations, and questions that can fleetingly point us to something of broader significance for understanding the multidirectional openness of the social life of Africans without presuming a constrictive universalizing framework. The hope was that the spirit, which is dynamic and cast bursting, would let us grasp the fluid, rhizomatic *how* of the African postcolony and not get caught in a calcifying, totalizing *what-is*. The story of the postcolony is too fragmentary to sustain a metanarrative or unified theory of African *situation* or political theology. The nature or spirit of the African postcolony appears to me to be "flung and scattered among [several traditions] like broken china in the sun."[1]

The notion of the sacred and the analyses of the tripartite cargo of transcripts (monstrosity, beauty, and ridiculous) have run on the grooves of the preceding six chapters, helping us to grasp the rhizomatic *how* of postcolonial Africa. In these six chapters, we saw the immurement in restlessness that pertains to human beings, pressed on every side but not destroyed or crushed, ever living in resistance to the closure of the horizon of existence. Yes, there are times we encountered the "incredible Pentecostals" and some of us wanted to state, like Hamm in Samuel Beckett's *Endgame*, "Use your head, can't you, use your head, you're on earth, there's no cure for that!"[2] At other times we encountered, endured, and enjoyed Africans living *adventally*, though not without *ressentiment*, the weeping and gnashing of teeth, and with a profound sense that everything important to human flourishing is *belated*. Thus, it bears repeating that the sacred has not been fair to Africans—or, more precisely, since the sacred is nonentitative, that Africans (and others) have not been fair to themselves. Their harvests from the universal urn of possibilities are meager, ugly, and lean. Their harvests have been few and difficult, and they do not equal the sleek and fat harvests of the peoples of the other continents. Possibilities for Africans are fragile and scarce. The set of possibilities that can grow human flourishing on the continent is at best very weak.

Possibility is the substance of the sacred; the sacred is the form of possibility. Possibilities are the infinite combinatorial arrangements of the vast and rich resources (including imagination) of a community and its people. The sacred is the possibility structure of the community. The performances of possibilities, the generation, extension, and interaction with possibilities, are what I refer to as transcripts of the sacred. A transcript is a union of determinate differentiations (different actual things)—that is, possibilities that are unified in moments of creativity and integration in the coursing of the sacred in the community. Each transcript not only serves as an actualization of possibilities but also transforms the possibility structure of the community. A transcript is the spatial-temporal mode

> that constitutes formal possibilities. The possibility structure of any date in the future is relative to the temporal modes of the past and the present. The past consists of all things that have been actualized and the present is the temporal mode in which past things are responded to, reconfigured, added to, and integrated into the new present reality. When that present moment of creative harmonization is finished, the result is a past actual thing. The future provides the possibilities for a present moment of creative harmonization relative to the past things with which it has to work. The present moment of creative

harmonization, it should be said, might be very destructive of past things and also lead to disastrous consequences; "harmonization" should not be assumed to be beneficent.[3]

A transcript is a creative harmonization of possibilities. It is the becoming of what has been actualized in the past, the becoming of past transcripts, so to speak. The sacred is an interaction of transcripts across three modes of time. Transcripts in a community roll along, drawing from and feeding on one another. The sacred is the transcripts' flow in a community. For the transcripts to flow together, they must be together. This togetherness is not a temporal togetherness; there is a context of mutual relevance that enables each of them to be together with the others. This togetherness is the sacred, the *human creative act*, or, simply, human creativity.[4]

In the preceding six chapters, I have described the structures of the sacred in the African postcolony, the life of the sacred as Africans experience it. Africans encounter and experience it as the monstrousness, ridiculousness, and beauty of social existence. We provided a rational account of the structure of reason, the moral choices, and the nature of society that make the experience of life of the sacred possible. The monstrous operates by the logic of *inclusive exclusion* (excluding insiders). It drives the good (that is, the actualization of human potentiality for increasing levels of human flourishing) out of society and relegates it to the outside. The possibilities of the actualization of human potentiality for members of the community are rendered out of reach by the power of the monstrous. The level of human flourishing that belongs to the community is driven out, and this act constricts the *possibility actualization frontiers* of community members. By this exclusion, the monstrous defines the limits that ground and curate the logic of the sacred operative in the community. The beautiful is characterized by exclusive inclusion (including outsiders): possibilities that are outside the realm of actualization are brought in and recognized by the virtue of desire, the unfinishedness of life, the perpetually longing for fulfillment.

The phrase *possibility actualization frontiers* (PAF) may sound novel, but it is rooted in a very familiar concept in economics, the *production possibilities frontiers* (hereafter PPF) of an economy. What economists call PPF is a graph (with a bowed-out curvature) that shows the most optimal allocation of resources in an economy given the effects of diminishing returns on production.[5] The graph shows how the total value of output will change as different allocations of land, labor, and capital are made. It plots out the output combinations at different allocation regimes of an economy's resources or factors of production. All points on and under the curve are attainable levels of production; those above it are not reachable given the limited supply of resources (capital, labor, technical know-how, management expertise, and so on).

Production levels that correspond to points on the PPF are theoretically considered efficient.[6] An efficient economy is considered to be producing at levels where there is no waste of resources. At such levels, producers can only increase the output of a product at the expense of another one—that is, by decreasing its production. Any attempt to increase the output of a product involves tradeoffs. But when the PPF of an economy shifts outward, not only can it increase the production of all items but it might even produce new ones. The PPF shifts outward when there are technical improvements in the economy.

If the PPF defines the boundary of the set of possibilities available for an economy to produce and manage its total output, then what is beyond this limit? Beyond the frontier (PPF) is a *void*. It is not a space; it is not conducive to "economic habitation" (to production and exchange). It is a nonplace, a nonexistent economic space. But as an economy expands and its constraints are loosened, it creates its own space. A cutting-edge economy creates the space into which it expands. With what forces does an expanding galaxy of economic activities unfurl the subsequent space it will inhabit? Technological breakthroughs and human capital improvements are two of the factors that usually shift the line (curve) outward.

I want to emphasize or reiterate one of the features of PPF's expansions: an economy creates the space into which it expands. Take, for instance, that decades ago there was no computer industry in the United States. There was no "there" of the computer industry into which the United States could move to expand its economy and increase its gross domestic product. It had to create this new space into which it would then go. The creation and movement into the new space is simultaneous, in the same way the universe expands by creating its own space and expanding into it.

The possibility actualization frontiers (PAF) *metaphorically* plot out the transcript combinations at different interplays of the potentiality-impotentiality regimes (scenarios) of a community's sacred (the universal set of possibilities). All points on and under the curve are attainable levels of actualization of human potentiality; those above it are not reachable given the current limits of the sacred. The more the PAF moves outward, the more possibilities in the universal, infinite set of possibilities (the sacred) the community has captured. If we identify the amount of possibility capture with the level of human flourishing (or crudely, economic development, human development), then the higher the level of human flourishing, the higher the concentration of the sacred in that community, so to speak.

So the further a community or nation pushes its PAF outward, the more of the sacred it has. Note once more, the sacred is not religion. Today, in many academic circles, because the sacred is seen restrictively as religion, "economically poor countries" (those with PAF curves close to the origins of the x and y axes, those that have captured fewer possibilities for human flourishing) are seen as having more of the presence of the sacred. What such poor countries have more of is religion, not the sacred. The portion of their sacred occupied, inhabited, or claimed by religion is quite high, but it does not mean the proportion of the global sacred they possess is high.

Religion is only a part of the sacred, a cluster of possibilities that arises from engaging certain transcendent, immanent, or transimmanent forces of existence.[7] As the PAF pushes outward, religion as a share of the sacred will tend to diminish even if the concern for it and its virtue might be increasing. So outward-moving PAF will lead to a decreasing share of religion in the total urn of possibilities. This has nothing to do with the secularization thesis. It is only an arithmetic of expanding sacred, the set of possibilities available to a society.

Let me also mention that decreasing the proportion of religion in the sacred might lower the "transaction cost" (the cost of the actualization of potentiality across a socially, ethologically, or "technologically" separable interface or the boundaries of possibilities) of expanding the PAF and lead to the expansion of the universal set of possibilities in cases where religious sentiments or norms inhibit the actualization of human potentialities. For instance, a religion that limits the education of women or confines them to the home front as just mothers will increase the transaction cost of increasing the overall frontiers of the sacred. There are times religion might actually lower the transaction cost of expanding PAF. For some groups or categories, religion provides the basis for trust and obligations. In certain cases, the reduction of trust due to the diminishment of religion might make it difficult for businesses or institutions to prosper and grow in scale and scope or for some members of a community to work with complete strangers.

On the whole, this book has been an attempt to provide a portraiture of the sacred in the African postcolony. Each chapter is a portrait of the sacred "designed to capture the richness, complexity, and dimensionality of human experience"[8] in the postcolonial context, conveying the experiences of people who are negotiating the hand that the sacred deals to them every day, the hand that their actions, successes, and failures daily create and recreate. The discoveries I have made in my probing and layered interpretations of the sacred in the African postcolony have all come from particularity and specific details of the individual contexts and cultural forms that each chapter records. Every one of them is shaped through a dialogue among analytical rigor, evocative language, and forms of representation that give voice to the lived experience of Africans in a particular context. Each chapter exemplifies the sacred, or at least the operativity of sacred, in the African postcolony, witnessing, representing, and referring to the character of the universal urn of possibilities that is set before Africans. Nelson Goodman defines *exemplification* as "possession plus reference," or the relation between a sample and what it refers to.[9] Every chapter is an exemplar of the sacred; it exemplifies properties of the sacred. Each chapter possesses and refers to a limited range of social experiences and character types (beautiful, monstrous, and ridiculous) reflecting the life of the sacred in the postcolony. Each reflects the burden of the sacred in Africa. Postcolonial Africa is burdened by the sacred. It is this burden that this book has interpreted in various ways, and the point is to change Africa, as Karl Marx is wont to put it.

Afterword: Plasticity of the Sacred

In the preceding pages, we examined alterations in the logic, dynamic, structure, or function in human communities owing to the development, experience, and deformation of potentiality and its various actualizations. In other words, we have been dealing with the plasticity of the sacred. The concept of plasticity is about how the sacred that courses through human societies is perceived to give, receive, and explode forms of flourishing in the social relationality. The sacred, as a network of potentiality, impotentiality, actualization of potentialities, and material and energetic flows engendered by billions of micro interaction rituals, is characterized by plasticity. This refers to three of its properties. It possesses "at once the capacity to *receive form* . . . and the capacity to *give form*. . . . But it must be remarked that plasticity is also the capacity to annihilate the very form it is able to receive or create."¹⁰ Buildings and bombs, sculptures and smithereens, ashes and fire, reification and fluidification, concrete and abstract, and suture and rupture are some of the shapes in which the sacred takes, animates, ruptures, transforms, gives, or receives form.

The concept of the transcript of the sacred is an attempt to name, understand, or interpret the plasticity of the sacred. Its purpose is to enable us to grasp what leads the sacred toward metamorphosis, to lay bare the metamorphic structure that undergirds its capacity to order, animate, or articulate transformation; to sustain the alterity of the sacred with regard to itself; or to perform exchanges with itself. In this sense, the sacred is nothing but the mutability, the plasticity of Being.¹¹ Indeed, a transcript is a new mode of discerning the forms the sacred assumes in the materiality of existence and a new imagination of the mode and modifications of the sacred itself.

Transcripts also function as synapses of the sacred (brain), the platform of connections. If a transcript belongs to a "circuit" of the sacred that is in high demand and traffic, with continual actualizations of potentialities, it tends to grow, its connectivity increases, and its synaptic efficacy increases. Transcripts that are not in frequent use, not in a dense circuit of connections, tend to die, becoming less efficacious over time. The metaphor of transcript as a synapse gives us a language to explain the gradual structuration, formation, modification, or molding of the sacred in a particular sociality under the influence of individual societal experiences. With time and more facility with theories of the sacred and transcripts (which are in themselves forms of circuits) in this book, we can, perhaps, precisely account for particularities and individual characteristics of the sacred in different communities. Each community makes its own sacred but does not know it is doing so. The sacred is a human capacity, "but it appears in wildly diverse forms among human beings."¹² A community does not create *the* sacred; it creates *a* sacred, and "so becomes [a community] in a distinctive and particular manner. That which is common to all is achieved only in ways that are not common to all."¹³ The sacred is the community's work, and the community does not know it. It is ignorant of its own plasticity, the plasticity of the sacred. The sacred is plastic, and the community does not know it. The creator made its own image and is ignorant of it, or the image is hidden from the creator. Transcripts (will) enable us to develop a paradigm of individuation that makes each instantiation of the sacred unique despite its conformity to a general model. The sacred is no longer immanence versus transcendence (transimmanence), but immanence, transimmanence, and plasticity—which enfolds, unfolds, and refolds the others.[14]

The sacred is an acentered system, a nonintegrative totality that is constituted by splits, by gaps, by breaks.[15] It is not a smooth, continuous space; there are gaps, cuts, and voids between any two transcripts, and a transcript itself is gapped. Because of "transcriptic gaps," information relating to potentiality and the actualization of potentiality "must cross voids, and something aleatory thus introduces itself between the emission and reception of a message, constituting the field of action of plasticity."[16]

NOTES

Preface

1. This epigraph was written by this writer. Let me hasten to add that the transcripts of the sacred are not limited to social practices. There are also traces of the sacred left behind on the surfaces of the human body or in the psyche. Such traces include the fragile moments of smiles, laughter, radiant faces, sweaty bodies, pleasures, feelings of elevation and empowerment, emotions, the sense of new possibilities, and so on. These kinds of traces at best remind us of the leftover glory of Jehovah that shone on Moses's face after he saw only God's back.
2. Catherine Keller, *Face of the Deep: A Theology of Becoming* (London: Routledge, 2003).
3. For a different kind of archive, see Toyin Falola, "Ritual Archives," in *The Palgrave Handbook of African Social Ethics*, ed. Nimi Wariboko and Toyin Falola (Cham, Switzerland: Palgrave Macmillan, 2020), 473–97.
4. Paul Tillich, *Systematic Theology* (Chicago: University of Chicago Press, 1951), 1:3–4.
5. F. W. J. Schelling, *Abyss of Freedom/Ages of the World* (second draft, 1813), trans. Judith Norman (Ann Arbor: University of Michigan Press, 1997).
6. See Catherine Keller, *Cloud of the Impossible: Negative Theology and Planetary Entanglement* (New York: Columbia University Press, 2014), 20, 26.
7. Ashon T. Crawley, *Blackpentecostal Breath: The Aesthetic of Possibility* (New York: Fordham University Press, 2017), 24.
8. Mark Lewis Taylor, *The Political and the Theological: On the Weight of the World* (Minneapolis: Fortress, 2011), 15.
9. Taylor, *Political and the Theological*, 15.
10. Taylor, *Political and the Theological*, 16.

Introduction

1. Paul Tillich, *Systematic Theology* (Chicago: University of Chicago Press, 1951), I:5.
2. My language of form and dynamics, power and meaning comes from Tillich, *Systematic Theology*, vol. 1. See also Tillich, *Systematic Theology*, vol. 3.
3. My language and ideas here are indebted to Theodore Schatzki, *Site of the Social: A Philosophical Account of the Constitution of Social Life and Change* (University Park: Pennsylvania State University Press, 2002).
4. For the definition of structural and motivational virtues, see Robert Merrihew Adams, *A Theory of Virtue: Excellence in Being for the Good* (Oxford: Oxford University Press, 2006), 31–35, 175–76.
5. For an argument about how concern for the good of persons is linked with caring for some activities for their own sake, see Adams, *Theory of Virtue*, 89–91.
6. Rudy Ruckers, *Infinity and the Mind: The Science and Philosophy of the Infinite* (Princeton, NJ: Princeton University Press, 1995), 50–51, 78, 203.

7. Ruckers, *Infinity of the Mind*, 145–48.

8. Calvin L. Warren, *Ontological Terror: Blackness, Nihilism and Emancipation* (Durham, NC: Duke University Press, 2018), 107, 108.

9. Ridiculous hope does not work to overcome the terror of possibilities, terrifying formlessness, for the monstrous sacred is part of the sacred, integral to the universal set of possibilities. A residue of the terror of possibilities will *always* remain in the world construction, in the unity of form and meaning of possibilities.

10. Quoting French authors Louis Althusser and Gilles Deleuze, Nicolas Bourriaud defines *assemblage [agencement]* as "a multiplicity which is made up of many heterogeneous terms and which establishes liaisons, relations between them. . . . Thus the assemblage's only unity is that of co-functioning: it is a symbiosis, a 'sympathy.'" Bourriaud, *The Radicant*, trans. James Gussen and Lili Porten (New York: Lukas and Sternberg, 2009), 155.

11. Bourriaud, *Radicant*, 22. See also Bourriaud, *Postproduction Culture as Screenplay: How Art Reprograms the World*, trans. Jeanine Herman (New York: Lukas and Sternberg, 2002), 51–53.

12. Devaka Premawardhana, *Faith in Flux: Pentecostalism and Mobility in Rural Mozambique* (Philadelphia: University of Pennsylvania Press, 2018).

13. Premawardhana, *Faith in Flux*, 20–21, 31, 57, 67, 102–5.

14. Premawardhana, *Faith in Flux*, 17–18.

15. Premawardhana, *Faith in Flux*, 18.

16. Note the allusion to Karl Marx, *Grundrisse: Foundations of the Critique of Political Economy* (New York: Penguin, 1993), 98.

17. Alexis de Tocqueville, *Democracy in America* (New York: Perennial Classics, 2001), 887 note c.

18. Premawardhana, *Faith in Flux*, 67.

19. Emmanuel Katongole, *The Sacrifice of Africa: A Political Theology for Africa* (Grand Rapids, MI: Eerdmans, 2011), 29.

20. Colin Campbell, *The Romantic Ethic and the Spirit of Modern Consumerism* (New York: Basil Blackwell, 1987), 205.

21. Campbell, *Romantic Ethic*, 205.

22. Thomas Sankara, *Thomas Sankara Speaks: The Burkina Faso Revolution*, trans. and ed. Samantha Anderson (New York: Pathfinder, 1988), 2.

23. Sankara, *Speaks*, 144.

24. Katongole, *Sacrifice of Africa*, 91–92.

25. Dayo Olopade, *The Bright Continent: Breaking Rules and Making Change in Modern Africa* (Boston: Mariner Books, 2014), 20, 22.

26. Robert Cummings Neville, *Ultimates: Philosophical Theology* (Albany: SUNY University Press, 2013), 1:70–73.

27. Richard Fenn, "Sociology and Religion: Searching for the Sacred," in *The Oxford Handbook of Religion and Science*, ed. Philip Clayton and Zachary Simpson (Oxford: Oxford University Press, 2006), 259 (italics in the original).

28. Akinwumi Ogundiran, *The Yoruba: A New History* (Bloomington: Indiana University Press, 2020), 409.

29. This way of formulating my thought is indebted to Jan Vasina, "Knowledge and Perceptions of the African Past," in *African Historiographies*, ed. Bogumil Jewsiewicki and David Newsbury (Beverly Hills: Sage, 1986), 28–41, quotation 28, quoted in Ogundiran, *Yoruba*, 412.

30. "Chinua Achebe: The Art of Fiction CXXXVIV," interview by Jerome Brooks, Paris Review, no. 133 (Winter 1994–95).
31. Peter van der Veer, *The Value of Comparison* (Durham, NC: Duke University Press, 2016), 1–47.
32. Clifford Geertz, *The Interpretation of Cultures* (New York: Basic Books, 1973), 15.
33. Tejumola Olaniyan, *Arrest the Music! Fela and His Rebel Art and Politics* (Bloomington: Indiana University Press, 2004), 2.
34. Hannah Arendt, *The Human Condition* (Chicago: University of Chicago Press, 1958), 246–47.
35. Robert Wright, *Nonzero: The Logic of Human Destiny* (New York: Vintage Books, 2001). See also Wright, *The Evolution of God* (New York: Little, Brown, 2009).
36. Nimi Wariboko, *The Pentecostal Principle: Ethical Methodology in New Spirit* (Grand Rapids, MI: Eerdmans, 2012), 164–65.
37. This sentence and the one before it were inspired by Giorgio Agamben, *The Kingdom and the Glory: For a Genealogy of Economy and Government*, trans. Lorenzo Chiesa (Stanford, CA: Stanford University Press, 2011), 233.
38. This way of putting across my ideas was inspired by Diana Taylor, *The Archive and the Repertoire: Performing Cultural Memory in the Americas* (Durham, NC: Duke University Press, 2007), 176–77.
39. Ronald M. Green, "Religious Ritual: A Kantian Perspective," *Journal of Religious Ethics* 7, no. 2 (1979): 229–38, quote 229.
40. David Little and Sumner B. Twiss, *Comparative Religious Ethics: A New Method* (San Francisco: Harper and Row, 1978), 59–60.
41. H. L. A. Hart, *The Concept of Law* (Oxford: Oxford University Press, 1961).
42. Little and Twiss, *Comparative Religious Ethics*, 77.
43. Little and Twiss, *Comparative Religious Ethics*, 78.
44. Little and Twiss, *Comparative Religious Ethics*, 78.
45. Pardon the allusion to Alfred North Whitehead here.

Interlude

1. Christopher Fynsk, foreword to *The Inoperative Community*, by Jean-Luc Nancy, trans. Peter Connor, Lisa Garbus, Michael Holland, and Simona Sawhney (Minneapolis: University of Minnesota Press, 1991), x, xxxvii.
2. This paragraph and the three that preceded it were inspired by Wesley J. Wildman, *Science and Religious Anthropology: A Spiritually Evocative Naturalist Interpretation of Human Life* (London: Routledge, 2009), xv–32.
3. Nimi Wariboko, *Nigerian Pentecostalism* (Rochester, NY: Rochester University Press, 2014).
4. Wariboko, *Nigerian Pentecostalism*, 145–65.
5. The discussions that follow are indebted to Achille Mbembe, *On the Postcolony* (Berkeley: University of California Press, 2001).
6. Mbembe, *On the Postcolony*, 109.
7. See Max Weber, *Economy and Society: An Outline of Interpretive Sociology*, ed. Guenther Roth and Claus Wittich (Berkeley: University of California Press, 1978), 53.
8. Hannah Arendt, *On Violence* (New York: Harcourt Brace Javanovich, 1970), 44.

9. Nimi Wariboko, *The Depth and Destiny of Work: An African Theological Interpretation* (Trenton, NJ: Africa World Press, 2008), 37–39. See also Robin Horton, *Kalabari Sculpture* (Lagos: Department of Antiquities, Federal Republic of Nigeria, 1965), 6, 10, 29.

10. Pentecostalism has revealed a deep-seated hunger among Africans for national, continental, and racial dignity. But I wonder if religion is best situated to play this role.

11. Friedrich W. Nietzsche, *On the Genealogy of Morality: A Polemic*, trans. Maudemarie Clark and Alan. J. Swensen (Indianapolis: Hackett, 1998).

12. David Oyedepo, *Pillars of Destiny: Exploring the Secrets of an Ever-Winning Life* (Canaan Land, Nigeria: Dominion, 2008), 7.

13. Slavoj Žižek, *The Sublime Object of Ideology* (London: Verso, 2008), 45.

14. Slavoj Žižek, *The Plague of Fantasies* (London: Verso, 1997), 7.

15. Žižek, *Sublime Object*, 30–31.

16. Mbembe, *On the Postcolony*, 108–9.

17. The analysis here is indebted to Abed Azzam, *Nietzsche versus Paul* (New York: Columbia University Press, 2015), 32–33.

18. Wariboko, *Nigerian Pentecostalism*, 221–57.

19. Clifford Geertz, "Religion as a Cultural System," in *The Interpretation of Cultures: Selected Essays* (London: Fontana, 1993), 87–125.

20. Geertz, "Religion as a Cultural System," 90.

21. Geertz, "Religion as a Cultural System," 98, 123–24.

22. Geertz, "Religion as a Cultural System," 115.

23. Geertz, "Religion as a Cultural System," 100.

24. Pardon my resort to Paul Tillich's language here.

25. This interpretation of the sacred was inspired by Robert Cummings Neville, *Ultimates: Philosophical Theology*, vol. 1 (Albany: SUNY Press, 2013).

26. Achille Mbembe, *Critique of Black Reason*, trans. Laurent Dubois (Durham, NC: Duke University Press, 2017), 8.

27. Theodore Schatzki, *The Site of the Social: A Philosophical Account of the Constitution of Social Life and Change* (University Park: Pennsylvania State University Press, 2002), xi.

28. Wildman, *Science and Religious Anthropology*, 204.

29. Wildman, *Science and Religious Anthropology*, 197–99.

30. Though in many places in this book my analyses are informed by continental philosophy as the best hermeneutical tool for understanding or interpreting the African experience, it is only a tool ready at hand for me.

31. This way of articulating my ideas is indebted to Kristine Suna-Koro, *In Counterpoint: Diaspora, Postcoloniality, and Sacramental Theology* (Eugene, OR: Pickwick, 2017), 249.

32. Peter Paris, *The Spirituality of African Peoples: The Search for a Common Moral Discourse* (Minneapolis: Fortress, 1995), 39.

33. Wildman, Science and Religious Anthropology, 211.

1. The Sacred as Im/possibility

1. Hannah Arendt, *The Origins of Totalitarianism* (New York: Schocken Books, 2004), 616. I have adapted her words to serve my purpose here.

2. Richard Fenn, "Sociology and Religion: Searching for the Sacred," in *The Oxford Handbook of Religion and Science*, ed. Philip Clayton and Zachary Simpson (Oxford: Oxford University Press, 2006), 259 (italics in the original).

3. Nimi Wariboko, *The Depth and Destiny of Work: An African Theological Interpretation* (Trenton, NJ: Africa World Press, 2008), 37–39.

4. *Agu-nsi* is an Igbo word that has been adopted in Kalabari. The Kalabari word for a carved or sculptured idol is *ẹkẹkẹ-tamụnọ*, and *ẹkẹkẹ* means "stone," "piece of stone or rock."

5. Robin Horton, *Kalabari Sculpture* (Lagos: Department of Antiquities, Federal Republic of Nigeria, 1965), 8–9; see also Robin Horton, "The Kalabari Worldview: An Outline and Interpretation," *Africa* 32, no. 3 (July 1962): 204. Horton relates the story of how a spirit who misbehaved was summoned before an assembly of its worshippers, found guilty, and fined. Robin Horton, "A Hundred Years of Change in Kalabari Religion," in *Black Africa: Its People and Their Cultures Today*, ed. John Middleton (New York: Macmillan, 1971), 194–98.

6. Horton, "Kalabari Worldview," 204. I have heard of at least two cases of gods that have been disrobed of their powers. One is the *Owu Akpana* (shark) cult, and the other is the *Ogboloma* (called *Kun-ma* in Okrika, also a Niger Delta community) cult.

7. Richard Fenn, *The Return of the Primitive: A New Sociological Theory of Religion* (Aldershot, UK: Ashgate, 2001), 59.

8. Fenn, *Return of the Primitive*, 60.

9. Fenn, *Return of the Primitive*, 60.

10. From here on I am going to adapt Richard Fenn's theory of religion as elucidated in his "Sociology and Religion," 253–70.

11. Fenn, "Sociology and Religion," 258.

12. Fenn, "Sociology and Religion," 259.

13. Fenn, "Sociology and Religion," 257–58.

14. If a person does not like the course of his or her life on earth, he or she goes to a diviner to change the *so* or *fiyeteboye*. The process of changing destiny is called *bibibari* (altering or nullifying the spoken word, recanting). The person visits a diviner to let Teme-órú (the supreme goddess) know that the person would like to change how he or she wants to live his or her life course on earth. Once the change of destiny is effected, the new *so* (which becomes a new point of fixity) determines the whole course of the person.

15. Slavoj Žižek, *Event: A Philosophical Journey through a Concept* (London: Penguin Books, 2014), 128.

16. Slavoj Žižek, *The Most Sublime Hysteric: Hegel with Lacan*, trans. Thomas Scott-Railton (Malden, MA: Polity, 2014), 157.

17. I have borrowed the term "mindful ignorance" (*docta ignorantia*) from Catherine Keller. See her *Cloud of the Impossible: Negative Theology and Planetary Entanglement* (New York: Columbia University Press, 2014), 165. By the term, Keller, relying on Nicholas Cusa, refers to "not only the maximum mystery but the misty unknowns of all relations." Catherine Keller, "The Entangled Cosmos: An Experiment in Physical Theopoetics," *Journal of Cosmology* 20 (September 2012): 2.

18. Slavoj Žižek, *The Fragile Absolute: Or, Why Is the Christianity Legacy Worth Fighting For?* (London: Verso, 2008), 89.

19. Jacques Lacan, *The Ego in Freud's Theory and in the Technique of Psychoanalysis, 1954–1955*, bk. 2 of *The Seminar of Jacques Lacan*, ed. Jacques-Alain Miller, trans. Sylvana Tomaselli (New York: W. W. Norton, 1991), 229, quoted in Žižek, *Most Sublime Hysteric*, 64.

20. Slavoj Žižek, "Christianity against the Sacred," in *God in Pain: Inversions of Apocalypse*, by Slavoj Žižek and Boris Gunjević (New York: Seven Stories, 2012), 58.

21. This sentence was inspired by Slavoj Žižek, *The Parallax View* (Cambridge, MA: MIT Press, 2009), 67.

22. G. W. F. Hegel, *Elements of the Philosophy of Right* (Cambridge: Cambridge University Press, 1991), 204–5, quoted in Žižek, *Parallax View*, 66.
23. Jeffrey Kripal, *Authors of the Impossible: The Paranormal and the Sacred* (Chicago: University of Chicago Press, 2010), 9.
24. Kripal, *Authors of the Impossible*, 9.
25. Mark C. Taylor and Carl Racshke, "About *About Religion*: A Conversation with Mark C. Taylor," accessed June 14, 2015, http://www.jcrt.org/archives/02.2/taylor_raschke.shtml, 2.
26. Taylor and Racshke, "About *About Religion*," 3.
27. Keller, *Cloud of the Impossible*.
28. I need to clarify this interpretation of her thinking. As a follower of Alfred North Whitehead, she will agree that in abstract form possibilities do function as "external objects," but as real possibilities/potentialities, they carry the relational density of the past.
29. Keller, *Cloud of the Impossible*, 188–92, quote on 188, see also 131–32, 145, 152–53, 164–65.
30. Keller, *Cloud of the Impossible*, 145.
31. Catherine Keller, *Face of the Deep: A Theology of Becoming* (London: Routledge, 2003).
32. Catherine Keller's preferred term is *Resolute*, not the Hegelian *Absolute*. It is a third place between Absolute and "Dissolute." See Keller, *On the Mystery: Discerning God in Process* (Minneapolis: Fortress, 2008), 173–76.
33. Keller, *Cloud of the Impossible*, 146. She is citing Charles Hartshrone here.
34. Slavoj Žižek, *In Defense of Lost Causes* (London: Verso, 2009), 140.
35. Slavoj Žižek, *Absolute Recoil: Towards a New Foundation of Dialectical Materialism* (London: Verso, 2014), 33. Žižek adds, "What characterizes a really great thinker is that they misrecognize the basic dimension of their own breakthrough" (34).
36. Keller, *Cloud of the Impossible*, 17.
37. Here I am applying the distinctions of Jacques-Alain Miller, "Le nom-du-père, s'en passer, s'en servir," https://www.lacan.com, quoted in Slavoj Žižek, *Defense of Lost Causes*, 327.
38. Žižek, *Defense of Lost Causes*, 327; see also Slavoj Žižek, *Less Than Nothing: Hegel and the Shadow of Dialectical Materialism* (London: Verso, 2012), 496.
39. Keller, *Cloud of the Impossible*, 148–50.
40. Keller, *Cloud of the Impossible*, 157.
41. The latter—no underlying oneness—more precisely represents the overall focus of her theological and philosophical thought over the years. For her, creativity would not be the One.
42. For the meaning of *en*, see Keller, *Cloud of the Impossible*, 177, 191. See also Keller, *Face of the Deep*.
43. In (en)? As we have shown earlier, the realm of the sacred exceeds what is religiously, doctrinally, and institutionally referred to as theistic God.
44. Nimi Wariboko, *The Pentecostal Principle: Ethical Methodology in New Spirit* (Grand Rapids, MI: Eerdmans, 2012), x, 131, 151, 186, 203.
45. See also Žižek, "Christianity against the Sacred," 50, where he relies on Giorgio Agamben to make the same point, that the profane is inherent to the sacred.
46. Giorgio Agamben, *Profanations*, trans. Jeff Fort (New York: Zone Books, 2007), 75.
47. Quentin Meillassoux, "Potentiality and Virtuality," *Collapse: Philosophic Research and Development* 2 (2007): 71–72.
48. Meillassoux, "Potentiality and Virtuality," 74.
49. Meillassoux, "Potentiality and Virtuality," 72.

50. Meillassoux, "Potentiality and Virtuality," 73n7.
51. Žižek, *Less Than Nothing*, 230.
52. Keller, *Cloud of the Impossible*, 138–42, 150–51. She certainly understands relationalism to be largely—but never entirely—subject to regulation. This is why she argues against intervention ex nihilo in her work.
53. For an excellent discussion of real presence, see Annalisa Butticci, *African Pentecostals in Catholic Europe: The Politics of Presence in the Twenty-First Century* (Cambridge, MA: Harvard University Press, 2016).
54. Gilles Deleuze, *The Logic of Sense*, trans. Mark Lester with Charles Stivale (New York: Columbia University Press, 1990).
55. Deleuze, *Logic of Sense*, 7.
56. Butticci, *Politics of Presence*.
57. Žižek, *Less Than Nothing*, 608.
58. In a different interpretation of her work, one could say that she overrides the distinction between the phenomenal and the noumenal through her focus on the materiality of human relationality. The inaccessibility of *Ding an sich* is not the apophatic for her, but the depth and margin of entanglement between things may be. But she does not trust anyone's claim to know the thing in itself, to master pure presence epistemically. She only respects conjectures and vivid, transformative glimpses, breakthroughs and breakouts. But she does not respect epistemic mastery of the mystery.
59. Žižek, *Less Than Nothing*, 609.
60. Alain Badiou, *Theoretical Writings* (London: Continuum, 2004), 43.
61. Alain Badiou, *Being and Event*, trans. Oliver Feltham (London: Continuum, 2005).
62. In the language or manner of Keller's thought, we should suspect any prophet who claims to have perceived the "full ply of possibilities," as in all of the Sacred.
63. Fenn, "Sociology and Religion," 259.
64. Meillassoux, "Potentiality and Virtuality," 67.
65. Meillassoux, "Potentiality and Virtuality," 73.
66. Meillassoux, "Potentiality and Virtuality," 69.
67. Meillassoux, "Potentiality and Virtuality," 73n7. The virtualizing power of time, its insubordination to any superior order, lets itself be known, or is phenomenalized, when there emerges a novelty that defeats all continuity between the past and the present. Every "miracle" thus becomes the manifestation of the inexistence of God, insofar as every radical rupture of the present in relation to the past becomes the manifestation of the absence of any order capable of overseeing the chaotic power of becoming.
68. There is, perhaps, what we may call a *Pentecostal unconscious* that has deep relations to the scared as the full plenum of possibilities along with its chaotic depths. The unconscious itself has been symbolized as an ocean, an oceanic plenum.

2. Demons as Guests

1. Nimi Wariboko, "West African Pentecostalism: A Survey of Everyday Theology," in *Global Renewal Christianity: Spirit-Empowered Movements, Past, Present and Future, Africa and Diaspora*, ed. Vinson Synan, Amos Yong, and Kwabena Asamoah-Gyadu (Lake Mary, FL: Charisma House, 2016), 1–18.
2. Nimi Wariboko, *The Split God: Pentecostalism and Critical Theory* (Albany: SUNY University Press, 2018), 133–53.

3. Wariboko, *Split God*, 133–53.
4. See chapter 1 of this book. See also Wariboko, *Split God*, 83–110.
5. Here I have borrowed the words of Shelly Rambo, *Spirit and Trauma: A Theology of Remaining* (Louisville: Westminster John Knox, 2010), 8; Serene Jones, *Feminist Theory and Christian Theology: Cartographies of Grace* (Minneapolis: Augsburg Fortress, 2000), 19.
6. Peter van der Veer, *The Value of Comparison* (Durham, NC: Duke University Press, 2016), 1–47.
7. Birgit Meyer, "Aesthetics of Persuasion: Global Christianity and Pentecostalism's Sensational Forms," *South Atlantic Quarterly* 109, no. 4 (2010): 741–63; Annalisa Butticci, *The Politics of Presence: African Pentecostalism and Roman Catholicism in the Twenty-First Century* (Cambridge, MA: Harvard University Press, 2016).
8. Meyer, "Aesthetics of Persuasion," 742 (italics in the original).
9. Meyer, "Aesthetics of Persuasion," 754.
10. Annalisa Butticci, "Crazy World, Crazy Faith! Prayer, Power and Transformation in a Nigerian Prayer City," *Annual Review of Sociology of Religion* 4 (2013): 254.
11. Butticci, "Crazy World," 256.
12. Steven Félix-Jäger, *Pentecostal Aesthetics: Theological Reflection in a Pentecostal Philosophy of Arts and Aesthetics* (Leiden: Brill, 2015).
13. Ashon T. Crawley, *Blackpentecostal Breath: Aesthetics of Possibility* (New York: Fordham University Press, 2016).
14. Daniel Olukoya, *Prayer Rain* (Lagos: Mountain of Fire and Miracles Ministries, 1999), 589 (italics added).
15. Daniel Olukoya, *Pray Your Way into 2016 and Prosperity Night Day Prayers* (Lagos: Mountain of Fire and Miracles Ministries, 2015), 14.
16. David Abram, *The Spell of the Sensuous* (New York: Vintage Books, 1996), 124, also 123–28.
17. Abram, *Spell of the Sensuous*, 125.
18. Abram, *Spell of the Sensuous*, 125.
19. Robin Horton, "The Kalabari Worldview: An Outline and Interpretation," *Africa* 32, no. 3 (July 1962): 204.
20. Nimi Wariboko, *The Pentecostal Principle: Ethical Methodology in New Spirit* (Grand Rapids, MI: Eerdmans, 2012), 67.
21. C. S. Lewis, *The Screwtape Letters* (New York: HarperOne, 2015). You could not call yourself born-again in Nigeria during the 1980s and 1990s unless you had read this book. It was that influential.
22. Robin Horton, *The Gods as Guests: An Aspect of Kalabari Religious Life* (Lagos: Nigerian Magazine, 1960).
23. Max Weber, "Religious Rejections of the World and Their Directions," in *From Max Weber: Essays in Sociology*, ed. H. H. Gerth and C. Wright Mills (London: Routledge and Kegan Paul, 1970), 323–59.
24. Jacques Rancière, *Disagreement: Politics and Philosophy*, trans. Julie Rose (Minneapolis: University of Minnesota Press, 1998). See also Jacques Rancière, *Dissensus: On Politics and Aesthetics*, ed. and trans. by Steven Corcoran (London: Continuum, 2010).
25. Meyer, "Aesthetics of Persuasion," 741–63.
26. Mark C. Taylor, *Confidence Games: Money and Markets in a World without Redemption* (Chicago: University of Chicago Press, 2004), 5.
27. Wariboko, *Split God*, 133–53.

28. Wariboko, *Split God*, 136.
29. Wariboko, *Split God*, 136.
30. Pentecostals sing, "My God is bigger than all my problems."
31. Pardon the allusion to the opening three sentences of Karl Marx and Friedrich Engels, *The Communist Manifesto* (Chicago: Charles H. Kerr and Company, 1912/1848).
32. Giorgio Agamben, *The Use of Bodies*, trans. Adam Kotsko (Stanford, CA: Stanford University Press, 2015), 81.
33. Walter Benjamin, "Notes toward a Work on the Category of Justice," trans. Peter Fenves in his *The Messianic Reduction: Walter Benjamin and the Shape of Time* (Stanford, CA: Stanford University Press, 2011), 257, quoted in Agamben, *Use of Bodies*, 81.
34. Richard Fenn, "Sociology and Religion: Searching for the Sacred," in *The Oxford Handbook of Religion and Science*, ed. Philip Clayton and Zachary Simpson (Oxford: Oxford University Press, 2006), 259.
35. On Pentecostalism and possibilities/new creation, see Wariboko, *Pentecostal Principle*.

3. The Pentecostal Incredible

This chapter was originally presented Friday, May 24, 2019, as "Governance as Trauma in Nigeria: Turning Evangelicalism into Pentecostal Incredible," at a conference on "Evangelical Christianity and the Transformation of Africa," Radcliffe Institute for Advanced Study at Harvard University, Cambridge, MA, May 23–24, 2019. Thanks to Professor Jacob Olupona, Harvard University, for facilitating my invitation to this conference.

1. Tejumola Olaniyan, *Arrest the Music! Fela and His Rebel Art and Politics* (Bloomington: Indiana University Press, 2004), 2.
2. This section is a slightly revised version of portions of chapter 4 of Nimi Wariboko, *Ethics and Society: Identity, History, and Political Theory* (Rochester, NY: University of Rochester Press, 2019), 73–97.
3. Shelly Rambo, *Spirit and Trauma: A Theology of Remaining* (Louisville, KY: Westminster John Knox, 2010).
4. Rambo, *Spirit and Trauma*, 20.
5. Wariboko, *Ethics and Society*, 19–34.
6. William T. Cavanaugh, *Torture and Eucharist* (Malden, MA: Blackwell, 1998).
7. Rambo, *Spirit and Trauma*, 20.
8. Dominick LaCapra, *Writing History, Writing Trauma* (Baltimore: Johns Hopkins University Press, 2001), 82.
9. Achille Mbembe, *On the Postcolony* (Berkeley: University of California Press, 2001), 13.
10. Hannah Arendt, *Between Past and Future: Eight Exercises in Political Thought* (New York: Penguin Books, 1968), 11.
11. This section is a slightly revised version of portions of chapter 4 of Wariboko, *Ethics and Society*, 73–97.
12. Olaniyan, *Arrest the Music*, 90.
13. This way of linking the dialogue to the moral situation of Nigeria was inspired by Hugh Hodges, "No, This Is Not Redemption: The Biafra War Legacy in Chris Abani's *GraceLand*," in *Writing the Nigeria-Biafra War*, ed. Toyin Falola and Ogechukwu Ezekwem (New York: James Currey, 2016), 380–99.
14. Chris Abani, *GraceLand* (New York: Farrar, Straus and Giroux, 2004), 147, 190.

15. Paul L. Lehman, *Ethics in a Christian Context* (Eugene, OR: Wipf and Stock, 1998), 24–25.
16. Jacques Rancière, *Dissensus: On Politics and Aesthetics*, ed. and trans. Steven Corcoran (London: Continuum, 2010), 184.
17. Abani, *GraceLand*, 306.
18. Olaniyan, *Arrest the Music*, 90.
19. Olaniyan, *Arrest the Music*, 96.
20. Olaniyan, *Arrest the Music*, 96.
21. Mbembe, *On the Postcolony*, 13.
22. Olaniyan, *Arrest the Music*, 2.
23. Cavanaugh, *Torture and Eucharist*.
24. Abani, *GraceLand*, 58.
25. The concept and discussion that follow were inspired by Patrick Chabal and Jean-Pascal Daloz, *Africa Works: Disorder as Political Instrument* (Oxford: James Currey, 1999).
26. See Luke Bretherton, *Christ and the Common Life: Political Theology and the Case for Democracy* (Grand Rapids, MI: Eerdmans, 2019).
27. Nimi Wariboko, "Pentecostal Paradigms of National Economic Prosperity in Africa," in *Pentecostalism and Prosperity: The Socio-economics of the Global Charismatic Movement*, Christianities of the World 1, ed. Amos Yong and Katy Attanasi (New York: Palgrave Macmillan, 2012), 35–59.
28. See Nimi Wariboko, *The Pentecostal Hypothesis: Christ Talks, They Decide* (Eugene, OR: Cascade Books, 2020).
29. Slavoj Žižek, *Violence: Six Sideways Reflections* (New York: Picador, 2008), 12–13.
30. This way of expressing my ideas was inspired by Žižek, *Violence*, 96.
31. Žižek, *Violence*, 136.
32. Žižek, *Violence*, 137.
33. Žižek inspired this paragraph, and I have borrowed his phrasing to express my ideas here in ways that he might not agree with. See Žižek, *Violence*, 170–71.
34. Cheryl Kirk-Duggan, *Exorcizing Evil: A Womanist Perspective on the Spirituals* (Maryknoll, NY: Orbis Books, 1997), 132.
35. We will come back to this claim and reassess it in the subsection where I discuss Paul Tillich's theorization of reason and emotionalism in Christian faith.
36. Richard K. Fenn, *Liturgies and Trials: The Secularization of Religious Language* (Oxford: Basil Blackwell, 1982), 71–78.
37. Robin Horton, *Patterns of Thought in Africa and the West: Essays on Magic, Religion and Science* (Cambridge: Cambridge University Press, 1993), 239.
38. Nimi Wariboko, *God and Money: A Theology of Money in a Globalizing World* (Lanham, MD: Lexington Books, 2008).
39. Nimi Wariboko, *The Split God: Pentecostalism and Critical Theory* (Albany: SUNY University Press, 2018).
40. Slavoj Žižek, *Less Than Nothing: Hegel and the Shadow of Dialectical Materialism* (London: Verso, 2012), 166.
41. Bretherton, *Christ and the Common Life*, 54.
42. Bretherton, *Christ and the Common Life*, 455.
43. Elias K. Bongmba, "What Has Kinshasa to Do with Athen? Methodological Perspective on Theology and Social Sciences in Search for a Political Theology," in *Faith in African Lived Christianity*, ed. Karen Lauterbach and Mika Vahakangas (Leiden, Netherlands: Brill, 2019), 195–223, quotation 213.

44. For an excellent critique of Bretherton's kind of approach to political theory that emphasizes the administration and coordination of interests rather than the irruptions and disruptions of politics, see Bonnie Honig, *Political Theory and the Displacement of Politics* (Ithaca, NY: Cornell University Press, 1993).

45. Here I am making an allusion to Delores S. Williams, "The Color of Feminism, or Speaking the Black Woman Tongue," in *Feminist Theological Ethics: A Reader*, ed. Lois K. Daly (Louisville: Westminster John Knox, 1994), 42–58.

46. In response to my essay, Bretherton has responded to some of these issues for a symposium on his book published by Syndicate, an online academic discussion forum, which is available at https://syndicate.network/symposia/theology/christ-and-the-common-life/.

47. Slavoj Žižek, *Violence*, 140. See also Honig, *Political Theory*.

48. For a detailed explanation of this ethics, see Nimi Wariboko, *Economics in Spirit and Truth: A Moral Philosophy of Finance* (New York: Palgrave Macmillan, 2014).

49. This is not to say that the version they have worked out is exactly benefiting them; nonetheless, it is a starting point for academic study.

50. Nimi Wariboko, *The Pentecostal Principle: Ethical Methodology in New Spirit* (Grand Rapids, MI: Eerdmans, 2012), 3–4, 25–26, 151–54; Wariboko, *Economics in Spirit and Truth*, xvi, 166.

51. Existential distortion is a distortion that penetrates into and affects the very existence of human beings or nations. See Paul Tillich, *Dynamics of Faith* (New York: Perennial Classic, 2001), 13.

52. Paul Tillich, *Systematic Theology*, vol. 1, *Reason and Revelation, Being, and God* (Chicago, University of Chicago Press, 1951), 72–77.

53. Tillich, *Systematic Theology*, 1:72.

54. Tillich, *Systematic Theology*, 1:90–92.

55. Tillich, *Systematic Theology*, 1:93.

56. Tillich, *Systematic Theology*, 1:93.

57. Tillich, *Dynamics of Faith*, 7.

58. Tillich, *Dynamics of Faith*, 133.

59. Tillich, *Dynamics of Faith*, 133.

60. Paul Tillich, *The Courage to Be* (New Haven, CT: Yale University Press, 2014), 39.

61. Tillich, *Courage to Be*, 39.

62. Tillich, *Courage to Be*, 39.

63. Tillich, *Courage to Be*, 139.

64. Tillich, *Courage to Be*, 138.

65. Tillich, *Courage to Be*, 138.

66. Tillich, *Courage to Be*, 138.

67. This paragraph was inspired by Tillich, *Courage to Be*, 141.

68. Tillich, *Courage to Be*, 136.

69. This paragraph is indebted to Tillich, *Dynamics of Faith*, 21–24.

70. Roberto Esposito, *Communitas: The Origin and Destiny of Community* (Stanford, CA: Stanford University Press, 2010), 139. I have with infinite liberty transposed Espositos's words about community to serve my purpose about promise.

71. This paragraph, including both the ideas and their phrasing, is inspired by Esposito, *Communitas*, 136–39.

72. Esposito, *Communitas*, 137.

73. I have manipulated Esposito's ideas about community to make my point here. See Esposito, *Communitas*, 136–39.
74. Jürgen Moltmann, *Theology of Hope* (Minneapolis: Fortress, 1993), 94–143.
75. Hannah Arendt, *The Human Condition*, 2nd ed. (Chicago: University of Chicago Press, 1998).
76. Bonnie Honig, *Emergency Politics: Paradox, Law and Democracy* (Princeton, NJ: Princeton University Press, 2009), 83–103.
77. Honig, *Emergency Politics*, 94.
78. Please pardon my excessive allusions to William Butler Yeats's poem "The Second Coming."
79. Bonnie Honig, *Political Theory and the Displacement of Politics* (Ithaca, NY: Cornell University Press, 1993), 194.
80. For the difference between virtue and *virtù*, see Honig, *Political Theory*, 1–17.
81. Honig, *Political Theory*, 2.
82. Honig, *Political Theory*, 15.
83. Arendt, *Human Condition*, 246–47.

4. Production of Violence in the Postcolony

1. Elaine Scarry, *Body in Pain: The Making and Unmaking of the World* (Oxford: Oxford University Press, 1985).
2. Jason K. Stearns, *Dancing in the Glory of Monsters: The Collapse of the Congo and the Great War of Africa* (New York: Public Affairs, 2012), 34–35.
3. Stearns, *Dancing in the Glory of Monsters*, 37.
4. Mahmood Mamdani, *When Victims Become Killers: Colonialism, Nativism, and the Genocide in Rwanda* (Princeton, NJ: Princeton University Press, 2001), 3.
5. Susan O'Brien, "Spirit Discipline: Gender, Islam, and Hierarchies of Treatment in Postcolonial Northern Nigeria," in *Discipline and the Other Body: Correction, Corporeality, Colonialism*, ed. Steven Pierce and Anupama Rao (Durham, NC: Duke University Press, 2006), 273–302, quotation 286–87.
6. Bjørn Enge Bertelsen, *Violent Becomings: State Formation, Sociality, and Power in Mozambique* (New York: Berghahn Books, 2016), 20–23.
7. Bertelsen, *Violent Becomings*, 22.
8. Bertelsen, *Violent Becomings*, 9–10.
9. Bertelsen, *Violent Becomings*, 22.
10. Laurent Magesa, *What Is Not Sacred? African Spirituality* (Maryknoll, NY: Orbis Books, 2013), 32 (italics in the original).
11. Magesa, *What Is Not Sacred*, 32 (italics added), see also 172.
12. Nimi Wariboko, *The Split God: Pentecostalism and Critical Theory* (Albany: SUNY Press, 2018), 83–110.
13. Here I am going to adapt the theory of religion as elucidated in Richard Fenn, "Sociology and Religion: Searching for the Sacred," in *The Oxford Handbook of Religion and Science*, ed. Philip Clayton and Zachary Simpson (Oxford: Oxford University Press, 2006), 253–70.
14. For an important insight into the disorder of the postcolony in Africa and elsewhere, see Jean Comaroff and John L. Comaroff, *Law and Disorder in the Postcolony* (Chicago: University of Chicago Press, 2006); for Africa, see especially the chapters by Peter Geschiere,

"Witchcraft and the Limits of the Law: Cameroun and South Africa," 219–46; Janet Roitman, "The Ethics of Illegality in the Chad Basin," 247–72.

15. This paragraph is indebted to Nimi Wariboko, *Ethics and Society in Nigeria: Identity, History, Political Theory* (Rochester, NY: University of Rochester Press, 2019), 73–97.

16. Abubakar Shekau, "Message to President Jonathan," YouTube, January 2012, https://www.youtube.com/watch?v=umjk5oSUzck, quoted in Alexander Thurston, *Boko Haram: The History of an African Jihadist Movement* (Princeton, NJ: Princeton University Press, 2018), 160.

17. Thurston, *Boko Haram*, 183.

18. This way of expressing my ideas was inspired by Catherine Keller, *Political Theology of the Earth: Our Planetary Emergency and the Struggle for a New Public* (New York: Columbia University Press, 2018), 80.

19. Keller, *Political Theology of the Earth*, 48.

20. "What distinguishes our age from the previous ages, the breach over which there is apparently no going back is existence that is contingent, dispersed, but reveals itself in the guise of arbitrariness and the absolute power to give death any time, anywhere, by any means, and for any reason." Achille Mbembe, *On the Postcolony* (Berkeley: University of California Press, 2001), 13.

21. Mbembe, *On the Postcolony*, 110.

22. For a history of violence and the Nigerian state, see Toyin Falola, *Violence in Nigeria: The Crisis of Religious Politics and Secular Ideologies* (Rochester, NY: University of Rochester Press, 1998); Toyin Falola, *Colonialism and Violence in Nigeria* (Bloomington: Indiana University Press, 2009).

23. Stearns, *Dancing in the Glory of Monsters*, 328. For an analysis of the crisis of the state in Africa, see relevant sections of Bruce Kapferer and Bjørn E. Bertelsen, eds., *Crisis of the State: War and Social Upheaval* (New York: Berghahn Books, 2009); Leo Panitch and Colin Leys, eds., *Fighting Identities: Race, Religion, and Ethno-nationalism* (London: Merlin, 2002).

24. Timothy Longman, *Memory and Justice in Post-genocide Rwanda* (Cambridge: Cambridge University Press, 2017), 4.

25. Longman, *Memory and Justice*, 68.

26. Emmanuel Katongole, *Born from Lament: The Theology and Politics of Hope in Africa* (Grand Rapids, MI: Eerdmans, 2017), 12.

27. Stearns, *Dancing in the Glory of Monsters*, 244.

28. Katongole, *Born from Lament*, 12–13. For an exemplary study of the significance of kings and other community leaders for the maintenance of peace and prevention of violence in their communities, see Simon Simonse, *Kings of Disaster: Dualism, Centralism and the Scapegoat King in Southeastern Sudan* (Kampala, Uganda: Fountain, 2017), 281, 289, 296–97, 345–46.

29. Stearns, *Dancing in the Glory of Monsters*, 244.

30. Stearns, *Dancing in the Glory of Monsters*, 256.

31. Stearns, *Dancing in the Glory of Monsters*, 257.

32. Karl Marx and Friedrich Engels, *The Communist Manifesto* (Chicago: Charles H. Kerr and Company, 1912/1848), 2.

33. Katongole, *Born from Lament*, 77.

34. This paragraph and the next were inspired by Gustav Mahler's song "Nun will die sonn," as translated by Martha C. Nussbaum, *Upheavals of Thought: The Intelligence of Emotions* (Cambridge: Cambridge University Press, 2001), 293–94.

35. Mahler, "Nun will die sonn," 294.

36. This paragraph is informed by Slavoj Žižek, *Violence* (New York: Picardo, 2008), 198–99.

37. See Eric Santner, *On the Psychotheology of Everyday Life* (Chicago: University of Chicago Press, 2001).

38. Žižek, *Violence*, 200.

39. Lest any reader think that this form of violence is peculiar to Black Africans, let me state that the roots of it are in the slave trade, colonialism, neocolonialism, and global capitalism.

5. Chosenness, Spirituality, and the Weight of Blackness

1. For a study of the "choseness" in three monotheistic religions—Judaism, Christianity, and Islam—see Avi Beker, *The Chosen: The History of an Idea, and the Anatomy of an Obsession* (New York: Palgrave Macmillan, 2008). It is often linked to the doctrine of the supersessionism and replacement of Isreal (Jews) or any other nation that lays claim to the title of chosenness.

2. Pastor Tony Rapu leads This Present Church.

3. A longer version of the fragment of the sermon is available on request.

4. The sermon was transcribed by my daughter Bele Wariboko of Westwood, Massachusetts, on October 12, 2011.

5. David Theo Goldberg, *The Threat of Race: Reflections on Racial Neoliberalism* (Oxford: Wiley-Blackwell, 2009), 8–9.

6. Matthew Ashimolowo, *What Is Wrong with Being Black? Celebrating Our Heritage, Confronting Our Challenges* (Shippensburg, PA: Destiny Image, 2007).

7. Ashimolowo, *What Is Wrong with Being Black?*, 63–93, 142.

8. Ashimolowo, *What Is Wrong with Being Black?*, 7.

9. Atei Beredugo, email interview, June 23, 2011.

10. Beredugo, email interview, June 23, 2011.

11. Beredugo, email interview, June 23, 2011.

12. Beredugo, email interview, June 23, 2011.

13. Paul Adefarasin said this in a sermon on salt as the change agent at the 9:15 a.m. service on July 24, 2011.

14. Michael O. Ojewale, *A Call to Prayer for Nigeria* (Lagos: Peace and Salvation, 1990), 35, 36–37.

15. Ruth Marshall, *Political Spiritualities: The Pentecostal Revolution in Nigeria* (Chicago: University of Chicago Press, 2009), 125.

16. Kevin Lewis O'Neil, *City of God: Christian Citizenship in Postwar Guatemala* (Berkeley: University of California Press, 2010).

17. O'Neil, *City of God*, 5.

18. See Nimi Wariboko, "Pentecostal Paradigms of National Prosperity in Africa," in *Pentecostalism and Prosperity: The Socio-economics of the Global Charismatic Movement*, Christianities of the World 1, ed. Amos Yong and Katy Attanasi (New York: Palgrave Macmillan, 2012), 35–59.

19. This kind of geocentrism is common in religions. It came to acquire a special name, the "omphalos" myth. This is the idea that "one's city or country of origin lay at the center or 'navel' [omphalos] of the world. . . . This geocentrism is found in both pagan and Jewish sources. To the Greeks, Delphi was the center or navel of the universe. . . . The author of

Jubilees makes the same claim for Jerusalem. . . . Philo of Alexandria makes a similar claim for Jerusalem." Mikeal C. Parson, *Body and Characters in Luke and Acts: The Subversion of Physiognomy in Early Christianity* (Waco, TX: Baylor University Press, 2011), 24–25.

20. Atei Beredugo, face-to-face and email interviews, June 2010 and June 2011.

21. Ogbu Uke Kalu, *Religions in Africa: Conflicts, Politics and Social Ethics*, ed. Wilhelmina J. Kalu, Nimi Wariboko, and Toyin Falola (Trenton: Africa World Press, 2010), 25.

22. Atei Beredugo, *The Mandate, the Man and the Message*, campaign brochure, Port Harcourt, Nigeria, 2010.

23. Michael Hardt and Antonio Negri, *Commonwealth* (Cambridge, MA: Harvard University Press, 2009), 32, 31.

24. Hardt and Negri, *Commonwealth*, 34.

25. Hardt and Negri, *Commonwealth*, 33.

26. Hardt and Negri, *Commonwealth*, 32.

27. I have traced this development in Nimi Wariboko, *Nigerian Pentecostalism* (Rochester, NY: University of Rochester Press, 2014), 221–57.

28. See J. Cameron Carter, *Race: A Theological Account* (Oxford: Oxford University Press, 2008); Willie James Jennings, *The Christian Imagination: Theology and the Origins of Race* (New Haven, CT: Yale University Press, 2010).

29. Carter, *Race*, 311.

30. Carter, *Race*, 309. This and the earlier quotations are from this page.

31. Carter, *Race*, 309.

32. Brian Bantum, *Redeeming Mulatto: A Theology of Race and Christian Hybridity* (Waco, TX: Baylor University Press, 2010).

33. Jennings, *Christian Imagination*, 58, 59, 63, 64, 289–90.

34. On the connection between Pentecostalism and the human capacity to begin something new, see Nimi Wariboko, *The Pentecostal Principle: Ethical Methodology in New Spirit* (Grand Rapids, MI: Eerdmans, 2012).

35. Michel Foucault, *Society Must Be Defended: Lectures at the College of France, 1975–1976* (New York: Picador, 1997), 237.

36. Foucault, *Society Must Be Defended*, 237.

6. Disruption and Promise

1. Joseph A. Bracken, *The Divine Matrix: Creativity as Link between East and West* (Delhi: Motilal Banarsidass, 1997), 19.

2. Richard Fenn, "Sociology and Religion: Searching for the Sacred," in *The Oxford Handbook of Religion and Science*, ed. Philip Clayton and Zachary Simpson (Oxford: Oxford University Press, 2006), 259 (italics in the original). See also Nimi Wariboko, *The Split God: Pentecostalism and Critical Theory* (Albany: SUNY University Press, 2018), 83–110.

3. Karl Marx and Frederick Engels, *The Communist Manifesto* (Chicago: Charles H. Kerr and Company, 1912).

4. Max Weber, *The Protestant Ethics and the Spirit of Capitalism*, trans. Talcott Parsons (London: Routledge, 1992).

5. Joseph Schumpeter, *Capitalism, Socialism, and Democracy* (New York: Harper and Row, 1942).

6. Hannah Arendt, *The Human Condition* (Chicago: University of Chicago Press, 1958).

7. Jean-Marie Dru, *Thank You for Disrupting: The Disruptive Business Philosophies of the World's Great Entrepreneurs* (Hoboken, NJ: John Wiley and Sons, 2019).

8. Rudolf Otto, *The Idea of the Holy: An Inquiry into the Non-rational Factor in the Idea of the Divine and Its Relation to the Rational* (Oxford: Oxford University Press, 1923).

9. For a definition of economy as "making provision for the future," see Nimi Wariboko, *The Split Economy: Saint Paul Goes to Wall Street* (Albany: SUNY University Press, 2020), 1–48.

10. Claude Ake, *Democracy and Development in Africa* (Washington, DC: Brookings Institution, 1996), 9.

11. Ake, *Democracy and Development*, 6, 7.

12. Ake, *Democracy and Development*, 7.

13. Summer Aku, "Nigerian Pastors Unite against Daddy Freeze: The Full Compilation of Pastors' Response s(Tithe Drama)," Summer Aku Vlogs, YouTube, April 18, 2018, https://www.youtube.com/watch?v=KzB2l3J-q38.

14. BellaNaija, "Pay Your Tithes Willingly and Not out of Fear—Bishop Mike Okonkwo," March 7, 2018, https://www.bellanaija.com/2018/03/pay-tithes-willingly-mike-okonkwo/.

15. I wish to acknowledge the assistance of Dr. Abimbola A. Adelakun in helping me to track down newspaper reports and online sources about the controversy.

16. Kehinde Olatunji, "You Have Talked about COZA, Now Talk about RUGA, Charly Boy, Other Protestors Urge Adeboye," *Guardian*, July 9, 2019, https://guardian.ng/news/you-have-talked-about-coza-now-talk-about-ruga-charly-boy-other-protesters-urge-adeboye/.

17. Victor Aselebe, "COZA: Pastor Adeboye Stirs Reactions Online with Comments," *Newswatch*, July 6, 2019, https://www.newswatch.ng/coza-pastor-adeboye-stirs-reactions-online-with-comments/.

18. Sahara Reporters, "Remember Samson and Delilah, Pastor Adeboye Warns Church Ministers While Speaking on Rape Scandal of COZA Fatoyinbo, Busola Dakolo," July 6, 2019, http://saharareporters.com/2019/07/06/remember-samson-and-delilah-pastor-adeboye-warns-church-ministers-while-speaking-rape.

19. Ike Uchechukwu, "Tithing Is a Scriptural Injunction, Mandatory, but Not Compulsory—Bishop Isong," Vanguard Nigeria, *Vanguard*, December 26, 2017, https://www.vanguardngr.com/2017/12/tithing-scriptural-injunction-mandatory-not-compulsory-bishop-isong/.

20. Femi Ibirogha et al., "Adeboye Leads 'Prayer Walk' as Christians Protest against Insecurity," *Guardian*, February 3, 2020, https://guardian.ng/news/adeboye-leads-prayer-walk-as-christians-protest-against-insecurity/.

21. Slavoj Žižek, *Event: A Philosophical Journey through a Concept* (London: Penguin Books, 2014), 70.

22. Wariboko, *Split God*, 128; see also William E. Connolly, *Capitalism and Christianity: American Style* (Durham, NC: Duke University Press, 2008).

23. Abimbola A. Adelakun, *Performing Power in Nigeria: Identity, Politics, and Pentecostalism* (Cambridge: Cambridge University Press, 2021). This brilliant book is partly a study of the emerging dissensus among Nigerian Pentecostals through the lens of performance studies.

24. Žižek, *Event*, 132.

25. James C. Scott, *Domination and the Arts of Resistance: Hidden Transcripts* (New Haven, CT: Yale University Press, 1990); James C. Scott, *Weapons of the Weak: Everyday Forms of Peasant Resistance* (New Haven, CT: Yale University Press, 1985).

26. Nimi Wariboko, "Christian-Muslim Relations and the Ethos of State Formation in West Africa," in *Dynamics of the Muslim Worlds: Regional, Theological, and Theological Perspectives*, ed. Evelyn Reisacher (Downers Grove, IL: IVP Academic, 2017), 57–81.

27. Ebenezer Obadare, *Pentecostal Republic: Religion and the Struggle for State Power in Nigeria* (London: Zed Books, 2018).

28. Žižek, *Event*, 119–20.

29. Nimi Wariboko, *The Pentecostal Principle: Ethical Methodology in New Spirit* (Grand Rapids, MI: Eerdmans, 2012).

30. Giorgio Agamben, *The Time That Remains: A Commentary on the Letter to the Romans*, trans. Patricia Dailey (Stanford, CA: Stanford University Press, 2005).

31. Agamben, *Time That Remains*, 23–24; see also Wariboko, *Pentecostal Principle*, 198–203.

32. Agamben, *Time That Remains*, 54–55.

33. This way of putting the matter was influenced by Ezra Delahaye, "About Chronos and Kairos: On Agamben's Interpretation of Pauline Temporality through Heidegger," *International Journal of Philosophy and Theology* 77, no. 3 (2016): 85–101.

34. Delahaye, "About Chronos and Kairos," 89.

35. Robin Horton, "A Hundred Years of Change in Kalabari Religion," in *Black Africa: Its People and Their Cultures Today*, ed. John Middleton (New York: Macmillan, 1971), 192–211.

36. Lewis S. Ford, *The Lure of God: A Biblical Background for Process Theism* (Philadelphia: Fortress, 1978), 63–66, 71–79, 100–101.

37. Paul Tillich, *Systematic Theology: Existence and the Christ* (Chicago: University of Chicago Press, 1957), 2:80, 119, 133–37, 150–53.

38. Paul Eisenstein and Todd McGowan, *Rupture: On the Emergence of the Political* (Evanston, IL: Northwestern University Press, 2012), 3.

39. Eisenstein and McGowan, *Rupture*, 4.

40. Eisenstein and McGowan, *Rupture*, 28.

41. Hannah Arendt, Between Past and Future: Eight Exercises in Political Thought (New York: Penguin, 2006), 13.

Conclusion

1. John Pepper Clark-Bekederemo, "Ibadan," in *Collected Poems, 1958–1988* (Washington, DC: Howard University Press, 1991), 14.

2. Samuel Beckett. *The Complete Dramatic Works, Endgame* (London: Faber and Faber, 2006), 125.

3. Robert Cummings Neville, *Ultimates: Philosophical Theology* (Albany: SUNY Press, 2013), 1:197–98.

4. I am here deeply indebted to Robert Cummings Neville, *Eternity and Time's Flow* (Albany: SUNY Press, 1993). See also Nimi Wariboko, *The Split Time: Economic Philosophy for Human Flourishing in African Perspective* (Albany: SUNY Press, 2022), chap. 1.

5. For a simple discussion of PPF, see Sean Masaki Flynn, *Economics for Dummies* (Hoboken, NJ: Wiley, 2005), 38–44.

6. It is important to add that points on the curve that are considered efficient by economists may not always be ethical, moral, or good for workers. Managers might have attained positions on the efficiency frontiers by paying very low wages or externalizing the costs of environmental pollution or ecological degradation.

7. As I noted in the introductory chapter, these "forces" are transcripts of the sacred that are restated at a higher level to acquire or embody certain attributes. When some transcripts are so transformed or restated, they are raised to the status of religion and come to constitute a superintending institution. David Little and Sumner B. Twiss, *Comparative Religious Ethics: A New Method* (San Francisco: Harper and Row, 1978), 59–60, 77–78.

8. Sara Lawrence-Lightfoot and Jessica Hoffman Davis, *The Art and Science of Portraiture* (San Francisco: John Wiley and Sons, 1997), 5.

9. Nelson Goodman, *The Language of Art* (Indianapolis: Hackett, 1967), 53.

10. Catherine Malabou, *What Should We Do with Our Brains?*, trans. Sebastian Rand (New York: Fordham University Press, 2008), 5 (italics in the original).

11. Is being not plasticity? See Malabou, *What Should We Do with Our Brains?* See also Catherine Malabou, *Plasticity at the Dusk of Writing: Dialectics, Destruction, Deconstruction*, trans. Carolyn Shread, foreword by Clayton Crockett (New York: Columbia University Press, 2010).

12. Anne Norton, "Pentecost: Democratic Sovereignty in Carl Schmitt," *Constellations* 18, no. 3 (2011): 389–402, see quotation on 397.

13. Norton, "Pentecost," 397.

14. This paragraph was inspired by Malabou, *What Should We Do with Our Brains?*, 6–8. For a way of interpreting the connections among (a) communality, (b) participation, and (c) participation as a theorization of the sacred as human work, see also Nimi Wariboko, *The Charismatic City and the Public Resurgence of Religion: A Pentecostal Social Ethics of Cosmopolitan Urban Life* (New York: Palgrave, 2014), 104–8, 151–52, 181–85.

15. This insight was inspired by Malabou, *What Should We Do with Our Brains?*, 36.

16. Malabou, *What Should We Do with Our Brains?*, 36.

BIBLIOGRAPHY

Abani, Chris. *GraceLand*. New York: Farrar, Straus and Giroux, 2004.
Abram, David. *The Spell of the Sensuous*. New York: Vintage Books, 1996.
Achebe, Chinua. "The Art of Fiction CXXXIV." Interview by Jerome Brooks. *Paris Review*, no. 133 (Winter 1994–95): 142–66.
Adams, Robert Merrihew. *A Theory of Virtue: Excellence in Being for the Good*. Oxford: Oxford University Press, 2006.
Adelakun, Abimbola A. *Performing Power in Nigeria: Identity, Politics, and Pentecostalism*. Cambridge: Cambridge University Press, 2021.
Agamben, Giorgio. *The Kingdom and the Glory: For a Genealogy of Economy and Government*. Translated by Lorenzo Chiesa. Stanford, CA: Stanford University Press, 2011.
———. *Profanations*. Translated by Jeff Fort. New York: Zone Books, 2007.
———. *The Time That Remains: A Commentary on the Letter to the Romans*. Translated by Patricia Dailey. Stanford, CA: Stanford University Press, 2005.
———. *The Use of Bodies*. Translated by Adam Kotsko. Stanford, CA: Stanford University Press, 2015.
Ake, Claude. *Democracy and Development in Africa*. Washington, DC: Brookings Institution, 1996.
Aku, Summer. "Nigerian Pastors Unite against Daddy Freeze: The Full Compilation of Pastors' Responses (Tithe Drama)." YouTube. *Summer Aku Vlogs*, April 18, 2018. https://www.youtube.com/watch?v=KzB2l3J-q38.
Arendt, Hannah. *Between Past and Future: Eight Exercises in Political Thought*. New York: Penguin Books, 1968.
———. *The Human Condition*. Chicago: University of Chicago Press, 1958.
———. *On Violence*. New York: Harcourt Bruce Javanovich, 1970.
———. *The Origins of Totalitarianism*. New York: Schocken Books, 2004.
Aselebe, Victor. "COZA: Pastor Adeboye Stirs Reactions Online with Comments." *Newswatch*, July 6, 2019. https://www.newswatch.ng/coza-pastor-adeboye-stirs-reactions-online-with-comments/.
Ashimolowo, Matthew. *What Is Wrong with Being Black? Celebrating Our Heritage, Confronting Our Challenges*. Shippensburg, PA: Destiny Image, 2007.
Azzam, Abed. *Nietzsche versus Paul*. New York: Columbia University Press, 2015.
Badiou, Alain. *Being and Event*. Translated by Oliver Feltham. London: Continuum, 2005.
———. *Theoretical Writings*. London: Continuum, 2004.
Bantum, Brian. *Redeeming Mulatto: A Theology of Race and Christian Hybridity*. Waco, TX, Baylor University Press, 2010.
Beckett, Samuel. *The Complete Dramatic Works, Endgame*. London: Faber and Faber, 2006.
Beker, Avi. *The Chosen: The History of an Idea, and the Anatomy of an Obsession*. New York: Palgrave Macmillan, 2008.
BellaNaija. "Pay Your Tithes Willingly and Not out of Fear—Bishop Mike Okonkwo." March 7, 2018. https://www.bellanaija.com/2018/03/pay-tithes-willingly-mike-okonkwo/.

Benjamin, Walter. "Notes toward a Work on the Category of Justice." Translated by Peter Fenves. In *The Messianic Reduction: Walter Benjamin and the Shape of Time*, by Peter Fenves, 257–58. Stanford, CA: Stanford University Press, 2011.

Bertelsen, Bjørn Enge. *Violent Becomings: State Formation, Sociality, and Power in Mozambique*. New York: Berghahn Books, 2016.

Bongmba, Elias K. "What Has Kinshasa to Do with Athen? Methodological Perspective on Theology and Social Sciences in Search for a Political Theology." In *Faith in African Lived Christianity*, edited by Karen Lauterbach and Mika Vahakangas, 195–223. Leiden: Brill, 2019.

Bourriaud, Nicolas. *Postproduction Culture as Screenplay: How Art Reprograms the World*. Translated by Jeannine Herman. New York: Lukas and Sternberg, 2002.

———. *The Radicant*. Translated by James Gussen and Lili Porten. New York: Lukas and Sternberg, 2009.

Bracken, Joseph A. *The Divine Matrix: Creativity as Link between East and West*. Delhi: Motilal Banarsidass, 1997.

Bretherton, Luke. "Christ and the Common Life." https://syndicate.network/symposia/theology/christ-and-the-common-life/.

———. *Christ and the Common Life: Political Theology and the Case for Democracy*. Grand Rapids, MI: Eerdmans, 2019.

Butticci, Annalisa. *African Pentecostals in Catholic Europe: The Politics of Presence in the Twenty-First Century*. Cambridge, MA: Harvard University Press, 2016.

———. "Crazy World, Crazy Faith! Prayer, Power and Transformation in a Nigerian Prayer City." *Annual Review of Sociology of Religion* 4 (2013): 243–61.

Campbell, Colin. *The Romantic Ethic and the Spirit of Modern Consumerism*. New York: Basil Blackwell, 1987.

Carter, J. Cameron. *Race: A Theological Account*. Oxford: Oxford University Press, 2008.

Cavanaugh, William T. *Torture and Eucharist*. Malden, MA: Blackwell, 1998.

Chabal, Patrick, and Jean-Pascal Daloz. *Africa Works: Disorder as Political Instrument*. Oxford: James Currey, 1999.

Clark-Bekederemo, John Pepper. "Ibadan." In *Collected Poems, 1958–1988*, 14. Washington, DC: Howard University Press, 1991.

Connolly, William E. *Capitalism and Christianity: American Style*. Durham, NC: Duke University Press, 2008.

Crawley, Ashon T. *Blackpentecostal Breath: Aesthetics of Possibility*. New York: Fordham University Press, 2016.

Delahaye, Ezra. "About Chronos and Kairos: On Agamben's Interpretation of Pauline Temporality through Heidegger." *International Journal of Philosophy and Theology* 77, no. 3 (2016): 85–101.

Deleuze, Gilles. *The Logic of Sense*. Translated by Mark Lester with Charles Stivale. New York: Columbia University Press, 1990.

Dru, Jean-Marie. *Thank You for Disrupting: The Disruptive Business Philosophies of the World's Great Entrepreneurs*. Hoboken, NJ: John Wiley and Sons, 2019.

Eisenstein, Paul, and Todd McGowan. *Rupture: On the Emergence of the Political*. Evanston, IL: Northwestern University Press, 2012.

Esposito, Roberto. *Communitas: The Origin and Destiny of Community*. Stanford, CA: Stanford University Press, 2010.

Falola, Toyin. *Colonialism and Violence in Nigeria*. Bloomington: Indiana University Press, 2009.

———. *Violence in Nigeria: The Crisis of Religious Politics and Secular Ideologies*. Rochester, NY: University of Rochester Press, 1998.
Félix-Jäger, Steven. *Pentecostal Aesthetics: Theological Reflection in a Pentecostal Philosophy of Arts and Aesthetics*. Leiden: Brill, 2015.
Fenn, Richard K. *Liturgies and Trials: The Secularization of Religious Language*. Oxford: Basil Blackwell, 1982.
———. *The Return of the Primitive: A New Sociological Theory of Religion*. Aldershot, UK: Ashgate, 2001.
———. "Sociology and Religion: Searching for the Sacred." In *The Oxford Handbook of Religion and Science*, edited by Philip Clayton and Zachary Simpson, 253–70. Oxford: Oxford University Press, 2006.
Fenves, Peter. *The Messianic Reduction: Walter Benjamin and the Shape of Time*. Stanford, CA: Stanford University Press, 2011.
Flynn, Sean Masaki. *Economics for Dummies*. Hoboken, NJ: Wiley, 2005.
Ford, Lewis S. *The Lure of God: A Biblical Background for Process Theism*. Philadelphia: Fortress, 1978.
Foucault, Michel. *Society Must Be Defended: Lectures at the College of France, 1975–1976*. New York: Picador, 1997.
Geertz, Clifford. *The Interpretation of Cultures*. New York: Basic Books, 1973.
Geschiere, Peter. "Witchcraft and the Limits of the Law: Cameroun and South Africa." In *Law and Disorder in the Postcolony*, edited by Jean Comaroff and John L. Comaroff, 219–46. Chicago: University of Chicago Press, 2006.
Goldberg, David Theo. *The Threat of Race: Reflections on Racial Neoliberalism*. Oxford: Wiley-Blackwell, 2009.
Goodman, Nelson. *The Language of Art*. Indianapolis: Hackett, 1967.
Green, Ronald M. "Religious Ritual: A Kantian Perspective." *Journal of Religious Ethics* 7, no. 2 (1979): 229–38.
Hardt, Michael, and Antonio Negri. *Commonwealth*. Cambridge, MA: Harvard University Press, 2009.
Hart, H. L. A. *The Concept of Law*. Oxford: Oxford University Press, 1961.
Hegel, G. W. F. *Elements of the Philosophy of Right*. Cambridge: Cambridge University Press, 1991.
Hodges, Hugh. "No, This Is Not Redemption: The Biafra War Legacy in Chris Abani's *GraceLand*." In *Writing the Nigeria-Biafra War*, edited by Toyin Falola and Ogechukwu Ezekwem, 380–99. New York: James Currey, 2016.
Honig, Bonnie. *Emergency Politics: Paradox, Law and Democracy*. Princeton, NJ: Princeton University Press, 2009.
———. *Political Theory and the Displacement of Politics*. Ithaca, NY: Cornell University Press, 1993.
Horton, Robin. *The Gods as Guests: An Aspect of Kalabari Religious Life*. Lagos: Nigerian Magazine, 1960.
———. "A Hundred Years of Change in Kalabari Religion." In *Black Africa: Its People and Their Cultures Today*, edited by John Middleton, 192–211. New York: Macmillan, 1971.
———. *Kalabari Sculpture*. Lagos: Department of Antiquities, Federal Republic of Nigeria, 1965.
———. "The Kalabari Worldview: An Outline and Interpretation." *Africa* 32, no. 3 (July 1962): 197–219.
———. *Patterns of Thought in Africa and the West: Essays on Magic, Religion and Science*. Cambridge: Cambridge University Press, 1993.

Ibirogha, Femi, et al. "Adeboye Leads 'Prayer Walk' as Christians Protest against Insecurity." *Guardian*, February 3, 2020. https://guardian.ng/news/adeboye-leads-prayer-walk-as-christians-protest-against-insecurity/.

Ike, Uchechukwu. "Tithing Is a Scriptural Injunction, Mandatory, but Not Compulsory—Bishop Isong." Vanguard Nigeria. *Vanguard*, December 26, 2017. https://www.vanguardngr.com/2017/12/tithing-scriptural-injunction-mandatory-not-compulsory-bishop-isong/.

Jennings, Willie James. *The Christian Imagination: Theology and the Origins of Race*. New Haven, CT: Yale University Press, 2010.

Jones, Serene. *Feminist Theory and Christian Theology: Cartographies of Grace*. Minneapolis: Augsburg Fortress, 2000.

Kalu, Ogbu Uke. *Religions in Africa: Conflicts, Politics and Social Ethics*. Edited by Wilhelmina J. Kalu, Nimi Wariboko, and Toyin Falola. Trenton: Africa World Press, 2010.

Kapferer, Bruce, and Bjørn E. Bertelsen, eds. *Crisis of the State: War and Social Upheaval*. New York: Berghahn Books, 2009.

Katongole, Emmanuel. *Born from Lament: The Theology and Politics of Hope in Africa*. Grand Rapids, MI: Eerdmans, 2017.

———. *The Sacrifice of Africa: A Political Theology for Africa*. Grand Rapids, MI: Eerdmans, 2011.

Keller, Catherine. *Cloud of the Impossible: Negative Theology and Planetary Entanglement*. New York: Columbia University Press, 2014.

———. "The Entangled Cosmos: An Experiment in Physical Theopoetics." *Journal of Cosmology* 20 (September 2012): 1–18.

———. *Face of the Deep: A Theology of Becoming*. London: Routledge, 2003.

———. *On the Mystery: Discerning God in Process*. Minneapolis: Fortress, 2008.

———. *Political Theology of the Earth: Our Planetary Emergency and the Struggle for a New Public*. New York: Columbia University Press, 2018.

Kirk-Duggan, Cheryl. *Exorcizing Evil: A Womanist Perspective on the Spirituals*. Maryknoll, NY: Orbis Books, 1997.

Kripal, Jeffrey. *Authors of the Impossible: The Paranormal and the Sacred*. Chicago: University of Chicago Press, 2010.

Lacan, Jacque. *The Ego in Freud's Theory and in the Technique of Psychoanalysis, 1954–1955*. Bk. 2 of *The Seminar of Jacques Lacan*, edited by Jacques-Alain Miller. Translated by Sylvana Tomaselli. New York: W. W. Norton, 1991.

Lawrence-Lightfoot, Sara, and Jessica Hoffman Davis. *The Art and Science of Portraiture*. San Francisco: John Wiley and Sons, 1997.

Lehman, Paul L. *Ethics in a Christian Context*. Eugene, OR: Wipf and Stock, 1998.

Lewis, C. S. *The Screwtape Letters*. New York: HarperOne, 2015.

Little, David, and Sumner B. Twiss. *Comparative Religious Ethics: A New Method*. San Francisco: Harper and Row, 1978.

Longman, Timothy. *Memory and Justice in Post-genocide Rwanda*. Cambridge: Cambridge University Press, 2017.

Magesa, Laurent. *What Is Not Sacred? African Spirituality*. Maryknoll, NY: Orbis Books, 2013.

Malabou, Catherine. *Plasticity at the Dusk of Writing: Dialectics, Destruction, Deconstruction*. Translated by Carolyn Shread, with a foreword by Clayton Crockett. New York: Columbia University Press, 2010.

———. *What Should We Do with Our Brains?* Translated by Sebastian Rand. New York: Fordham University Press, 2008.
Mamdani, Mahmood. *When Victims Become Killers: Colonialism, Nativism, and the Genocide in Rwanda*. Princeton, NJ: Princeton University Press, 2001.
Marshall, Ruth. *Political Spiritualities: The Pentecostal Revolution in Nigeria*. Chicago: University of Chicago Press, 2009.
Marx, Karl. *Grundrisse: Foundations of the Critique of Political Economy*. New York: Penguin, 1993.
Marx, Karl, and Friedrich Engels. *The Communist Manifesto*. Chicago: Charles H. Kerr and Company, 1912/1848.
———. *Manifesto of the Communist Party*. Radford, VA: Wilder, 2007.
Mbembe, Achille. *Critique of Black Reason*. Translated by Laurent Dubois. Durham, NC: Duke University Press, 2017.
———. *On the Postcolony*. Berkeley: University of California Press, 2001.
Meillassoux, Quentin. "Potentiality and Virtuality." *Collapse: Philosophic Research and Development* 2 (2007): 55–81.
Meyer, Birgit. "Aesthetics of Persuasion: Global Christianity and Pentecostalism's Sensational Forms." *South Atlantic Quarterly* 109, no. 4 (2010): 741–63.
Moltmann, Jürgen. *Theology of Hope*. Minneapolis: Fortress, 1993.
Nancy, Jean-Luc. *The Inoperative Community*. Translated by Peter Connor, Lisa Garbus, Michael Holland, and Simona Sawhney. Minneapolis: University of Minnesota Press, 1991.
Neville, Robert Cummings. *Eternity and Time's Flow*. Albany: SUNY Press, 1993.
———. *Ultimates: Philosophical Theology*. Vol. 1. Albany: SUNY Press, 2013.
Nietzsche, Friedrich W. *On the Genealogy of Morality: A Polemic*. Translated by Maudemarie Clark and Alan. J. Swensen. Indianapolis: Hackett, 1998.
Norton, Anne. "Pentecost: Democratic Sovereignty in Carl Schmitt." *Constellations* 18, no. 3 (2011): 389–402.
Nussbaum, Martha C. *Upheavals of Thought: The Intelligence of Emotions*. Cambridge: Cambridge University Press, 2001.
Obadare, Ebenezer. *Pentecostal Republic: Religion and the Struggle for State Power in Nigeria*. London: Zed Books, 2018.
O'Brien, Susan. "Spirit Discipline: Gender, Islam, and Hierarchies of Treatment in Postcolonial Northern Nigeria." In *Discipline and the Other Body: Correction, Corporeality, Colonialism*, edited by Steven Pierce and Anupama Rao, 273–302. Durham, NC: Duke University Press, 2006.
Ogundiran, Akinwumi. *The Yoruba: A New History*. Bloomington: Indiana University Press, 2020.
Ojewale, Michael O. *A Call to Prayer for Nigeria*. Lagos: Peace and Salvation, 1990.
Olaniyan, Tejumola. *Arrest the Music! Fela and His Rebel Art and Politics*. Bloomington: Indiana University Press, 2004.
Olatunji, Kehinde. "You Have Talked about COZA, Now Talk about RUGA, Charly Boy, Other Protestors Urge Adeboye." *Guardian*, July 9, 2019. https://guardian.ng/news/you-have-talked-about-coza-now-talk-about-ruga-charly-boy-other-protesters-urge-adeboye/.
Olopade, Dayo. *The Bright Continent: Breaking Rules and Making Change in Modern Africa*. Boston: Mariner Books, 2014.

Olukoya, Daniel. *Prayer Rain*. Lagos: Mountain of Fire and Miracles Ministries, 1999.

———. *Pray Your Way into 2016 and Prosperity Night Day Prayers*. Lagos: Mountain of Fire and Miracles Ministries, 2015.

O'Neil, Kevin Lewis. *City of God: Christian Citizenship in Postwar Guatemala*. Berkeley: University of California Press, 2010.

Otto, Rudolf. *The Idea of the Holy: An Inquiry into the Non-rational Factor in the Idea of the Divine and Its Relation to the Rational*. Oxford: Oxford University Press, 1923.

Oyedepo, David. *Pillars of Destiny: Exploring the Secrets of an Ever-Winning Life*. Canaan Land, Nigeria: Dominion, 2008.

Panitch, Leo, and Colin Leys, eds. *Fighting Identities: Race, Religion, and Ethno-nationalism*. London: Merlin, 2002.

Paris, Peter. *The Spirituality of African Peoples: The Search for a Common Moral Discourse*. Minneapolis: Fortress, 1995.

Parson, Mikeal C. *Body and Characters in Luke and Acts: The Subversion of Physiognomy in Early Christianity*. Waco, TX: Baylor University Press, 2011.

Premawardhana, Devaka. *Faith in Flux: Pentecostalism and Mobility in Rural Mozambique*. Philadelphia: University of Pennsylvania Press, 2018.

Rambo, Shelly. *Spirit and Trauma: A Theology of Remaining*. Louisville: Westminster John Knox, 2010.

Rancière, Jacques. *Disagreement: Politics and Philosophy*. Translated by Julie Rose. Minneapolis: University of Minnesota Press, 1998.

———. *Dissensus: On Politics and Aesthetics*. Edited and translated by Steven Corcoran. London: Continuum, 2010.

Roitman, Janet. "The Ethics of Illegality in the Chad Basin." In *Law and Disorder in the Postcolony*, edited by Jean Comaroff and John L. Comaroff, 247–72. Chicago: University of Chicago Press, 2006.

Ruckers, Rudy. *Infinity and the Mind: The Science and Philosophy of the Infinite*. Princeton, NJ: Princeton University Press, 1995.

Sahara Reporters. "Remember Samson and Delilah, Pastor Adeboye Warns Church Ministers While Speaking on Rape Scandal of COZA Fatoyinbo, Busola Dakolo." July 6, 2019. http://saharareporters.com/2019/07/06/remember-samson-and-delilah-pastor-adeboye-warns-church-ministers-while-speaking-rape.

Sankara, Thomas. *Thomas Sankara Speaks: The Burkina Faso Revolution*. Translated and edited by Samantha Anderson. New York: Pathfinder, 1988.

Santner, Eric. *On the Psychotheology of Everyday Life*. Chicago: University of Chicago Press, 2001.

Scarry, Elaine. *Body in Pain: The Making and Unmaking of the World*. Oxford: Oxford University Press, 1985.

Schatzki, Theodore. *Site of the Social: A Philosophical Account of the Constitution of Social Life and Change*. University Park: Pennsylvania State University Press, 2002.

Schumpeter, Joseph. *Capitalism, Socialism, and Democracy*. New York: Harper and Row, 1942.

Scott, James C. *Domination and the Arts of Resistance: Hidden Transcripts*. New Haven, CT: Yale University Press, 1990.

———. *Weapons of the Weak: Everyday Forms of Peasant Resistance*. New Haven, CT: Yale University Press, 1985.

Simonse, Simon. *Kings of Disaster: Dualism, Centralism and the Scapegoat King in Southeastern Sudan*. Kampala, Uganda: Fountain, 2017.

Stearns, Jason K. *Dancing in the Glory of Monsters: The Collapse of the Congo and the Great War of Africa*. New York: Public Affairs, 2012.
Suna-Koro, Kristine. *In Counterpoint: Diaspora, Postcoloniality, and Sacramental Theology*. Eugene, OR: Pickwick, 2017.
Taylor, Diana. *The Archive and the Repertoire: Performing Cultural Memory in the Americas*. Durham, NC: Duke University Press, 2007.
Taylor, Mark C. *Confidence Games: Money and Markets in a World without Redemption*. Chicago: University of Chicago Press, 2004.
Taylor, Mark C., and Carl Racshke. "About *About Religion*: A Conversation with Mark C. Taylor." *Journal for Cultural and Religious Theory* Archives. Accessed June 14, 2015, http://www.jcrt.org/archives/02.2/taylor_raschke.shtml.
Taylor, Mark Lewis. *The Political and the Theological: On the Weight of the World*. Minneapolis: Fortress, 2011.
Thurston, Alexander. *Boko Haram: The History of an African Jihadist Movement*. Princeton, NJ: Princeton University Press, 2018.
Tillich, Paul. *The Courage to Be*. New Haven, CT: Yale University Press, 2014.
———. *Dynamics of Faith*. New York: Perennial Classic, 2001.
———. *Systematic Theology*. Vol. 1, *Reason and Revelation, Being and God*. Chicago: University of Chicago Press, 1951.
———. *Systematic Theology*. Vol. 2, *Existence and the Christ*. Chicago: University of Chicago Press, 1957.
———. *Systematic Theology*. Vol. 3, *Life and the Spirit*. Chicago: University of Chicago, 1965.
Tocqueville, Alexis de. *Democracy in America*. New York: Perennial Classics, 2001.
van der Veer, Peter. *The Value of Comparison*. Durham, NC: Duke University Press, 2016.
Vasina, Jan. "Knowledge and Perceptions of the African Past." In *African Historiographies*, edited by Bogumil Jewsiewicki and David Newsbury, 28–41. Beverly Hills: Sage, 1986.
Wariboko, Nimi. *The Charismatic City and the Public Resurgence of Religion: A Pentecostal Social Ethics of Cosmopolitan Urban Life*. New York: Palgrave, 2014.
———. "Christian-Muslim Relations and the Ethos of State Formation in West Africa." In *Dynamics of the Muslim Worlds: Regional, Theological, and Theological Perspectives*, edited by Evelyn Reisacher, 57–81. Downers Grove, IL: IVP Academic, 2017.
———. *The Depth and Destiny of Work: An African Theological Interpretation*. Trenton, NJ: Africa World Press, 2008.
———. *Economics in Spirit and Truth: A Moral Philosophy of Finance*. New York: Palgrave Macmillan, 2014.
———. *Ethics and Society: Identity, History, and Political Theory*. Rochester, NY: University of Rochester Press, 2019.
———. *God and Money: A Theology of Money in a Globalizing World*. Lanham, MD: Lexington Books, 2008.
———. *Nigerian Pentecostalism*. Rochester, NY: University of Rochester Press, 2014.
———. *The Pentecostal Hypothesis: Christ Talks, They Decide*. Eugene, OR: Cascade Books, 2020.
———. "Pentecostal Paradigms of National Economic Prosperity in Africa." In *Pentecostalism and Prosperity: The Socio-economics of the Global Charismatic Movement*, Christianities of the World 1, edited by Amos Yong and Katy Attanasi, 35–59. New York: Palgrave Macmillan, 2012.
———. *The Pentecostal Principle: Ethical Methodology in New Spirit*. Grand Rapids, MI: Eerdmans, 2012.

———. *The Split Economy: Saint Paul Goes to Wall Street*. Albany: SUNY University Press, 2020.

———. *The Split God: Pentecostalism and Critical Theory*. Albany: SUNY University Press, 2018.

———. *The Split Time: Economic Philosophy for Human Flourishing in African Perspective*. Albany: SUNY Press, 2022.

———. "West African Pentecostalism: A Survey of Everyday Theology." In *Global Renewal Christianity: Spirit-Empowered Movements, Past, Present and Future, Africa and Diaspora*, edited by Vinson Synan, Amos Yong, and Kwabena Asamoah-Gyadu, 1–18. Lake Mary, FL: Charisma House, 2016.

Warren, Calvin L. *Ontological Terror: Blackness, Nihilism and Emancipation*. Durham, NC: Duke University Press, 2018.

Weber, Max. *Economy and Society: An Outline of Interpretive Sociology*. Edited by Guenther Roth and Claus Wittich. Berkeley: University of California Press, 1978.

———. "Religious Rejections of the World and Their Directions." In *Max Weber: Essays in Sociology*, edited by H. H. Gerth and C. Wright Mills, 323–59. London: Routledge and Kegan Paul, 1970.

Wildman, Wesley J. *Science and Religious Anthropology: A Spiritually Evocative Naturalist Interpretation of Human Life*. London: Routledge, 2009.

Williams, Delores S. "The Color of Feminism, or Speaking the Black Woman Tongue." In *Feminist Theological Ethics: A Reader*, edited by Lois K. Daly, 42–58. Louisville: Westminster John Knox, 1994.

Wright, Robert. *The Evolution of God*. New York: Little, Brown, 2009.

———. *Nonzero: The Logic of Human Destiny*. New York: Vintage Books, 2001.

Žižek, Slavoj. *Absolute Recoil: Towards a New Foundation of Dialectical Materialism*. London: Verso, 2014.

———. "Christianity against the Sacred." In *God in Pain: Inversions of Apocalypse*, by Slavoj Žižek and Boris Gunjević, 43–71. New York: Seven Stories, 2012.

———. *Event: A Philosophical Journey through a Concept*. London: Penguin Books, 2014.

———. *The Fragile Absolute, or Why Is the Christianity Legacy Worth Fighting For?* London: Verso, 2008.

———. *In Defense of Lost Causes*. London: Verso, 2009.

———. *Less Than Nothing: Hegel and the Shadow of Dialectical Materialism*. London: Verso, 2012.

———. *The Most Sublime Hysteric: Hegel with Lacan*. Translated by Thomas Scott-Railton. Malden, MA: Polity, 2014.

———. *The Parallax View*. Cambridge, MA: MIT Press, 2009.

———. *The Plague of Fantasies*. London: Verso, 1997.

———. *The Sublime Object of Ideology*. London: Verso, 2008.

———. *Violence: Six Sideways Reflections*. New York: Picador, 2008.

INDEX

Abani, Chris, 100–102
Absolute, 53–54, 61
Achebe, Chinua, 16
actualization of potentialities, 4–5, 7–8, 13, 15, 22, 27, 37–38, 41, 46, 53, 89–90, 117, 164, 187, 190–92
Adeboye, Enoch, 151, 154, 178–79
Adefarasin, Paul, 157–58
aesthetics, 4, 67–93
African traditional religion (ATR), 20, 28, 40, 69–70, 81–83, 92, 185
Agamben, Giorgio, 89–90, 184, 202n45
agency, human, 41
Ake, Claude, 173–74
angels, 73–74, 78, 81
Anikulapo-Kuti, Fela, 102–3
anti-flourishment, 2, 6, 8
antifragility, 117
anxiety, 24, 88, 98, 118–23
archives, definition of, xii
Arendt, Hannah, 20, 31, 124, 126, 128–29, 169, 188
Aristotle, 27, 112
Ashimolowo, Matthew, 155–58

Baal, 79
Badiou, Alain, 63, 66
Bantum, Brian, 166
beauty, xii, 3–5, 8, 10–11, 188, 190–91
Beckett, Samuel, 190
Belewa, Tafawa, 100
Benjamin, Walter, 90, 116
Beredugo, Atei, 156–57, 160–62
Bertelsen, Bjørn Enge, 133
bibibari, 46–48, 201n14
Bible. *See* scripture
Blackness, 148–67
body, bodies, 162–64
Boehme, Jacob, 109
Boko Haram (BH), 137–40, 146, 178

bonds, 31, 44
Bongmba, Elias Kifon, 115
Bourriaud, Nicolas, 9
Bretherton, Luke, 115–16, 207n44, 207n46
Butticci, Annalisa, 61, 70–72, 84–86

Campaoré, Blaise, 11
Cantor, Georg, 63
Carter, J. Cameron, 165–66
Chabal, Patrick, 104
change makers, 185–88
chaos, 33, 48, 65, 104, 114, 123, 135–43, 147, 171
chief, 143–44
chosenness, 19, 34, 148–67
church, 10–11
circulation, 10
commons, 94–95, 117
community; common life, 13–14, 22, 27, 44, 56, 65, 77, 100, 104–5, 110–11, 122–29, 135, 143–46, 186–88, 190–93, 195
Connolly, William, 179
construction, 116–17
cooperativeness, 21
Crawley, Ashon, 71–72
creativity, 4, 7–8, 12, 36–37, 41, 49–50, 53–54, 56, 67, 116–17, 168, 190–91
culture, 35
Cusa, Nicholas, 201n17

Daddy Freeze. *See* Olarinde, Ifedayo
Dakolo, Busola, 178, 181
Daloz, Jean-Pascal, 104
death, 3, 97, 120, 131, 139
de Certeau, Michel, 61
deeds, 111–12
Deleuze, Gilles, 46, 60, 62
democracy, 115–16, 183–84
demons, 67–93, 132
desire(s), 29–34, 94, 112
destiny, 44–48, 201n14

223

destruction, 7–8, 67, 116
development, 168–88
disorder, 17, 104–5, 111–12, 114, 120, 135
disruption, 168–88
domination, 6, 31, 148–49
Dostoevsky, Fyodor, 107
Dru, Jean-Marie, 169
Durkheim, Emile, 44

economics, xiii–xiv, 18–20, 28, 32, 45, 65, 101, 104–5, 110, 135, 139, 149–50, 155–62, 168–88, 191–93
emancipation, 116–17, 157, 172, 181
emotionalism, 119
ends, 87–89. *See also* telos
enhancement of life. *See* flourishing, human
enrichment, 5
epistemology, 13, 17, 29, 31–32, 34, 37–38, 94–129, 148
eros, 5, 21
ethics, 9, 85, 92, 100–101, 108
evangelization, 19, 34, 149, 161, 163
existence, 21–22, 125, 190

faith, 78, 80, 95–96, 107–8, 112, 119–22, 125–26, 130, 151
Fanon, Frantz, 133
fantasy, 32–34, 148
Fatoyinbo, Biodun, 178
Fawehinmi, Gani, 161
fear, 32, 50, 124, 144, 176
Félix-Jäger, Steven, 71
Fenn, Richard, 15, 42, 46, 64
fire, 77–78
First World War, 98
flourishing, human, xi, 3–5, 7, 11, 16, 22, 27, 85, 92, 103, 106, 115–17, 160, 168, 171, 190–93
Ford, Lewis S., 187
Foucault, Michel, 163
fragments, 16–21
freedom, 7, 41, 48, 117, 122
Freud, Sigmund, 98
future, 6, 7, 11, 76, 96–98, 145, 149, 164, 175, 188; inventing the, 11–12

Geertz, Clifford, 34–35
genocide, 141–43

God, 53–56, 58–60, 66, 73–81, 86–88, 91, 95, 108, 120–21, 126, 149, 154, 156–57, 160–61, 163–64, 187
gods, 32, 43, 69–70, 81–83, 147, 156, 201n6
good, 4; of the sacred, 5
Goodman, Nelson, 194
governance, 18, 136, 145; as trauma, 95, 97–102, 104–6, 115–18, 120–21, 125, 127, 136, 140
grace, 7–8, 42, 117
Green, Ronald, 23
gross national product, 155

Hagin, Kenneth, 151
Hardt, Michael, 162–63
Hart, H. L. A., 24
healing, 96, 127, 158
Hegel, Georg Wilhelm Friedrich, 50, 61
Heidegger, Martin, 124
history, 6
Hobbes, Thomas, 124
Holy Spirit, 68, 70–74, 83, 85, 110, 113, 151, 154–55, 161
Honig, Bonnie, 128
hope, 4, 8–9, 20, 50, 124, 145, 149, 198n9
Horton, Robin, 43, 77, 81–82, 112, 186–87, 201n5
hypothesis, Pentecostal, 105

Ideh, Elishama, 151–54, 160
identity, x, 31–32, 44, 143–44, 151, 164–66; split, 34, 148
ideology, 32–33, 179
imagination, xiii, 8, 29, 76, 131, 165; moral, 21; religious, 65
impossibility, xi, xiii, 1, 7, 27, 36–37, 41–66
im/possibility, xi, 1, 17, 27, 36, 41–66, 67, 168
incredible: Pentecostal, 93, 94–129, 183, 186; postcolonial, 99–108, 115–18, 120–21, 125–26, 136, 143–44, 186
individuals, 27, 77, 123, 129, 135
injustice, 145, 156
inversion, 60–61
Ison, Emmah, 179

Jehu, 79
Jennings, Willie James, 165–66

Jesus Christ, 19, 34, 80, 94–95, 114, 116, 121, 125, 149, 161, 164–66, 187
Job, 79
Jonathan, Goodluck, 137–38
justice, 4, 89–90, 181, 183

Kalabari, 41, 43–47, 49, 57–58, 77, 81–82, 186–88, 201n4
Kalu, Ogbu, 161
Kant, Immanuel, 48, 83, 86–87, 89
Katongole, Emmanuel, 10–12, 143–44
Keller, Catherine, 51–63, 139, 201n17, 202n32, 203n62
Kirk-Duggan, Cheryl, 109
knowledge, 29, 105, 108–10; false, 33
Kripal, Jeffrey, 50–52

LaCapra, Dominick, 98
law, 42–43, 100
leaders, 29–31, 172–74, 178–85
Lewis, C. S., 81
liberation, 19, 164
life, 3, 97
limitation, 45–48, 192
Little, David, 24
logic of sense, 60–61
Longman, Timothy, 141–42

Magesa, Laurent, 134, 137
Makhuwa-Kaveya, 9–10
Mamdami, Mahmood, 131–32
manifestation, 4, 6, 13, 24, 53, 65–66, 72–74, 84–86, 90–92, 110, 118–19
Marley, Bob, 181
Marshall, Ruth, 158
Marx, Karl, 169, 194
Mbembe, Achille, 30, 34, 102, 139–40
means, 87–89
Meillassoux, Quentin, 57–58, 64–66
Meyer, Bridget, 70–72, 83–86
miracle, 63, 66, 87, 106, 112, 203n67
mobility, 9–10
Moltmann, Jürgen, 125
monstrosity, xii–xiii, 6–7, 8, 10, 94–129, 130–47, 167, 190–91, 198n9
morality, 22–25, 100–101, 112, 159
Munroe, Myles, 161

mutuality, 21

Naluindu, Francois, 143–44
natality, 7, 14, 20, 22, 129
Negri, Antonio, 162–63
Nietzsche, Friedrich, 32, 125
nihilism, 100–101, 103, 124
non-zero-sumness, 21
noumenal, 62
novum, 8, 24, 49, 56
numen, 44

Obadare, Ebenezer, 181, 183
Obisakin, Lawrence Olufemi, 157–58
O'Brien, Susan, 132
Ojewale, Michael, 158
Okonkwo, Mike, 176
Olaniyan, Tejumola, 18, 95, 103
Olarinde, Ifedayo, 176
Olopade, Dayo, 12
Olukoya, Daniel, 74–75
O'Neil, Kevin Lewis, 159
Otto, Rudolf, 141, 170
Oyedepo, Bishop David, 32

pain, 130–31
past, 6, 15, 48, 76, 96–98, 110
Paul, 80, 184
philosophy, continental, 38–40
Plato, 60
play, 21, 57
political, the, 29, 104, 106, 115–16, 172, 173–75, 188; definition of, xiv, 27
poor, the, 30
possibility, xi, xiii–xiv, 1–3, 6–8, 13, 27, 35, 37–38, 41–66, 67, 90, 91–92, 136, 140, 168, 190–93, 198n9; critique of, 3; definition of, 5, 35–36; formlessness of, 6; form of, 3–4; otherwise, 18; sacred as, 41–44, 135; unfulfilled, 1, 15, 42–43, 46, 90
postcolony, ix–x, 1–2, 16, 26–40, 94, 115, 120–23, 127, 129, 130–47, 149, 167, 171, 183, 189–91, 194
potentiality. *See* possibility
poverty, ix, 34, 145–46, 156, 161
power, ix–x, 2, 5, 29–31, 33–36, 61, 67, 94, 105, 120, 130–47, 173–74; of gods, 43–44

powerlessness, ix, 61
prayer, 17, 67–93
Premawardhana, Devaka, 9–10
presence, real, 59, 61, 68–69, 82–88, 90, 92
present, 6, 15, 48, 76, 96–98, 110
privilege, 31–32
profane, 56, 58–59
promise, 124–29, 168–88
prosperity gospel, 11, 32, 163, 175

race, 148–67
radicant, 9
Rambo, Shelly, 98
Rancière, Jacques, 83–84, 90
reality, 3
reason, 118–19, 123
reciprocity, 21
recognition, 31–32, 94. See also identity: split
reflection principle, 5
relationships, 52–53, 59
religion, 2, 10, 20, 22–25, 35, 52–53, 63–65, 83, 94, 120, 123, 134, 168–88, 193, 200n10
remnant, 184–85
repetition, 2
ridiculous, xiii, 7–12, 190–91
ritual, 23–24
rules, 24

sacrament, 14
sacred, x–xi, 12–15, 90, 92, 94, 130–47, 148–50, 168, 190–96; critique of, 2–3; definition, xi, 1, 26–27, 35–36; movements of the, 12; parts of the, 36, 194; as transcendent other, 26; truth of the, 5
Sankara, Thomas, 11–12
Sartre, Jean-Paul, 121
Satan, 79–81
Schatzki, Theodore, 37
Schmitt, Carl, 42, 138
Schumpeter, Joseph, 169
Scott, James, 61
scripture, 79–80, 108, 111–12, 165
Second Coming, 149–50
secularity, 18, 63–65, 130–47, 193
self-consciousness, 50
Shekau, Abubakar, 137–39

sin, 81, 159
So, 44–45, 48–50, 186–87
so, 45, 201n14
sovereignty, 102, 124, 135, 138–40, 163, 171
speech, 111–12
spheres, 29
spiritual, the, 29
spirituality, 9, 19, 67, 88, 91, 106, 148–67, 171, 183; African, 39, 134
stasis, 6, 8
Stearns, Jason, 140, 143–44
supersessionism, 166, 210n1
superstition, 156
symbols, 130–31; transcripts as, xi
synesthesia, 75–76

Tamuno, 46, 82
Taylor, Mark C., 51
teleology, 68
telos, 45, 86, 88
theology, 155; of chaosmosic life, 114, 117, 123–29; geographical, 160; negative, 51–53, 55; political, 106, 113–14, 115–18
therapy, 77
Thurston, Alexander, 138
Tillich, Paul, 3, 119–20, 187, 206n35
time, 6, 22–23, 65, 74, 76, 91–92, 96–97, 99, 203n67
transcripts, 12–15, 22–24, 37–40, 67–93, 148–50, 168–69, 190–91, 195, 197n1 (preface), 214n7; definition of, xi–xii, 13
trauma, 6, 76, 95–99, 104–7, 115, 145; historical, 98–99; micro, 98–99; structural, 98–99
Tutuola, Amos, 89
Twiss, Sumner B., 24

van der Veer, Peter, 70
violence, ix, 6, 18, 31, 97, 104, 107, 111, 130–47; emancipatory, 116; sexual, 139–40
virtue, 117
von Schelling, Friedrich Wilhelm Joseph, 48

warfare, 174; spiritual, 2, 17, 67–93
wealth, ix
Weber, Max, 83, 169
Whitehead, Alfred North, 199n45, 202n28
Wildman, Wesley, 40
women, 131–32

worship, 43–44, 60–61, 69, 72, 78, 87–89; space, 75, 77–79
Wright, Robert, 21

Yeats, W. B., 99
Yusuf, Muhammad, 138

Žižek, Slavoj, 33, 48–50, 55–56, 58, 60

NIMI WARIBOKO is Walter G. Muelder Professor of Social Ethics at Boston University. His recent books include *Social Ethics and Governance in Contemporary African Writing* (2023) and *The Split Time: Economic Philosophy for Human Flourishing in African Perspective* (2022).

For Indiana University Press

Brian Carroll, Rights Manager
Gary Dunham, Acquisitions Editor and Director
Anna Francis, Assistant Acquisitions Editor
Brenna Hosman, Production Coordinator
Katie Huggins, Production Manager
David Miller, Lead Project Manager/Editor
Dan Pyle, Online Publishing Manager
Nancy Smith, Artist and Book Designer
Stephen Williams, Marketing and Publicity Manager

www.ingramcontent.com/pod-product-compliance
Lightning Source LLC
Chambersburg PA
CBHW021352300426
44114CB00012B/1191